Post-Digital Book Cultures

POST-DIGITAL BOOK CULTURES

Australian Perspectives

Edited by Alexandra Dane and Millicent Weber

MONASH
UNIVERSITY
PUBLISHING

Monash University Publishing
Matheson Library Annexe
40 Exhibition Walk
Monash University
Clayton, Victoria 3800, Australia
publishing.monash.edu/

Monash University Publishing brings to the world publications which advance the best traditions of humane and enlightened thought.

ISBN: 9781922464330 (paperback)
ISBN: 9781922464347 (pdf)
ISBN: 9781922464354 (epub)

Design: Les Thomas
Typesetting: Jo Mullins

A catalogue record for this book is available from the National Library of Australia.

Contents

Editors' Acknowledgements

We would like to thank the copyeditors – Chloe Agius, Sophia Benjamin, James Cummings, Lydia McClelland, Lucinda Naughton, Ethan Patrick, Chloe Salecker, Poppy Willis and Jon Worthen – who copyedited this book with care, skill and intelligence.

We would also like to thank everyone at Monash University Publishing for their support of this project.

Chapter 1

Post-Digital Book Cultures

An Introduction

Alexandra Dane and Millicent Weber

In the introduction to *The Digital Literary Sphere*, Simone Murray considers the enduring 'unfortunate legacy' of 1990s scholarly technophoria/technophobia and the ways in which debates around the printed versus the digital codex has distracted researchers 'from considering the surprising resilience of literary discussion on the internet'.[1] Murray's observation is simultaneously a criticism of contemporary publishing studies and a call to action for researchers of twenty-first century book cultures, a call that can be understood as a need to shift from a digital to a post-digital scholarly paradigm wherein researchers examine and seek to understand the publishing field that exists beyond the initial disruption of computerisation and digitisation.[2] The essays in this volume exist within this contemporary paradigm and demonstrate the ontological opportunities that moving into the post-digital affords.

Rather than being separate to or 'after' digital technologies, the notion of post-digital publishing can be understood as being the expansion of digital: the second (or even third) wave of digital publishing, wherein digital and analogue book technologies exist with simultaneous relevance.[3] Posting images of printed books on Instagram, reviewing a title on biblio-social networking site Goodreads, and supporting a Kickstarter fund for the publication of an art book that showcases a designer's experimental typography and compositions are all examples of participation in the post-digital publishing field, and offer researchers the opportunity to observe and explore the production and circulation of literary culture like never before.

Post–digital Book Cultures is a collection that aligns with the disciplinary aims and approaches of twenty-first century book studies. Rachel Noorda and Stevie Marsden describe the intentions of the discipline as wide-ranging, engaging with the 'radical changes to the production, dissemination and transmission of ideas'[4] that characterise contemporary book publishing and book cultures. The research published in this volume echoes these ideas by bringing diverse methodological approaches into play with cross-disciplinary theoretical frameworks[5] to interrogate the ever-expanding modes by which book cultures exist within current contexts.

This volume explores book cultures from an Australian perspective, in as much as the perspectives come from scholars situated in Australia, published by an Australian publisher. Twenty-first century book studies and research examining the post-digital complicates the notion of 'national' literatures and book cultures as digital technologies establish connections that serve to erode borders between nations. This erosion is evident in the research published in this collection, and study of the production and circulation of literary culture that moves equally within and beyond national borders.[6]

Writing on the notion of the transformative reading experience afforded by (post)digital publishing practices, Anouk Lang observes the ever-evolving relational structures that define contemporary book cultures: 'Texts are positioned within and constituted by multiple frameworks of social meaning, entering into a diverse array of relations with readers'.[7] In highlighting this, Lang inspires us to interrogate this structure and the role that digital technologies play in the way readers relate to texts. This relationship, and the complex structure that defines it, is a touchpoint that recurs in the essays in this volume. In editing this collection, we looked to the structure Lang describes and the publishing communications circuit (both the digital[8] and pre-digital iteration[9]) as a launch pad for further exploration. The chapters that follow are clustered around three major themes that connect with this structure in both tacit and explicit ways: interrogating contemporary post-digital literary reception; exploring post-digital literary worlds; and understanding a new paradigm of literary production.

Interrogating Post-Digital Literary Reception

Digital and non-digital reading contexts collide in 'Online Reading During the COVID-19 Pandemic', wherein Millicent Weber analyses Goodreads 'book talk' and the effects of the pandemic on readers' relationship with particular literary texts. Weber explores the way collective tumultuous experiences intersect with texts with similar or associated themes, and how readers use their experiences of living through the pandemic as an interpretive lens. Weber looks at reader reviews of 36 titles on the Goodreads platform over the 'first wave' of the COVID-19 pandemic, observing the influence of the pandemic on readers' understandings of particular titles and the influence of particular titles on readers' understanding of the pandemic.

In 'Goodreads Reviewers and Affective Fan Labour', Alexandra Dane posits a framework for understanding the work of amateur Goodreads reviewers within the contemporary publishing circuit of value. This essay argues that the work of reviewers on Goodreads should be understood as a form of affective fan labour, enclosed within capitalist media platforms, that serves the financial interests of multitudinous agents within the publishing sector. While the focus of this essay is the Goodreads platform, many of the practices explored in Dane's essay could be applied to other social networking platforms and digital spaces. The production and circulation of book culture within platform ecosystems is an evolving practice that provides nuanced insights into literary trends and the intersection between physical and virtual book worlds.

Kenna MacTavish's essay, 'The Emerging Power of the Bookstagrammer: Reading #bookstagram as a Post-Digital Site of Book Culture' charts the rise of the literary influencer on Instagram and establishes the methodological and interpretive foundation for a study of Instagram as a platform that facilitates the production of literary tastes. MacTavish establishes a framework for understanding the role of the bookstagrammer as a cultural intermediary and presents a taxonomy of posts to demonstrate and evaluate the influence of both the platform and its users.

Exploring Post-Digital Literary Worlds

The diverse contexts and ecosystem that constitute the global publishing industry have been characterised by continuous change and evolution. Digital technologies have established new modes of production and reception and offer new ways to understand the intricate networks and relational scaffolding that ensures the continued circulation of book culture. In 'The Australian Digital Publishing Bubble, 2012–2016: An Insider Perspective', Kate Cuthbert takes an autoethnographic approach to the study of the phosphorescent life cycle of romance genre digital imprints within the Australian market. Cuthbert's essay examines the ways in which romance publishing was (and remains) at the forefront of publishing's technological advancements, how the particularities of the Australian market failed to support the expansion of a romance digital imprint, and the tension that exists between traditional approaches to publishing practice that are embedded within publishing houses and the self-publishing successes experienced by many entrepreneurial romance authors. The world of romance fiction publishing is a fertile case study for understanding the changing nature of publishing practice and the shifting sites of power.

Airlie Lawson's essay 'Digital Literary Cartography: Not a Metaphor, a Methodology', offers not just a methodology for conceptualising publishing worlds, but an exploration of various worlds (both geo-cultural and conceptual), providing new insights into the ways in which processes and practices move within sectors and beyond national borders. This essay looks not only at the flow of book culture, but why and how this flow occurs and the structural factors that influence literary movement. Lawson's essay uses innovative digital methods to establish new ways of understanding literary worlds and conceptions of value.

Understanding a New Paradigm of Literary Production

The post-digital publishing field is not simply a space for the circulation of book cultures, it also establishes new ways for the production of literary texts and new understandings of what form/s these texts can take. Claire Parnell's 'Crowdfunding Book Publishing Through Creativity and Connectivity on Kickstarter: A Case Study of a Small Publisher' explores the introduction of the Kickstarter platform to the publishing field, and the ways in which platformised crowdfunding is influencing the production of books. Against the backdrop of decreasing government support for literary production, Parnell raises poignant questions about crowdfunding, platform capitalism and the role of the platform algorithm in shaping successful Kickstarter campaigns.

The final two essays in this collection explore the ways in which creators are bypassing traditional modes and means of literary production, engaging with more experimental digital and post-digital forms, and pushing conceptions of the literary beyond the traditional bound codex. In 'Converging Margins: Punk Publishing Beyond the Codex', Sarah Layton explores new transmedial texts, 'web-first' literature and the ways in which small punk publishers are pushing contemporary perceptions of the digital-print divide. Using the case study of Instar Books' *Videogames for Humans* and Viz Media's *Homestruck*, Layton interrogates the role of digital hardware, software, platforms and printed books in post-digital literary production and the future of book cultures.

In the final chapter of this volume, 'Undisciplined Creation: Poetry on Tumblr as Autoethnographic and Authorial Practice', Eloise Faichney explores creative practice authorial subjectivity on social networking site Tumblr and within the Tumblr Writing Community.

This creative-scholarly essay is part critical analysis and part exegesis and interrogates the possibilities of amateur digital creative practice as a site of both scholarly exploration and of literary experimentation.

One central theme re-emerges throughout this collection of essays: the future of post-digital book cultures. These essays demonstrate what is possible – in terms of both creative practice and scholarly research – within the post-digital paradigm, and the challenges we must consider as we embrace these possibilities.

Endnotes

1   Simone Murray, *The Digital Literary Sphere: Reading, Writing, and Selling Books in the Internet Era* (Baltimore: John Hopkins University Press, 2019), 5.
2   Florian Cramer, 'What is "Post-Digital"?' *APRJA* 3, no. 1 (2014): 13.
3   Beth Driscoll, 'Book Blogs as Tastemakers,' *Participations* 16, no. 1 (May 2019): 280–305; Cramer, 'What is "Post-Digital"?'.
4   Rachel Noorda and Stevie Marsden 'Twenty-First Century Book Studies: The State of the Discipline,' *Book History* 22 (2019): 372.
5   Noorda and Marsden, 'Twenty-First Century Book Studies,' 390.
6   Pascale Casanova, 'Literature as a World', *New Left Review* 31 (Jan–Feb 2005): 71–90.
7   Anouk Lang 'Introduction: Transforming Reading' in *From Codex to Hypertext: Reading at the turn of the Twenty-First Century*, ed. Anouk Lang (Amherst, Boston: University of Massachusetts Press, 2012), 2.
8   Padmini Ray Murray and Claire Squires, 'The Digital Publishing Communications Circuit', *Book 2.0*, 3, no. 1 (2013): 3–24.
9   Robert Darnton, 'What is the History of Books?' *Deadalus*, 111, no. 3 (1982): 65–83.

Bibliography

Casanova, Pascale. 'Literature as a World,' *New Left Review* 31 (Jan–Feb 2005): 71–90.
Cramer, Florien. 'What is "Post-Digital"?' *APRJA* 3, no. 1 (2014): 11–24.
Darnton, Robert. 'What is the History of Books?' *Deadalus*, 111, no. 3 (1982): 65–83.

Driscoll, Beth. 'Book Blogs as Tastemakers,' *Participations* 16, no. 1 (May 2019): 280–305.

Lang, Anouk. 'Introduction: Transforming Reading,' in *From Codex to Hypertext: Reading at the turn of the Twenty-First Century.* Edited by Anouk Lang. Amherst, Boston: University of Massachusetts Press, 2012, 1–27.

Murray, Simone. *The Digital Literary Sphere: Reading, Writing, and Selling Books in the Internet Era.* Baltimore: John Hopkins University Press, 2019.

Noorda, Rachel and Marsden, Stevie. 'Twenty-First Century Book Studies: The State of the Discipline,'*Book History* 22 (2019): 370–397.

Ray Murray, Padmini and Squires, Claire. 'The Digital Publishing Communications Circuit,' *Book 2.0,* 3, no. 1 (2013): 3–24.

Part 1:

Interrogating Post-Digital Literary Reception

CHAPTER 2

Online Reading
During the COVID-19 Pandemic

MILLICENT WEBER

Introduction

In Semester One, 2020, I was teaching first-year university literature. We read Shakespeare, Austen, Dickens; the final text for the semester was Virginia Woolf's *Mrs Dalloway*. *Mrs Dalloway* is a book that in my experience delights and challenges undergraduates in equal measure. Like many Modernist texts, it fits hand-in-glove with a demonstration of how literary close reading operates; it presents immediate challenges with its lack of chapter structure and its flowing, stream-of-consciousness narration, but through these it offers deep, perceptive portraits of complex characters. Published in 1925 and set in post-World War One London, *Mrs Dalloway* explicitly depicts the aftermath of the War, most notably with the inclusion of the shell-shocked character Septimus Warren Smith as a counterpart to titular protagonist Clarissa Dalloway. While like most Modernist interwar novels, *Mrs Dalloway* does not explore the Spanish flu as an explicit theme, its "atmosphere of malaise and enervation … encode[s] a miasmic modernism at the heart of the era", with depiction of the pandemic's "ghostly presence" comprised of "fragmented traces".[1] As Outka argues, although *Mrs Dalloway* is rarely read as a novel that centres on influenza, it is in fact a work which "shows how language and our perceptions of reality are shaped by disease".[2] Reading and talking about *Mrs Dalloway* in May 2020, after two months' sustained isolation and weekly Zoom tutorials, was a very different experience to discussing it in classrooms in May 2018, or indeed when I read it during my own undergraduate studies a decade earlier. Students remarked on the setting of the novel, and its relationship to the Spanish flu; they noticed, and remembered the two brief mentions of Clarissa's own experience of influenza.[3] Class discussion included a focus on the determined joys of public gathering and public walking in post-influenza London, as well as the contrast between the explicitly named trauma of war embodied by the male Septimus, and the invisible and ongoing domestic incursions of pandemic illness on the female Clarissa.

On 11 March 2020 the World Health Organisation declared COVID-19 a global pandemic.[4] On 23 March 2020 substantial shutdown measures came into force in Australia, including the suspension of all non-essential services, the closure of public spaces, and extreme restrictions around physical interaction.[5] Similar measures were taking place around the world, albeit unevenly. It would, consequently, be something of an understatement to say that COVID-19 impacted collective social experiences of cultural participation.

In this essay, I seek to explore the intersection between experiences of COVID-19 and reading, as articulated in online discussion of books, through measuring and analysing discussions of sample titles on Goodreads over the period 1 April 2020–1 June 2020. I benchmark patterns of reading on Goodreads over this period, and analyse how these conversations compare to the kinds of online book talk engaged in at less tumultuous times. I contextualise this discussion against a bigger conversation about the history and practice of reading, and about Goodreads reading in particular. Recognising the Australian production context of the collection in which this essay is situated, I also seek to contextualise my analysis through consideration of the conversations about the arts taking place in Australia over this period. While Goodreads is of course an international platform, through this I hope to offer a concrete and contained example of other kinds of conversations taking place – in political, industry and media environments – concurrently with readers' discussions.

COVID-19 and the Book Industry

In the short term, media and government attention on the impacts of COVID-19 on Australian culture has largely focused on production rather than consumption. Federal government emergency relief for the arts in Australia, belatedly announced 25 June 2020, included $75 million in grants for productions and events; $50 million for local film productions and $35 million for "significant commonwealth-funded arts and culture organisations" already impacted by COVID-19; and $90 million in concessional loans to help support new productions and events.[6] State and territory governments were quicker to provide support. While generally more wide-ranging in their remits than the federal government package, their support still largely focuses on major organisations, with Victoria's grants to individual artists a notable exception.[7] Industry concerns with the support provided, aside from the insufficient amount disproportionate to other stimulus schemes and the size of the industry, include the focus of the support on medium and large-scale operations to the detriment of casual and freelance workers in the arts, many of whom are likewise ineligible for other government schemes such as JobKeeper income support.[8]

Broader concerns with the government support made available are directly relevant to Australian publishing, particularly considering the high rates of casual and freelance employment in the book sector, and writers' already low rates of pay.[9] Some packages, like the Copyright Agency's additional $375,000 in emergency funding for creators,[10] directly support writers and publishers, but otherwise publishing and adjacent industries rely on the major funding sources listed above. This is despite the "vital role that books play in society", and calls from major advocacy organisations for governments to adopt "economic stimulus packages to sustain their respective publishing sectors and the value chains that surround them".[11] While all cultural industries face similar struggles to articulate simultaneously their economic and less tangible value to society, publishing and adjacent industries are particularly vulnerable in this regard. In part this is because of the "intrinsic invisibility" of much of the labour that takes place in publishing and publicising a book,[12] and in part for more pragmatic reasons. In particular, this includes the difficulty of collectively articulating an agenda in a sector largely comprised of independent workers such as writers, and largely consumed individually and privately.

Although some online booksellers report increases in book sales, especially of ebooks and audiobooks,[13] overall the book sector appears weakened by COVID-19. While Nielsen reported a spike in book sales revenue in Australia of $2.6 million in the week immediately following the announcement of a lockdown (22–28 March), this was followed by a substantial drop in sales (based on metrics including reporting by major bookstores like Dymocks).[14] This was attributed to a range of factors, including bookstore closures, and the halting of promotional events such as writers' talks. This is despite many chain and independent booksellers around Australia trialling solutions such as free delivery to customers,[15] and despite international department stores like Walmart and Target reporting increased sales.[16] As a result, a number of Australian publishers adjusted publication schedules and cut hours and salaries for staff in response to the weakened book sector. Hardie Grant, Allen & Unwin, Lonely Planet and Scribe all reported having to cut salaries or hours, or implementing redundancies.[17] Both HarperCollins and Hachette reported moving publication dates for some titles.[18]

While these reports speak to sales insomuch as they necessarily underpin the production of books, they are unable to articulate shifts in reading experience – that is, books' reception more than their immediate "consumption". But despite the grim situation that these figures suggest, there appear to have been some interesting developments in book culture over this period. My research in this essay was initially prompted by publishers "… reporting booming sales for books whose fictional plots revolve around pandemics, including Albert Camus's *The Plague* and Ling Ma's *Severance*".[19] The proliferating news articles in March and April 2020 that spoke directly to these shifts in reading habits prompted me to enquire whether there were any deeper or more subtle shifts in readers' engagement with books and their experiences of reading at this particular time.

Understanding Reading

It is helpful to first contextualise these conversations in relation to existing understandings of reading. As part of a broader pushback against new critical modes of literary scholarship, research into reading began to gain strength in the 1960s and 1970s. Such research asserted the significance of a reader's engagement with a text in creating that text's meaning: as reading scholar Roger Chartier succinctly puts it, "a text does not exist except for a reader who gives it signification".[20] Research in this vein ranges from the theoretical to the empirical, with researchers at one end of the spectrum positing a range of possible readers that might interpret a text in a particular way, and at the other extreme conducting experimental or documentary studies of specific readers' practices. This perspective continues to inform contemporary "reception-informed critical practice", which is "the idea that all texts are designed for an audience, and only become meaningful when they are read, viewed or listened to".[21] Ika Willis argues this practice has three key components: considering "the real-life practices of historical and contemporary readers", "attending to the many different things that people do with texts", and "challeng[ing] the idea that texts are self-contained … [which] involves us in big questions about the nature of interpretation, language and meaning".[22]

These "big questions" Willis refers to incorporate a range of under-standings of how reading operates as an act or practice. Different theorists emphasise specific influencing factors and outcomes of reading – focusing on the effects of things like personal choice and disposition, affiliation with specific demographics or communities, or the role of cultural authorities; and exploring how these might affect choices, motivations, pleasures, or interpretations. Wolfgang Iser's "phenomenological approach" to the reading process defines a relationship between the text – that is, the literal words on a page; the realisation of the text by a reader; and the work, which resides somewhere between the two.[23] For Iser, this concept of the work is important because it gives rise to a dynamic and recursive situation where the reader operates on the text at the same time as the text operates on the reader:

> Herein lies the dialectical structure of reading. The need to decipher gives us the change to formulate our own deciphering capacity... The production of the meaning of literary texts ... does not merely entail the discovery of the unformulated, which can then be taken over by the active imagination of the reader; it also entails the possibility that we may formulate ourselves and so discover what had previously seemed to elude our consciousness.[24]

By this formulation, the act of reading is both personal and experiential. For other theorists, reading is a social and interpretive act. Stanley Fish argues for the importance of "interpretive communities", collective assumptions and understandings about a text and communally agreed strategies for interpreting them.[25] Indeed, Fish asserts that "interpretation is the only game in town", arguing that even attempts to focus on, for example, the pleasure of reading a poem line-by-line, are themselves interpretive constructs in that they stipulate "where the value and the significance of a poem are to be located".[26]

Fish's work is a useful starting point when thinking about Goodreads discussions, as it recognises the significance of community in predetermining which kinds of responses to a text are "acceptable", and which are not. But readers can also read against the grain, using practices that are "playful, protesting, fugitive".[27] Michel de Certeau proposes the concept of "reading as poaching", in which readers push back against meanings inscribed by the literary elite, and engage in their own "advances and retreats, tactics and games played with the text".[28]

This leads to consideration of an important question: what motivates people to read? Answers to this question include a range of functional, pleasurable, aesthetic, and social reasons that might prompt readers to engage with a book. Elizabeth Long's work on women's reading groups explores how participants contextualise their reading and their involvement in the groups as "voluntary participation in an enjoyable activity".[29] Here, the scaffolding around reading is both social and pleasurable, with the "enjoyable activity" of reading extended to the "book discussions […which] are very free, or in their [the participants'] term, 'playful'" as well.[30] Homing in on a specific genre, for Janice Radway, romance books meet a range of social and psychological needs. Through exploring and articulating these functions, Radway validates the popular cultural form of the romance, pushing back against those "who teach reading and control access to it in our society", who she sees as "frown[ing] with particular dourness on those books that exist solely to produce the pleasures of laughter, tears, shudders, and sexual arousal".[31] Both Radway and Long have been deeply influential in extending the consideration of women's reading practices, and reading outside academic spheres of influence. Their work therefore usefully contextualises analysis of Goodreads discussions, which likewise take place outside the academy, although with some awareness of it; likewise are heavily feminised, with the majority of readers on Goodreads women; and like Long's book groups, extend the "voluntary" and "enjoyable" features of leisure reading to that of participation in social discussion about it.

Radway's work, in particular, also informs broader discussions about the distinction between cognitive and affective modes of reading. Karin

Littau argues that reading needs to be simultaneously understood as both sense-making and sensuous, but that centuries of criticism first pathologised and then subsequently ignored affective responses to books.[32] Through this reconceptualisation, Littau argues that scholars can "approach reading from the ground upwards, from the moment of 'sensation which feels the moment in the moment' and not just from the moment of 'cognition which recognizes the moment only after the moment'".[33] Littau's work demarcates clearly the boundaries of the kinds of analysis that I am able to undertake here, with the practice of writing a review on Goodreads taking place solidly in this realm of after-the-fact reflection on reading – although not necessarily solely invoking or reflecting on cognitive responses to that reading.

This kind of twofold understanding of reading is also knitted together and instrumentalised by "bibliotherapy", which is "the directed use of books or other media for the resolution of human ills and conditions".[34] Nick Canty describes bibliotherapy as incorporating three stages: identification, followed by catharsis, followed by insight; he argues that, as a result, one of the important uses of literature is in supporting readers' wellbeing.[35] Although the discussions I explore in this essay do not take place within the context of bibliotherapy explicitly named, reading as a response to collective trauma has received increasing attention in recent years.[36] Indeed, the idea of reading operating as a form of therapy to enhance emotional wellbeing has been a recurring theme in public reading programs run during the COVID-19 pandemic.[37]

Online Reading

As I have noted above, this essay seeks to explore readers' engagement with and experiences of reading through inquiring specifically into individuals' reading habits as reported on the website Goodreads. As Simone Murray describes, "Online reading formations facilitate the entry of enthused but typically amateur readers into public literary discussion, fostering communities of interest that can be as geographically inclusive as they are selective in their preferred reading material".[38] Users of a site like Goodreads participate in social exchange about books and reading, while also constructing and performing their experiences of reading through these sites and exchanges. Despite minimal evolution in site mechanics and design since its launch in 2007, Goodreads remains the largest social media platform dedicated to books and reading, with its still-growing userbase numbering approximately 90 million registered users in 2019.[39]

Goodreads functions as part of a broader culture of recommendations and reviews, and combines a range of features that come with this. Bronwen Thomas explains how these include a desire to display reading tastes and practices to a broader social group; direct comparison and competition with others within these social groups; and functional features, including organising, tracking, and prioritising one's own reading.[40] Corinna Norrick-Rühl has argued that these competitive display functions are key to the success of sites like Goodreads at a time of increased digital engagement with culture: "It is possible to have an impressive book collection on an e-reader, but it is only visible to you, hidden on a hard drive. Therefore, other ways of presentation must be found to emanate authority and impress others".[41]

Goodreads is an extremely important social formation in contemporary book culture,[42] a period characterised by complex interdependencies in print, digital, and in-person modes of engagement between writers, readers and books.[43] Since at least the early 1990s, commentators have expressed concern that electronic literature and online reading practices would detract from pre-digital modes of reading, and particularly the kinds of long-form careful attention assumed by practices like "close reading" that predominate in literary scholarship.[44] Despite these fears, however, online engagement with books and reading, including "literary" reading, has flourished, such that "the visible participation of wider groups of people in discussions around the literary is becoming harder to ignore and is provoking renewed debates around notions of literary taste and value".[45] Indeed, Jim Collins has argued that "the complete redefinition of what literary reading means within the heart of electronic culture" has been "the most profound change in literary America after the rise of postmodern fiction".[46] For Collins, this shift has meant "a new set of players, locations, rituals, and use values for reading literary fiction".[47]

Looking specifically at the "rituals and use values" described by Goodreads readers, Beth Driscoll and DeNel Rehberg Sedo have argued that reading practices on the platform are characterised by "layers of connection and reflection".[48] Through analysing Goodreads reviews of seven titles, Driscoll and Rehberg Sedo demonstrated that experiential discussion of reading, which "links the book not to objective or external criteria but to the lived experience of the reader", was more prominent even than evaluative discussions.[49] Breaking this down into "temporal, intellectual, emotional, and physical" experiences, emotional experiences were by far the most common.[50]

COVID-19 drastically compounded the significance of online social spaces to an already post-digital period of book culture. During COVID-19 lockdowns, the vast majority of social interaction and self-expression has been necessarily mediated and digital. Without access to the usual in-person social and shared environments that support engagement with book culture (like book groups, libraries, bookshops, or talks), digital access to spaces like Goodreads is arguably more important than ever. On this basis, I understand Goodreads as a site of fieldwork that offers an understanding of concerns that shape contemporary book culture, and simultaneously as a valuable object of study in its own right, while still acknowledging that as a digital platform it necessarily places obvious limits around participation in terms of technological access and literacy.

Methods

My data collection and analysis are divided into two parts. The first measures "engagement" with thirty-six books on Goodreads during a period that coincides with the majority of countries' first experiences of the COVID-19 lockdown in quantitative terms, and the second explores readers' "experiences" of three titles through content analysis of reviews. The term "engagement" is taken in its most general sense in my discussion of quantitative measures of reading, as meaning simply participation or involvement in something. The exploration of "experience" in the analysis of reader discussions draws for its terminology and conceptualisation on the theoretical discussion in the earlier sections of this essay.

The titles analysed in the quantitative part of this essay were chosen to enable identification of some of the possible changes that might have taken place in reading habits during the lockdown period. Title selection was informed by popular media discourse about pandemic reading, both Australian and international – thematic lists of "pandemic novels"[51] and "dystopian reading lists" of "books to enjoy while in quarantine"[52] – and supplemented to enable enquiry into broader patterns of reading than these lists comprehend. Title selection began, then, with a range of possible changes to reading habits over the period:

a) that people were reading more books which were directly on the topic of the pandemic;

b) that people were treating isolation as an opportunity to read more difficult or "bucket list" titles – for example classic works of literature;

c) that people would look to escapist literature as a result of feeling particularly stressed or overwhelmed with the state of the world, in which case engagement with popular fiction might increase;

d) that there would be no or minimal changes;

e) that all reading across the board would increase or decrease.

In order to explore these changes, I looked at titles about pandemics, viruses, and social isolation, as well as a mixture of classic and recent titles, including titles that might be considered popular or genre fiction, and titles that might be considered literary. I deliberately included Australian and international titles in each of these categories as part of contextualising this discussion against Australian book culture and Australian responses to COVID-19, as noted above. Two titles with March/April 2020 publication dates – that is, coinciding with the data collection period – were included in the list. The resulting title selection was intended to be diverse, rather than representative, enabling me to explore trends in engagement with a range of distinct texts on Goodreads. The final title list (ordered by date) is given as Table 1.

In order to measure engagement with these titles, I collated the overall star rating, number of ratings, and number of reviews for each title at weekly intervals. I collated this data for ten weeks beginning 1 April 2020 and ending 4 June 2020. I did this by creating a list of the URLs for the public Goodreads page for each title, and then scraping this information using the program OutWit Hub.

I then obtained qualitative data for three titles: Camus' *The Plague*, Brooks' *Year of Wonders*, and Harper's *The Lost Man*. *The Plague* was selected because, as I discuss before, it was the title that showed the most significant change in reading patterns in quantitative terms over the period of the early COVID-19 lockdown. *Year of Wonders* was selected because of its equally thematically relevant content, and because it offered an Australian-authored point of comparison. I also chose to include *The Lost Man* as a counter-example – a recent and popular title, Australian but successful internationally as well, with no apparent thematic relevance to COVID-19.

I collated all publicly available reviews for each title posted between 1 April 2020 and 9 June 2020. These were collected on 9 June 2020. As Goodreads only makes the 300 most recent reviews from each star rating available, and as there were more than 300 5-star and 4-star reviews for *The Plague* over this period, this meant that this does not represent the entire dataset.[53] I used OutWit Hub to collect the full text and date of reviews, as well as the number of "likes" each review had received. An outline of the total number of reviews collected for each title is in Table 2.

The forms of reception studied for this research are published and made publicly available. However, I recognise that there are still ethical considerations relating to the use of these reviews as data, as reviewers might not anticipate their reviews forming part of academic study.[54] Consequently, I adopt established principles for academic work with Goodreads reviews. The Association of Internet Researchers' ethics guidelines differentiate between information that is publicly available and information sought from closed groups or private online communities.[55] I also draw from the work of Langer and Beckman, which adopts established research ethics used for content analysis (for example, of reader letters in newspapers) in public media.[56] As such, I view these online reviews as public documents but remove identifying information wherever possible.[57] However, since Goodreads reviews are publicly available, I use some direct quotes, paraphrase information as much as possible, and do not link quotes to any specific Goodreads users.[58]

Following leads from other researchers of Goodreads communities, like Driscoll and Rehberg Sedo, I am interested in readers' own articulations of their experiences of reading. My primary focus is on what these articulations suggest about how readers' experiences of these titles have been shaped by COVID-19, but I am likewise interested in how this relates to bigger conversations about the kinds of intimate and social reading practices that take place online, as well as to the long-standing discussions about the relationship between interpretation and experience noted above.

Table 1: Titles selected for quantitative data collection

Author	Title	Date	Nation	Notes about text
Tolstoy	*War and Peace*	1865	Russia	Classic; lengthy project read. (Published as serial 1865–67; first published as novel 1869; first English translation 1899.)
Proust	*Swann's Way*	1913	France	Classic; lengthy project read (Published in French 1913; first English translation 1922.)
Fitzgerald	*The Great Gatsby*	1925	USA	American classic
Huxley	*Brave New World*	1932	England	Dystopia
Camus	*The Plague*	1947	France	Pandemic novel (Published in French 1947; first English translation 1948.)
Orwell	*1984*	1949	England	Dystopia
Tolkien	*The Fellowship of the Ring*	1954	England	Classic fantasy
White	*Voss*	1957	Australia	Miles Franklin Award
Plath	*The Bell Jar*	1963	USA	Identity; mental health
García Márquez	*One Hundred Years of Solitude*	1967	Colombia	Magic realism; family novel; isolation/solitude major theme (Published in Spanish 1967; first English translation 1970.)
King	*The Stand*	1978	USA	Pandemic novel
Atwood	*The Handmaid's Tale*	1985	Canada	Dystopia; adaptation released 2017-present
García Márquez	*Love in the Time of Cholera*	1985	Colombia	Romance; disease major theme (Published in Spanish 1985; first English translation 1988.)
Morrison	*Beloved*	1987	USA	Multi-award winning; Morrison died 2019

Author	Title	Date	Nation	Notes about text
Winton	*Cloudstreet*	1991	Australia	Miles Franklin Award
Wallace	*Infinite Jest*	1996	USA	Lengthy project read
Brooks	*Year of Wonders*	2001	Australia	Pandemic novel
Wright	*Carpentaria*	2006	Australia	Miles Franklin Award
Tartt	*The Goldfinch*	2013	USA	Pulitzer Prize; bestseller across US, UK
Flanagan	*The Narrow Road to the Deep North*	2014	Australia	Booker Prize
Pascoe	*Dark Emu*	2014	Australia	Multiple prizes/ adaptations 2016–2020; history wars controversy 2019–20
Yanagihara	*A Little Life*	2015	USA	Lengthy project read
Saunders	*Lincoln in the Bardo*	2017	USA	Booker Prize
Boochani	*No Friend but the Mountains*	2018	Iran	Victorian Premier's Prize
Dalton	*Boy Swallows Universe*	2018	Australia	Bestseller
Hammer	*Scrublands*	2018	Australia	Crime novel
Harper	*The Lost Man*	2018	Australia	Harper's newest release
Lucashenko	*Too Much Lip*	2018	Australia	Miles Franklin Award
Moriarty	*Nine Perfect Strangers*	2018	Australia	Bestseller; Moriarty's newest release
Owens	*Where the Crawdads Sing*	2018	USA	Top *NY Times* bestseller for 30 weeks in 2019 and 2020
Rooney	*Normal People*	2018	Ireland	TV adaptation released April 2020
Evaristo	*Girl Woman Other*	2019	England	Booker Prize
Simsion	*The Rosie Result*	2019	Australia	Simsion's newest release; final Rosie trilogy novel
Cummins	*American Dirt*	2020	USA	Author identity scandal
Mantel	*The Mirror and the Light*	2020	England	Final Cromwell trilogy novel
King	*If It Bleeds*	2020	USA	Horror novella collection

Table 2: Number of reviews collected

Reviews	*The Plague*	*Year of Wonders*	*The Lost Man*
5 star reviews	300	89	157
4 star reviews	300	132	200
3 star reviews	225	62	67
2 star reviews	44	14	10
1 star reviews	12	2	4
Total reviews collected	881	299	438

The Extent of Engagement

At the start of the data collection period, the selected titles had been collectively rated 16,734,479 times, and reviewed 608,563 times; by the end of this period, the number of ratings had grown by 734,368 (approximately 4.4% of the original figure), and reviews had grown by 43,833 (approximately 7.2%). This growth is shown title-by-title in Table 3. The most-rated titles at the beginning of the period were *The Great Gatsby*, *1984*, *The Fellowship of the Ring*, *Brave New World*, and *The Handmaid's Tale*; and the least-rated were *If It Bleeds* (which was not yet published), *Carpentaria*, *The Mirror and the Light*, *Too Much Lip*, and *Voss*.

Table 3: Increase in ratings and reviews
(actual figures and as percentage of original);
novels about pandemics/disease shaded

Title	New ratings	New reviews	Ratings growth %	Reviews growth %
War and Peace	4874	350	2	3
Swann's Way	1449	127	3	4
The Great Gatsby	87615	1318	2	2
Brave New World	29480	881	2	3
The Plague	12369	1400	9	27
1984	89461	2170	3	3

Title	New ratings	New reviews	Ratings growth %	Reviews growth %
The Fellowship of the Ring	43001	752	2	4
Voss	45	4	2	2
The Bell Jar	13043	699	2	3
One Hundred Years of Solitude	16502	882	2	3
The Stand	11936	936	2	5
The Handmaid's Tale	51226	1975	4	3
Love in the Time of Cholera	10296	833	3	5
Beloved	6775	456	2	4
Cloudstreet	406	30	2	2
Infinite Jest	1427	164	2	2
Year of Wonders	2954	315	2	3
Carpentaria	16	0	2	0
The Goldfinch	20600	1449	3	3
The Narrow Road to the Deep North	784	84	2	1
Dark Emu	684	91	14	11
A Little Life	12541	1750	7	7
Lincoln in the Bardo	3651	429	3	2
No Friend but the Mountains	550	115	18	20
Boy Swallows Universe	4038	351	14	12
Scrublands	1525	123	15	10
The Lost Man	4158	425	9	7
Too Much Lip	323	34	14	13
Nine Perfect Strangers	18149	1290	9	7
Where the Crawdads Sing	120806	8955	19	14
Normal People	83332	6626	42	36
Girl Woman Other	15544	1545	82	61
The Rosie Result	2389	191	12	8
American Dirt	43866	4228	118	70
The Mirror and the Light	6534	1138	535	463
If It Bleeds	12019	1717	42925	11447

Over the ten-week data collection period, the titles which received the most ratings were *Where the Crawdads Sing*, *1984*, *The Great Gatsby*, *Normal People*, and *The Handmaid's Tale*, and the most-reviewed titles were *Where the Crawdads Sing*, *Normal People*, *American Dirt*, *1984*, and *The Handmaid's Tale*. In other words, the books getting the most attention, in these raw figures, comprise a mixture of contemporary international bestsellers (*Normal People*; *Crawdads*) as well as titles with demonstrated popular longevity (*Gatsby*; *1984*; *Handmaid's Tale*). As Beth Driscoll and DeNel Rehberg Sedo have observed, "online reception is intertwined with a book's bestseller status".[59] Owens' *Crawdads* has been a *New York Times* bestseller in 30 weeks since its 2018 publication, while Rooney's *Normal People* combines bestseller status with the buzz generated by a television adaptation released in April 2020. Looking not at the raw number of ratings and reviews but at the percentage increase in both, King's *If It Bleeds* and Mantel's *The Mirror and the Light*, both released in the data collection period, are wildly in front. Both are eagerly anticipated new releases by well-known authors, and both had very few reviews, most shared by readers with Advanced Reading Copies, at the beginning of the data collection period.

Albert Camus' 1947 pandemic novel *The Plague* saw the starkest increase, in relative terms, in reviews during the early COVID-19 lockdown period. Included on crowd-sourced Goodreads lists like "Best Books of the 20th Century" and "Best Books Ever", 1400 of the 6613 reviews *The Plague* has received over Goodreads' entire 14-year history were contributed in the ten-week data collection period – with the total corpus of reviews for *The Plague* increasing by 27% during this time.[60] Ratings of *The Plague* increased by 9% over the period. By contrast, reviews for *all* other titles in the dataset published in 2013 or earlier increased by at most 5% – and both of the pre-2013 titles that saw a 5% increase in reviews, King's 1978 *The Stand* and García Márquez' 1985 *Love in the Time of Cholera*, were also included in the dataset for their thematically relevant content.

The final way of breaking down this data that I want to consider before moving on to discuss the qualitative results is the ratio between ratings and reviews. Table 4 shows the number of ratings per review as at 1 April, and the same ratio for the period of data collection.

**Table 4: Number of ratings per review;
novels about pandemics/disease shaded**

Title	Ratings/reviews 1 April	Ratings/reviews 1 April – 4 June
War and Peace	24	14
Swann's Way	13	11
The Great Gatsby	56	66
Brave New World	49	33
The Plague	28	9
1984	45	41
The Fellowship of the Ring	108	57
Voss	11	11
The Bell Jar	26	19
One Hundred Years of Solitude	25	19
The Stand	32	13
The Handmaid's Tale	20	26
Love in the Time of Cholera	21	12
Beloved	27	15
Cloudstreet	14	14
Infinite Jest	8	9
Year of Wonders	14	9
Carpentaria	6	N/A
The Goldfinch	12	14
The Narrow Road to the Deep North	8	9
Dark Emu	6	8
A Little Life	7	7
Lincoln in the Bardo	6	9
No Friend but the Mountains	6	5

Title	Ratings/reviews 1 April	Ratings/reviews 1 April – 4 June
Boy Swallows Universe	9	12
Scrublands	8	12
The Lost Man	8	10
Too Much Lip	9	10
Nine Perfect Strangers	10	14
Where the Crawdads Sing	10	13
Normal People	11	13
Girl Woman Other	8	10
The Rosie Result	9	13
American Dirt	6	10
If It Bleeds	2	7
The Mirror and the Light	5	6

The ratio between ratings and reviews is a slightly more complex measure of readers' engagement with books, as it relates at least in broad terms to the extent of contemplation that each individual reading a title and adding it to Goodreads chooses to display on the platform.[61] This is not to say that this gives us a measure of readers' experiences of engaging with these titles prior to reviewing them – explored in more detail in the following section in relation to qualitative discussion of review content – but of the level of time and effort that has gone into showcasing these experiences through Goodreads.[62]

Looking at the dataset as a whole, the average number of ratings per review is 18 (calculated as the mean of all 'ratings/reviews' figures at 1 April). If we look just at the period of data collection, the average number of ratings per review is 16, suggesting that users have overall spent a slightly higher-than-average amount of time showcasing engagement on Goodreads. While this might be reflective of a greater amount of time spent dedicated to reading and/or reflecting on reading during COVID-19 lockdowns, it could also reflect longer-term patterns of engagement with Goodreads – for example, readers 'bulk' adding titles with ratings but not reviews when first setting up accounts.

Indeed, the clearest pattern in these figures is that newer titles tend to have a lower number of ratings per review, that is, their readers have, on the whole, put in more time and effort to showcasing their reading of these titles, whereas the older titles have been rated far more times than they have actually been reviewed. Intuitively, there are several reasons why this might be the case. Most sales and media discussion of a text take place soon after its publication, with marketing, prizes, any attendant scandals, and the resulting public discussion all part of this process. Other cultural events – such as the release of an adaptation – can likewise catalyse sales and discussion. Goodreads' system of ratings and reviews operates as a recommendations engine, and readers might see higher value in reviews of newer texts where popular opinion is not yet formed. Lastly, all readers of, say, *If It Bleeds* who have added it to Goodreads have by virtue of its 2020 publication date read it in the last few months – so their recollections of their experience of the book will be more detailed than those of a book they read twenty years ago and are just adding to Goodreads now.

Looking, again, at pre-2013 titles, there are a wide range of different figures here. The title with by far the highest number of ratings per review at 1 April was *The Fellowship of the Ring* (and this happens to be one of the most rated titles overall, too). By contrast, the titles that readers have usually tended to allocate the most time to publicly discussing are Alexis Wright's *Carpentaria* and David Foster Wallace's *Infinite Jest*. Scholars have argued that Wright's *Carpentaria* is a text that demands reading through "the paradigm of radical uncertainty", in order to foster a "reading practice … that allows *Carpentaria* its difference, its strangeness, and which points to the necessary estrangement of white readers".[63] While this doesn't make for a popular title on Goodreads, with *Carpentaria* among the least rated and reviewed texts considered here, these features tally with the fact that readers who *have* chosen to read and post *Carpentaria* to Goodreads are more likely to write a review – that is, they have tended to allocate more substantial time to consider it. *Infinite Jest* has a reputation for being deeply insular, navel-gazing, and pretentious,[64] and its cultural status is aptly described by Simone Murray as "an all-too-frequently-unread bookshelf marker of aspirations to cultural capital".[65] In other words, there is a perception of a certain type of cultural cred attached to having actually read, and being seen to have read, *Infinite Jest*, which again could be seen as a justification for the high number of reviews compared to ratings.

The four titles related to pandemics sit in the middle of this spectrum, with less time ordinarily accorded to reviewing them than more contemporary or more deeply aspirational books, but readers likely to accord more time to reviewing them than to the overall most popular titles on the site. During the period studied, however, *The Plague* and *Year of Wonders* had the equal lowest number of ratings per review of any pre-2013 titles, corresponding with an increase in the amount of time readers were more likely to spend thinking about them as part of adding them to Goodreads. Indeed, while the majority of pre-2013 titles, including the four related to pandemics, saw the number of ratings per review decrease, by far the most substantial decreases were for *The Plague* and *The Stand* (see Table 5).

These data are complex, and only partially able to illuminate changes in reading habits during COVID-19 lockdowns. However, two key findings emerge from reviewing quantitative levels of engagement on Goodreads with titles relating to pandemics, in comparison with engagement on Goodreads with other titles. Firstly, reported sales spikes in books related to pandemics appear to correlate with readers' engagement with those titles. And secondly, these readers have been more likely than they ordinarily would be to spend time writing reflections on these books for Goodreads.

Table 5: Percentage change in number of ratings per review for pre-2013 titles; novels about pandemics/disease shaded

Title	% change in ratings/reviews
The Plague	-68
The Stand	-59
The Fellowship of the Ring	-47
Beloved	-44
Love in the Time of Cholera	-43
War and Peace	-42
Year of Wonders	-36
Brave New World	-33
The Bell Jar	-27
One Hundred Years of Solitude	-24
Swann's Way	-15
1984	-9
Voss	0
Cloudstreet	0
Infinite Jest	13
The Great Gatsby	18
The Handmaid's Tale	30
Carpentaria	N/A

Overlapping Experiences of Reading and COVID-19 Lockdowns

As well as analysing in quantitative terms patterns in engagement with books on Goodreads during COVID-19 lockdowns, I was interested in exploring the specific nature of that engagement: readers' experiences of specific titles and how this overlapped with their experiences of COVID-19. For the reasons discussed above, the titles chosen for this analysis were *The Plague*, *Year of Wonders*, and *The Lost Man*.

I sorted reviews of these three titles according to language, and for practical reasons I only consider the English language reviews in my analysis. Of the three titles, *The Plague* had the largest number of multilingual reviews, unsurprising for an originally French-language, highly translated classic. The initial corpus of 881 reviews of *The Plague* comprised 550 English-language reviews (62%), with reviews in 23 additional languages as well – the most prominent were Spanish (94), Dutch (32), Arabic (30), French (28), Portuguese (23), Italian (20) and Persian (20). 189 (or 35%) of the English-language reviews of *The Plague* explicitly mention "covid" or "coronavirus". 292 of *Year of Wonders'* initial corpus of 299 reviews were in English (98%), with five in Italian, one in Spanish, and one in Russian. 68 (or 23%) of the English-language reviews of *Year of Wonders* explicitly mention "covid" or "coronavirus". As a point of contrast, I was also looking at reviews of *The Lost Man*, a recent release with no obvious specific relevance to COVID-19. Of the 438 reviews initially collected, 416 were in English (95%), with single-digit reviews in eight other languages. This corpus contained only five specific mentions of "covid" or "coronavirus"; about 1% of reviews.

I collated every explicit mention of "covid" or "coronavirus" in these reviews, and then coded these mentions. The codes align with the focus of this research, which is the nexus of experiences of reading and experiences of COVID-19, and they were devised following a preliminary read-through of the dataset to determine prominent recurring themes. I applied codes to the sentence which explicitly mentioned "covid" or "coronavirus"; where a code could not be inferred from the sentence, I also took into account the sentences on either side. Where "covid" or "coronavirus" appear twice in a sentence, I only coded once. In order to try and ensure that the codes had been consistently applied, I applied these codes to each review, re-applied the codes without looking at the first process of coding, and then compared and reconciled the small number of discrepancies.

I selected this method to enable me to home in on discussions of the relationship between experiences of COVID-19 and experiences of reading (although I acknowledge that this approach captures only explicit mentions of the pandemic). As discussed in the setting up of this essay, my focus is primarily on the way that these experiences of COVID-19 and of reading are understood by readers to intersect with one another, with a secondary focus on the way that this intersection is articulated in online discussions about reading. De Certeau cautions that "it is always good to remind ourselves that we mustn't take people for fools" (1984: 176), and in adopting this approach I am following the prompts of the Goodreads readers themselves in order to identify where experiences of COVID-19 are most relevant to their discussions of these books.

A list of the codes and a breakdown of how they were applied to reviews of the three titles is included in Table 6. As noted above, while both my research focus and the theoretical work discussed above inform the focus of these codes, the specific codes themselves were iteratively developed through a close reading of reviewers' descriptions of the relationship between experiences of COVID-19 and experiences of reading each title. They are therefore to be taken as interpretive of the dataset in and of themselves, as suggestive of the range of different kinds of descriptions reviewers give of this relationship. Below, I offer some further interpretation of the range of responses collected under each of the codes.

As the descriptive titles I have given to these codes suggest, two relate very specifically to explicit discussions of overlapping experience – "COVID-19 affected the reading experience" and "Reading the book affected or informed the reader's experience of COVID-19". One relates to the influence of COVID-19 on selection: specific mentions of whether or how "COVID-19 prompted the decision to read the book".

The next code, broken into subgroups, has an explicit interpretive edge – reviews in this category make a "Direct comparison between

COVID-19 and the content of the book" – but, as close examination of the reviews below reveals, these interpretations are based on a wide range of reading experiences, including emotional, social, and cognitive responses to the texts.

There are separate codes for mentions of COVID-19 without an explicit connection between COVID-19 and the book being made by the reader, and for the specific opinion that "the book predicted COVID-19"; lastly, two reviews (both discussed below) have also been coded as "Other", as none of these codes were applicable.

Table 6: Codes applied to *The Plague, Year of Wonders,* and *The Lost Man*

Code	Secondary code	*The Plague*	*Year of Wonders*	*The Lost Man*
COVID-19 affected the reading experience		43 (23%)	14 (21%)	0
Reading the book affected or informed the reader's experience of COVID-19		19 (10%)	5 (7%)	1 (20%)
COVID-19 prompted the decision to read the book		20 (11%)	5 (7%)	0
Direct comparison between COVID-19 and the content of the book	Relevance	25 (13%)	21 (31%)	0
	Irrelevance	3 (2%)	1 (1%)	0
	Similarities	55 (29%)	16 (24%)	4 (80%)
	Dissimilarity	7 (4%)	2 (3%)	0
Reader does not make explicit a connection between COVID-19 and the book (but both are mentioned)		10 (5%)	4 (6%)	0
The book predicted COVID-19		5 (3%)	0	0
Other		2 (1%)	0	0
Total		189	68	5

The Lost Man has not been considered in the discussions below, as the data collected were not substantial enough to warrant direct comparison to *The Plague* or *Year of Wonders*. One reviewer of *The Lost Man* joked that "Hopefully my Groundhog day of COVID-19 experience so far is because I took so long to finish this book" – the joke being a deliberately inaccurate portrayal of the effect of their experience of reading the book on their experience of the COVID-19 lockdown. The other four described similarities between depictions of isolation and loneliness in the novel, and feelings of isolation experienced during the pandemic.

COVID-19 Affected the Reading Experience

The first of these codes relates to how COVID-19 directly impacted the experience of reading *The Plague* or *Year of Wonders*. This code accounts for 23% (N=43) of mentions of COVID-19 in reviews of *The Plague*, and 21% (N=14) of mentions of COVID-19 in reviews of *Year of Wonders*.

Reviews in this category include a range of evaluative descriptions of the experience as "interesting" or "fascinating", as well as multiple discussions of the "relatable" nature of the text as a result of this reading context. These speak directly to existing framings of reading on Goodreads as both forming part of recommendation culture, and of "intimate" experiences with both social and emotional components.[66]

In a small number of these reviews readers engaged in more elaborate reflection on their experiences of these texts. These include lengthy descriptions of strong emotional and social responses to the each of the novels, contextualised in relation to readers' specific experiences of the pandemic and its own emotional and social effects. An exemplary reader writing in this mode comments that:

> In the context of COVID-19, all the meditations and perspectives on separation and hope had a unique weight--reading it almost felt like a type of mourning, allowing me to join in with the

communal suffering that I am at once separate from and yet united to while in self-isolation.

Other reviews combine discussion of their experiences with cognitive interpretative strategies. One such reader explains that "Reading this in the midst of the pandemic COVID-19, I found the narration to be a profound social commentary". However, as other readers note, experiences of COVID-19 also overshadow the established allegorical interpretation of *The Plague*:

> I completely failed to realise that this book was an allegory on the Nazi occupation of France. Reading it in the time of Covid-19, I was quite happy to compare the characters' responses with those of us here today. In that regard Camus perfectly captures those feelings of isolation and suspension we've got to know this year. The narrative of human behaviour and the wide-ranging reactions to the escalating crisis and the eventual emergence from lockdown could have been written today about coronavirus, which leads the reader away from the apparent sub-narrative of how the French people reacted to being ruled by the Germans during the occupation in WW2.

As these examples demonstrate, for these readers, the re-contextualising of *The Plague* that occurs as a result of reading it during a COVID-19 lockdown effectively decouples it from its historical context. This occurs even for some readers who are aware of this context and of established readings of the novel. These two example readers, both of whom are aware of or have sought out and deliberately invoke "acceptable" (per Fish) established interpretations of the text, both connect this directly to their personal experiences of COVID-19, with the first example in particular drawing on their emotional responses to both the pandemic and the novel.

Reading the Book Affected or Informed the Reader's Experience of COVID-19

A number of readers of *The Plague* and *Year of Wonders* also described the effects of their reading on their experiences of or responses to COVID-19. This code accounts for 10% (N=19) of mentions of COVID-19 in reviews of *The Plague*, and 7% (N=5) of mentions of COVID-19 in reviews of *Year of Wonders*.

Reviews that are part of this category describe specific learning experiences which were seen to be helpful or positive, both factual and emotional, ultimately tying in directly with framings of reading as offering readers "bibliotherapy", as discussed above.

One reader, for example, describes how "I read this as a way of learning how other generations of people have dealt with a plague in light of Covid 19". For this reader, the historical fiction *Year of Wonders* might contain information about possible responses to the current situation. Other readers describe how reading *The Plague* "was like being given the language to describe what I, myself, am experiencing", or suggest that:

> Despite the millions of words that have been and will be written on the various aspects of Covid-19, to understand the state of the human condition in a pandemic, we return to a novel published over 70 years ago.

Each reveals readers' experiences of *The Plague* offering them access to models for personal, emotional responses and empathetic understanding of others' responses that inform and have the potential to guide their experiences of COVID-19.

The inverse of these responses is a small number of reviews in which readers joke about learning about the plague putting their experiences of COVID-19 into perspective. One comments that "It made me very grateful that the coronavirus doesn't cause bleeding boils, so at least there's that", while another slightly bizarrely berates other possible readers looking to emulate the town of Oran's responses to the plague:

How many idiots are going to read this book and then start Zoom conference war rooms with their boring buddies trying to figure out how to lead their communities through the COVID-19 crisis? Just go back to playing video games and leave everyone alone you nerds.

As with discussion of the effect of COVID-19 on the reader's experience, these responses share many of the hallmarks of other reader discussions on Goodreads, offering social and empathetic experiences in the form of connections to "other generations of people" or to "the human condition" and offering informational experiences – "learning", "the language to describe" and "understand". The joking responses, although less earnest in their register, likewise exhibit well-acknowledged features of contemporary book-talk. As Collins notes in his discussion of book-talk on Oprah, "talking the talk of reading literary books … [comprises] rocketing back and forth between reverence for the classic and ironic undercutting of any seriousness".[67] This is encapsulated by the reader of *The Plague* who simultaneously jokes about the COVID-19 context for their reading, while also demonstrating their understanding of the novel's key plot points.

COVID-19 Prompted the Decision to Read the Book

11% (N=20) of mentions of COVID-19 in reviews of *The Plague* and 7% (N=5) of mentions in reviews of *Year of Wonders* explained that their motivation for reading the book was a direct response to the current pandemic situation. Such reviews of *The Plague* ranged from direct statements of fact, to situational descriptions – "Someone sent me a quote from this book at the start of the COVID-19 pandemic and I found myself irresistibly drawn to read this" – to tongue-in-cheek quips. For example, one reader writes:

CORONAVIRUS; Oh good, now I've got your attention. I figured I'd go ahead and mention what's on everyone's minds and what was the obvious reason I chose now to be the moment that I'd pick up this book that's been sitting on my shelf for at least a year.

By contrast, such mentions of reading *Year of Wonders* tended to be relatively direct statements (with one joking rhetorical question: "Who but a crazy woman would read a novel about The Plague during the Covid19 pandemic? Me, I guess"). Further, two reviewers of *Year of Wonders* (included under other codes, as this was not their primary focus) mentioned that reading the book was "random" or "coincidental" despite the relevance of the subject matter. The differences in these responses showcases a perception that anyone reading *The Plague* during the lockdown would by necessity be doing so in response to COVID-19; whereas this was a major but not the *only* reason for reading the less canonical (and also less obviously titled) *Year of Wonders.*

Other Direct Comparison between COVID-19 and the Content of the Book

The majority of other mentions of COVID-19 offered direct comparisons between the content of the novels, and the current pandemic situation. Sub-categories under this code included discussion of relevance; irrelevance; similarities; and dissimilarity. Readers of *The Plague* and *Year of Wonders* were interested in both relevance and similarities. 13% (N=25) of mentions of COVID-19 in reviews of *The Plague* and 31% (N=21) of mentions of COVID-19 in reviews of *Year of Wonders* predominantly focused on the relevance of these texts to the pandemic, while 29% (N=55) of mentions of COVID-19 in reviews of *The Plague* and 24% (N=16) of mentions of COVID-19 in reviews of *Year of Wonders* discuss similarities between the book and the current situation. Reviewers of *Year of Wonders* within the sample were far more likely than reviewers of *The Plague* to describe it as relevant to the current situation – perhaps a result of *Year of Wonders*' less complicated generic status as a work of historical fiction. Discussions of the reverse, irrelevance and dissimilarity, were also present in reviews of each title, although at a much lower rate. Irrelevance accounted for 2% (N=3) of the sample for *The Plague* and 1% (N=1) of the sample for *Year of Wonders*, and dissimilarity 4% (N=7) of the sample for *The Plague* and 3% (N=2) of the sample for *Year of Wonders*.

The key difference between codes "relevance" and "similarities" was a sense of "use-value" present in the idea of relevance – similarities were often also discussed in reviews coded under this category, but this additional sense of usefulness or productiveness in the reading of the text was also conveyed. Relevance therefore might be as simple as inclusions of descriptions of either novel as "timely" or "appropriate". The opposite was irrelevance, for example, "The death rate back then was so much higher than for today's coronavirus, and today's world is so much more interconnected, I'm not sure there are too many useful parallels to be drawn". By contrast, reviews coded at similarities very frequently included specific phrases such as "parallels include …", with the opposite, dissimilarities, including statements such as "I read it while in the midst of the COVID-19 quarantine and it makes that look like a walk through the park".

In an interesting example of the kinds of sociability that Goodreads reviews invoke, the code of "relevance" also included exhortations to other readers to read each novel:

> Like reading and playing Renaissance lute from French tablature of its day, "Year of Wonders" is like touching the fingertips of those who came before us by centuries, long dead, from a world we cannot visit, but who felt and experienced and loved exactly as we do. If you are living through COVID-19 and have never experienced another pandemic, and especially if you're a Millennial, this is the book for you.

This example draws on the relevance of the novel as part of its warm recommendation towards other readers. It invokes a specific audience or community for this review – explicitly framed as Millennials or alternatively people who have not previously experienced a pandemic. Importantly, it also ventures this recommendation on the book's ability to facilitate strong, intimate connections with other individuals – "like touching the fingertips of those who came before us" – through shared emotional experiences of feeling and loving. In other words, as I note above, while the prominence of "direct comparisons" suggests a predominantly interpretive framework for understanding the relationship between the two, readers' experiences directly infuse their discussions, and do so in ways that are directly congruous with framings of Goodreads as a space for social and emotional experiences.

Other Codes

The two remaining codes are "Reader does not make explicit a connection between COVID-19 and the book (but both are mentioned)" and "The book predicted COVID-19". Both are applicable to a relatively small number of reviews compared to the other codes discussed thus far. 5% (N=10) of mentions of COVID-19 in reviews of *The Plague* and 6% (N=4) of mentions of COVID-19 in reviews of *Year of Wonders* do not make explicit a connection between COVID-19 and the book. 3% (N=5) of mentions of COVID-19 in reviews of *The Plague* and no reviews of *Year of Wonders* directly state that the book predicted COVID-19; lastly, 1% (N=2) of reviews of *The Plague* and no reviews of *Year of Wonders* are in the final category of "Other".

Reviews categorised under the first of these codes contain primarily direct statements of fact ("I read this book during the April-May, 2020 coronavirus pandemic"). They also include several messages addressed to other readers that do not engage with the book, for example:

> COVID-19 is ravaging the world at this present moment. I do not know where you are or what has already happened to you. But I do hope in these troubled times that you are safe, that you have good health, and more importantly that you feel the warmth

of humanity who has already done so much for each other. We are getting through this.

Like the reviews quoted above, this invokes a warm, intimate connection with an imagined other person. This connection is deeply personal in its direct second-person address to the reader of the review. For this reviewer, however, the connection is not framed through the shared experience of reading, but through an assumed shared experience of COVID-19. Reading *The Plague* might be what has driven the initial moment of contact between the author and implied reader of this review, but the author takes it as given that there is another shared life experience between the two, and this is their primary focus.

I chose to separately code reviews which describe *The Plague* as "prescient" or "uncanny" in its "predictions" of COVID-19. Although this code applies only to a small number of reviews, the presence of these reviews does suggest that meaning of the text is shifting, as a result of readers' new lived experiences of the pandemic. This is also one of the codes which showcases reviewers' sense of humour: "Wholly unoriginal – I am of course referring to Covid-19 and our collective response to it/'the absurd', which obviously plagiarize the 1947 fiction". This ties in directly with the combination of nods to authoritative interpretations and playful resistance of them, discussed above in relation to Collins' work on literary fiction. It is useful to note too, however, that preliminary research into responses to COVID-19 suggests that play and playfulness are important and transformative coping mechanisms, and these certainly feature in the reviews explored.[68]

Finally, despite my best efforts to code all of the reviews, I ended up applying the code "Other" to two reviews of *The Plague*. The first is aspirational and celebratory: "Extra star just for that last chapter on celebrations, contemplations when the plague ends and city doors open. How I wish that day comes soon in our lives and we survive this dirty Covid!". The second opines that "Camus would be delighted to see how popular his novel has become during the COVID-19 lockdown".

Conclusion

Goodreads data are useful and interesting to researchers exploring contemporary book culture. Unlike sales data, they show us not just what people are *buying* but what people are *reading*; what they are thinking about, deciding to read, and deciding is worthy of particular kinds of attention. While a partial record of contemporary book culture, Goodreads is consequently an important site to readers, authors, and researchers in enabling and shaping the public discussion of books in the twenty-first century. In the context of COVID-19, Goodreads is particularly important because it continued to perform this function when so many of the other social apparatus of book culture – such as book clubs, festivals, and author talks – were suspended.

In the broader cultural scene, one of the most significant conversations taking place during the COVID-19 lockdown period was about understanding and promoting the value of the arts to our communities. Again, at a time when so much of the social apparatus that we rely on was stripped away, the basic components of cultural activities like reading, watching television or films, or listening to music remained accessible.

Readers read for many purposes: for education or enlightenment, for social connection, for emotional release. Goodreads is likewise multi-faceted – recommendation engine, social media, public platform, space for personal exploration. Exploring how readers used Goodreads during a ten-week period of the COVID-19 lockdown in 2020 demonstrates that COVID-19 directly informed readers' experiences of books about pandemics – and that these books were sought out and read in direct response to the pandemic. Readers framed their experiences of COVID-19 through their readings of books about pandemics, as well as seeing their experiences and interpretations of these books as directly shaped by COVID-19. These responses ranged from earnest to playful, from intellectual to deeply emotional, and from straightforward to completely bizarre. Components of practices like bibliotherapy came through strongly in some of these responses, suggesting wellbeing as promoted by reading as a potential avenue for more directed exploration in future research. For the book industry, both Australian and international, the relevance of reading during this period should be heartening. The diverse experiences of reading articulated on sites like Goodreads could help inform specific articulations of the value of reading.

This is not, however, to say that readers' discussions of COVID-19 on Goodreads were necessarily greatly different from other discussions of reading on Goodreads. The reviews analysed in this essay demonstrated many of the hallmarks of reader discussion noted by other scholars, including the kinds of evaluative responses typical to recommendation culture, the social and emotional responses typical to practices of intimacy in online reading, and the bent towards simultaneously acknowledging and undercutting existing authoritative interpretations of a literary text, in particular.

But while the practices of reading haven't drastically shifted, if we understand a text's meaning to be rooted in its reception – that is, to return to Chartier, "a text does not exist except for a reader who gives it signification" – then, based on my analysis of these reviews, I would argue that the *meaning* of specific books, like *The Plague* or *Year of Wonders*, has shifted radically at this point in time.[69] Ika Willis notes that "From the structure of human brains and the personal histories of individual readers to the material, economic and social structures which influence the production and distribution of texts, a vast number of interdependent factors are involved in acts of reception".[70] Teasing out the effect of any one such factor is difficult, and COVID-19 has inarguably impacted many, perhaps all, of these factors.

COVID-19 is an event of massive global collective significance. As this essay has shown, it is also thematically resonant with a number of texts that pre-date it. Some readers take these texts to be an expression of these events – the meaning that they get from reading these texts is predetermined by this particular experience. Even in discussion of texts like *The Lost Man*, which thematically have no clear connection to COVID-19, these events are (albeit infrequently) invoked in readers' discussions. By adding an experience that is deeply emotional, communal, and that has directly and massively impacted people's lived experiences, COVID-19 has refashioned the range of possible points of reference outside the text, and in doing so has changed the scope of possible experiences, interpretations, and meanings constructed through readers' encounters with these texts.

Endnotes

1   Outka, Elizabeth, *Viral Modernism: The Influenza Pandemic and Interwar Literature* (New York: Columbia University Press, 2019), 7–8.
2   Ibid., 104.
3   Virginia Woolf, *Mrs Dalloway* (London: Penguin Books, 2000), 4, 116.
4   World Health Organisation, 'Timeline of WHO's Response to COVID-19,' June 29, 2020, https://www.who.int/news-room/detail/29-06-2020-covidtimeline.
5   Prime Minister of Australia, 'Update on Coronavirus Measures,' (Prime Minister of Australia, March 22, 2020), https://www.pm.gov.au/media/update-coronavirus-measures-220320.
6   Katharine Murphy, 'Australian Arts and Culture to Get $250m Rescue Package from Morrison Government,' *The Guardian*, June 24, 2020, https://www.theguardian.com/australia-news/2020/jun/25/australian-arts-and-culture-to-get-250m-rescue-package-from-morrison-government.
7   Ben Eltham, 'Australia's Cultural Sector Is Haemorrhaging Money, but the Federal Government Isn't Interested in Stemming the Flow,' *The Guardian*, May 26, 2020, https://www.theguardian.com/culture/2020/may/26/australias-cultural-sector-is-haemorrhaging-money-but-its-not-the-federal-government-stemming-the-flow.
8   Eltham, 'Australia's Cultural Sector,' 2020; Gina Fairley, 'What the Arts Sector Says about the Fed Government's $250M Relief Package,' ArtsHub, June 25, 2020, https://www.artshub.com.au/news-article/opinions-and-analysis/covid-19/gina-fairley/what-the-arts-sector-says-about-the-fed-governments-250m-relief-package-260620.
9   Hannah Reich, '"The 'Cancellation Apocalypse": How Coronavirus Is Threatening Australian Writers,' *ABC News*, March 29, 2020,

https://www.abc.net.au/news/2020-03-29/coronavirus-covid-19-australian-writers-livelihoods/12093816.

10   Copyright Agency, 'Copyright Agency Releases $375,000 and Brings Forward $1.8m in Cultural Fund Grants in COVID-19 Support,' April 6, 2020, https://www.copyright.com.au/2020/04/covid-19-support-program/.

11   International Publishers Association, 'World Book Day: Authors, Publishers and Booksellers Call for International Support,' April 22, 2020, https://www.internationalpublishers.org/news/971-world-book-day-authors-publishers-and-booksellers-call-for-international-support.

12   Anne Richards, 'Coming Out: Reframing the Public Face of Publishing,' in *The Return of Print? Contemporary Australian Publishing*, ed. Aaron Mannion and Emmett Stinson (Melbourne: Monash University Publishing, 2016), 3.

13   Katie Knibbs, 'The Coronavirus Pandemic Is Changing How People Buy Books,' *Wired*, April 27, 2020, https://www.wired.com/story/coronavirus-book-sales-indie/.

14   Jason Steger, 'Australian Book Industry Faces Strife after Brief Boost in Sales,' *The Sydney Morning Herald*, April 3, 2020, https://www.smh.com.au/culture/books/australian-book-industry-faces-strife-after-brief-boost-in-sales-20200403-p54gvs.html.

15   *Books+Publishing*, 'Australian Bookshops Respond to Covid-19,' March 18, 2020, https://www.booksandpublishing.com.au/articles/2020/03/18/147865/australian-bookshops-respond-to-covid-19/.

16   Elizabeth A. Harris, 'How to Sell Books in 2020: Put Them Near the Toilet Paper,' *The New York Times*, July 22, 2020, https://www.nytimes.com/2020/07/22/books/books-coronavirus-retail-walmart-target-costco.html.

17   ArtsHub, 'Job Cuts Hit Publishing Industry,' April 9, 2020, https://www.artshub.com.au/news-article/news/covid-19/staff-writer/job-cuts-hit-publishing-industry-260178; Steger, 'Australian Book Industry Faces Strife,' 2020.

18   Steger, 'Australian Book Industry Faces Strife.' 2020.

19   Joumana Khatib et al., 'Your Quarantine Reader,' *The New York Times*, March 12, 2020, https://www.nytimes.com/2020/03/12/books/coronavirus-reading.html.

20   Roger Chartier, 'Laborers and Voyagers: From the Text to the Reader'. *Diacritics* 22, no. 2 (1992): 50.

21   Ika Willis, *Reception* (Abingdon: Routledge, 2018), 1.

22   Ibid., 2.

23   Wolfgang Iser, 'The Reading Process: A Phenomenological Approach,' *New Literary History* 3, no. 2 (1972): 279–99.

24   Ibid., 299.

25 Stanley Fish, 'Interpreting the "Variorum",' *Critical Inquiry* 2, no. 3 (1976): 465–85; Stanley Fish, *Is There a Text in This Class? The Authority of Interpretive Communities* (Cambridge MA: Harvard University Press, 1980).

26 Fish, *Is There a Text in This Class*, 355, 354.

27 Michel de Certeau, *The Practice of Everyday Life*, trans. Steven Rendall (Berkeley: University of California Press, 1984), 175.

28 Ibid., 175.

29 Elizabeth Long, 'Women, Reading, and Cultural Authority: Some Implications of the Audience Perspective in Cultural Studies,' *American Quarterly* 38, no. 4 (1986): 603.

30 Ibid., 603.

31 Janice Radway, *A Feeling for Books: The Book-of-the-Month Club, Literary Taste, and Middle-Class Desire* (Chapel Hill: University of North Carolina Press, 1997), 44.

32 Karin Littau, *Theories of Reading: Books, Bodies, and Bibliomania* (Cambridge: Polity Press, 2006).

33 Ibid., 157.

34 Nick Canty, 'Bibliotherapy: Its Processes and Benefits and Application in Clinical and Developmental Settings,' *Logos* 28, no. 3 (2017): 32–33.

35 Ibid., 35, 39.

36 Sara Haslam, Edmund King, and Siobhan Campbell, 'Bibliotherapy: How Reading and Writing Have Been Healing Trauma since World War I,' *The Conversation*, November 15, 2018, http://theconversation. com/bibliotherapy-how-reading-and-writing-have-been-healing-trauma-since-world-war-i-106626.

37 Shelley Hepworth, '95 Books and Counting: Finding Solace in Reading through the Year of Covid,' *The Guardian*, October 2, 2020, https://www. theguardian.com/books/2020/oct/03/take-me-away-from-all-this-how-books-save-our-souls-during-difficult-times.

38 Simone Murray, *The Digital Literary Sphere: Reading, Writing, and Selling Books in the Internet Era* (Baltimore: Johns Hopkins University Press, 2018), 142.

39 Steph Coelho, 'The Current State and Future of Goodreads' Book Riot, November 7, 2019, https://bookriot.com/future-of-goodreads/; Goodreads, 'About Goodreads,' n.d., https://www.goodreads.com/about/ us; Statista, 'Number of Registered Members on Goodreads from May 2011 to July 2019', 2019, https://www.statista.com/statistics/252986/ number-of-registered-members-on-goodreadscom/.

40 Bronwen Thomas, *Literature and Social Media* (Abingdon: Routledge, 2020), 77.

41 Corinna Norrick-Rühl, '(Furniture) Books and Book Furniture as Markers of Authority,' *TXT* 1 (2016): 6.

42 Beth Driscoll and DeNel Rehberg Sedo, 'Faraway, So Close: Seeing the Intimacy in Goodreads Reviews,' *Qualitative Inquiry* 25, no. 3 (2019): 248–59; Beth Driscoll and DeNel Rehberg Sedo, 'The Transnational Reception of Bestselling Books between Canada and Australia,' *Global Media and Communication* 16, no. 2 (2020): 243–58; Lisa Nakamura, '"Words with Friends": Socially Networked Reading on Goodreads,' *PMLA* 128, no. 1 (2013): 238–43.

43 Simone Murray, *The Digital Literary Sphere: Reading, Writing, and Selling Books in the Internet Era* (Baltimore: Johns Hopkins University Press, 2018); see also Simone Murray and Millicent Weber, '"Live and Local?": The Significance of Digital Media for Writers' Festivals,' *Convergence* 23, no. 1 (2017): 61–78; and Millicent Weber and Mark Davis, 'Feminism in the Troll Space: Clementine Ford's Fight Like a Girl, Social Media, and the Networked Book,' *Feminist Media Studies* 20, no. 7 (2020): 944–65.

44 For an overview and assessment of this debate, see N Katherine Hayles, 'How We Read: Close, Hyper, Machine,' *ADE Bulletin* 150 (2010): 62–79.

45 Thomas, *Literature and Social Media*, 119.

46 Jim Collins, *Bring on the Books for Everybody: How Literary Culture Became Popular Culture* (Durham: Duke University Press, 2010), 3.

47 Ibid., 3.

48 Driscoll and Rehberg Sedo, 'Faraway So Close.' 257.

49 Ibid., 252.

50 Ibid., 252.

51 Joumana Khatib et al., 'Your Quarantine Reader,' *The New York Times*, March 12, 2020, https://www.nytimes.com/2020/03/12/books/coronavirus-reading.html.

52 Lois Beckett, 'A Dystopian Reading List: Books to Enjoy While in Quarantine,' *The Guardian*, March 16, 2020, http://www.theguardian.com/books/2020/mar/15/books-to-read-while-quarantined-coronavirus.

53 This feature of Goodreads also means that it is unfortunately not possible to take a sample of reviews from directly before the COVID-19 lockdown for comparison. Likewise, it is not possible to use Goodreads to track the number of ratings and reviews given to a title for a particular timeframe outside of this '300 newest' (or '300 oldest' or '300 top') posts.

54 The approach outlined here was approved by the ANU Human Research Ethics Committee, protocol 2020/355.

55 aline shakti franzke et al., 'Internet Research: Ethical Guidelines 3.0,' (Association of Internet Researchers, 2020), https://aoir.org/ethics/.

56 Roy Langer and Suzanne C. Beckmann, 'Sensitive Research Topics: Netnography Revisited,' *Qualitative Market Research* 8, no. 2 (2005): 189–203.

57 Lisa Sugiura, Rosemary Wiles, and Catherine Pope, 'Ethical Challenges in Online Research: Public/Private Perceptions,' *Research Ethics* 13, no. 3–4 (2017): 184–99; Rose Wiles and Janet Boddy, 'Introduction to the Special Issue: Research Ethics in Challenging Contexts,' *Methodological Innovations Online* 8, no. 2 (2013): 1–5.

58 Nicholas Hookway, '"Entering the Blogosphere": Some Strategies for Using Blogs in Social Research,' *Qualitative Research* 8, no. 1 (2008): 91–113; James M. Hudson and Amy Bruckman, '"Go Away": Participant Objections to Being Studied and the Ethics of Chatroom Research,' *The Information Society* 20, no. 2 (2004): 127–39.

59 Driscoll and Rehberg Sedo, 'The Transnational Reception of Bestselling Books,' 252.

60 Available at https://www.goodreads.com/list/show/6.Best_Books_of_ the_20th_Century and https://www.goodreads.com/list/show/1.Best_ Books_Ever.

61 Information about the length of reviews would also add greatly to this metric; unfortunately, without having access to the full-text of all reviews, this blunter measurement is substituted.

62 As the figures given correspond to the number of ratings divided by the number of reviews, it is useful to explicitly note that a lower number corresponds to a higher number of reviews compared to ratings – that is, the lower the number, the greater the time and effort spent by readers in showcasing their engagement with a title on Goodreads.

63 Alison Ravenscroft, 'Dreaming of Others: Carpentaria and Its Critics,' *Cultural Studies Review* 16, no. 2 (2010): 197–8.

64 See, for example, Dana Schwartz, 'What I Learned From Pretending to Be a Pretentious Lit Bro for 5 Years,' *LitHub*, November 7, 2019, https:// lithub.com/what-i-learned-from-pretending-to-be-a-pretentious-lit-bro-for-5-years/.

65 Simone Murray, *The Digital Literary Sphere: Reading, Writing, and Selling Books in the Internet Era* (Baltimore: Johns Hopkins University Press, 2018), 159.

66 See discussion above, particularly in relation to Driscoll and Rehberg Sedo, 'Faraway, So Close,' and Norrick-Rühl, '(Furniture) Books and Book Furniture'.

67   Collins, *Bring on the Books*, 98.
68   Karen Alison Tonkin and Julia Whitaker, 'Play and Playfulness for Health and Wellbeing: A Panacea for Mitigating the Impact of Coronavirus (COVID 19),' SSRN Scholarly Paper (Rochester, NY: Social Science Research Network, May 5, 2020), https://doi.org/10.2139/ssrn.3584412.
69   Chartier, 'Laborers and Voyagers,' 50.
70   Willis, *Reception*, 7.

Bibliography

Arts Hub. 'Job Cuts Hit Publishing Industry,' 9 April, 2020. https://www.artshub.com.au/news-article/news/covid-19/staff-writer/job-cuts-hit-publishing-industry-260178.

Beckett, Lois. 'A Dystopian Reading List: Books to Enjoy While in Quarantine,' *The Guardian*, 16 March, 2020. http://www.theguardian.com/books/2020/mar/15/books-to-read-while-quarantined-coronavirus.

Books+Publishing. 'Australian Bookshops Respond to Covid-19,' 18 March, 2020. https://www.booksandpublishing.com.au/articles/2020/03/18/147865/australian-bookshops-respond-to-covid-19/.

Canty, Nick. 'Bibliotherapy: Its Processes and Benefits and Application in Clinical and Developmental Settings,' *Logos* 28, no. 3 (2017): 32–40.

Chartier, Roger. 'Laborers and Voyagers: From the Text to the Reader,' *Diacritics* 22, no. 2 (1992): 49–61.

Coelho, Steph. 'The Current State and Future of Goodreads,' Book Riot, 7 November, 2019. https://bookriot.com/future-of-goodreads/.

Collins, Jim. *Bring on the Books for Everybody: How Literary Culture Became Popular Culture*. Durham: Duke University Press, 2010.

Copyright Agency. 'Copyright Agency Releases $375,000 and Brings Forward $1.8m in Cultural Fund Grants in COVID-19 Support,' 6 April, 2020. https://www.copyright.com.au/2020/04/covid-19-support-program/.

de Certeau, Michel. *The Practice of Everyday Life*. Translated by Steven Rendall. Berkeley: University of California Press, 1984.

Driscoll, Beth, and DeNel Rehberg Sedo. 'Faraway, So Close: Seeing the Intimacy in Goodreads Reviews,' *Qualitative Inquiry* 25, no. 3 (2019): 248–59.

Driscoll, Beth, and DeNel Rehberg Sedo. 'The Transnational Reception of Bestselling Books between Canada and Australia,' *Global Media and Communication* 16, no. 2 (2020): 243–58.

Eltham, Ben. 'Australia's Cultural Sector Is Haemorrhaging Money, but the Federal Government Isn't Interested in Stemming the Flow,' *The Guardian*, 26 May, 2020. https://www.theguardian.com/culture/2020/may/26/australias-cultural-sector-is-haemorrhaging-money-but-its-not-the-federal-government-stemming-the-flow.

Fairley, Gina. 'What the Arts Sector Says about the Fed Government's $250M Relief Package,' *ArtsHub*, 25 June, 2020. https://www.artshub.com.au/news-article/opinions-and-analysis/covid-19/gina-fairley/what-the-arts-sector-says-about-the-fed-governments-250m-relief-package-260620.

Fish, Stanley. 'Interpreting the "Variorum",' *Critical Inquiry* 2, no. 3 (1976): 465–85.

Fish, Stanley. *Is There a Text in This Class? The Authority of Interpretive Communities*. Cambridge MA: Harvard University Press, 1980.

Flood, Alison. 'Publishers Report Sales Boom in Novels about Fictional Epidemics,' *The Guardian*, 5 March, 2020. http://www.theguardian.com/books/2020/mar/05/publishers-report-sales-boom-in-novels-about-fictional-epidemics-camus-the-plague-dean-koontz.

franzke, aline shakti, Anja Bechmann, Michael Zimmer, Charles M Ess, and Association of Internet Researchers. 'Internet Research: Ethical Guidelines 3.0,' Association of Internet Researchers, 2020. https://aoir.org/ethics/.

Goodreads. 'About Goodreads,' n.d. https://www.goodreads.com/about/us.

Harris, Elizabeth A. 'How to Sell Books in 2020: Put Them Near the Toilet Paper,' *The New York Times*, 22 July, 2020. https://www.nytimes.com/2020/07/22/books/books-coronavirus-retail-walmart-target-costco.html.

Haslam, Sara, Edmund King, and Siobhan Campbell. 'Bibliotherapy: How Reading and Writing Have Been Healing Trauma since World War I,' *The Conversation*, 15 November, 2018. http://theconversation.com/bibliotherapy-how-reading-and-writing-have-been-healing-trauma-since-world-war-i-106626.

Hayles, N Katherine. 'How We Read: Close, Hyper, Machine,' *ADE Bulletin* 150 (2010): 62–79.

Hepworth, Shelley. '95 Books and Counting: Finding Solace in Reading through the Year of Covid,' *The Guardian*, 2 October, 2020. https://www.theguardian.com/books/2020/oct/03/take-me-away-from-all-this-how-books-save-our-souls-during-difficult-times.

Hookway, Nicholas. '"Entering the Blogosphere": Some Strategies for Using Blogs in Social Research,' *Qualitative Research* 8, no. 1 (2008): 91–113.

Hudson, James M., and Amy Bruckman. '"Go Away": Participant Objections to Being Studied and the Ethics of Chatroom Research,' *The Information Society* 20, no. 2 (2004): 127–39.

International Publishers Association. 'World Book Day: Authors, Publishers and Booksellers Call for International Support,' International Publishers Association, 22 April, 2020. https://www.internationalpublishers.org/news/971-world-book-day-authors-publishers-and-booksellers-call-for-international-support.

Iser, Wolfgang. 'The Reading Process: A Phenomenological Approach,' *New Literary History* 3, no. 2 (1972): 279–99.

Khatib, Joumana, Concepción de León, Tammy Tarng, and Alexandra Alter. 'Your Quarantine Reader,' *The New York Times*, 12 March, 2020. https://www.nytimes.com/2020/03/12/books/coronavirus-reading.html.

Knibbs, Katie. 'The Coronavirus Pandemic Is Changing How People Buy Books,' *Wired*, 27 April, 2020. https://www.wired.com/story/coronavirus-book-sales-indie/.

Langer, Roy, and Suzanne C. Beckmann. 'Sensitive Research Topics: Netnography Revisited,' *Qualitative Market Research* 8, no. 2 (2005): 189–203.

Littau, Karin. *Theories of Reading: Books, Bodies, and Bibliomania.* Cambridge: Polity Press, 2006.

Long, Elizabeth. 'Women, Reading, and Cultural Authority: Some Implications of the Audience Perspective in Cultural Studies,' *American Quarterly* 38, no. 4 (1986): 591–612.

Murphy, Katharine. 'Australian Arts and Culture to Get $250m Rescue Package from Morrison Government,' *The Guardian*, 24 June, 2020. https://www.theguardian.com/australia-news/2020/jun/25/australian-arts-and-culture-to-get-250m-rescue-package-from-morrison-government.

Murray, Simone. *The Digital Literary Sphere: Reading, Writing, and Selling Books in the Internet Era.* Baltimore: Johns Hopkins University Press, 2018.

Murray, Simone, and Millicent Weber. '"Live and Local"? The Significance of Digital Media for Writers' Festivals,' *Convergence* 23, no. 1 (2017): 61–78.

Nakamura, Lisa. '"Words with Friends": Socially Networked Reading on Goodreads,' *PMLA* 128, no. 1 (2013): 238–43.

Norrick-Rühl, Corinna. '(Furniture) Books and Book Furniture as Markers of Authority,' *TXT* 1 (2016): 3–8.

Outka, Elizabeth. *Viral Modernism: The Influenza Pandemic and Interwar Literature.* New York: Columbia University Press, 2019.

Prime Minister of Australia. 'Update on Coronavirus Measures,' Prime Minister of Australia, 22 March, 2020. https://www.pm.gov.au/media/update-coronavirus-measures-220320.

Radway, Janice. *A Feeling for Books: The Book-of-the-Month Club, Literary Taste, and Middle-Class Desire.* Chapel Hill: University of North Carolina Press, 1997.

Ravenscroft, Alison. 'Dreaming of Others: Carpentaria and Its Critics,' *Cultural Studies Review* 16, no. 2 (2010): 194–224.

Reich, Hannah. 'The "Cancellation Apocalypse": How Coronavirus Is Threatening Australian Writers,' *ABC News*, 29 March, 2020. https://www.abc.net.au/news/2020-03-29/coronavirus-covid-19-australian-writers-livelihoods/12093816.

Richards, Anne. 'Coming Out: Reframing the Public Face of Publishing,' In *The Return of Print? Contemporary Australian Publishing*, edited by Aaron Mannion and Emmett Stinson, 163–87. Melbourne: Monash University Publishing, 2016. Available from https://bridges.monash.edu/articles/monograph/The_Return_of_Print_Contemporary_Australian_Publishing/12821435.

'Roundtable: Publishing and Editing Literary Criticism,' Presented at the Association for the Study of Australian Literature 2020 Virtual Conference, 2 July, 2020.

Schwartz, Dana. 'What I Learned From Pretending to Be a Pretentious Lit Bro for 5 Years,' *LitHub*, 7 November, 2019. https://lithub.com/what-i-learned-from-pretending-to-be-a-pretentious-lit-bro-for-5-years/.

Statista. 'Number of Registered Members on Goodreads from May 2011 to July 2019,' 2019. https://www.statista.com/statistics/252986/number-of-registered-members-on-goodreadscom/.

Steger, Jason. 'Australian Book Industry Faces Strife after Brief Boost in Sales,' *The Sydney Morning Herald*, 3 April, 2020. https://www.smh.com.au/culture/books/australian-book-industry-faces-strife-after-brief-boost-in-sales-20200403-p54gvs.html.

Sugiura, Lisa, Rosemary Wiles, and Catherine Pope. 'Ethical Challenges in Online Research: Public/Private Perceptions,' *Research Ethics* 13, no. 3–4 (2017): 184–99.

Thomas, Bronwen. *Literature and Social Media*. Abingdon: Routledge, 2020.

Tonkin, Karen Alison, and Julia Whitaker. 'Play and Playfulness for Health and Wellbeing: A Panacea for Mitigating the Impact of Coronavirus (COVID 19),' SSRN Scholarly Paper. Rochester, NY: Social Science Research Network, 5 May, 2020. https://doi.org/10.2139/ssrn.3584412.

Weber, Millicent, and Mark Davis. 'Feminism in the Troll Space: Clementine Ford's Fight Like a Girl, Social Media, and the Networked Book,' *Feminist Media Studies* 20, no. 7 (2020): 944–65.

Wiles, Rose, and Janet Boddy. 'Introduction to the Special Issue: Research Ethics in Challenging Contexts,' *Methodological Innovations Online* 8, no. 2 (2013): 1–5.

Willis, Ika. *Reception*. Abingdon: Routledge, 2018.

Woolf, Virginia. *Mrs Dalloway*. London: Penguin Books, 2000.

World Health Organisation. 'Timeline of WHO's Response to COVID-19,' 29 June, 2020. https://www.who.int/news-room/detail/29-06-2020-covidtimeline.

Chapter 3

Goodreads Reviewers
and Affective Fan Labour

Alexandra Dane

According to their company slogan, biblio-centric social networking platform Goodreads offers its users the opportunity to meet their 'next favourite book'.[1] Inherent in this slogan is an acknowledgement of the promotional role that the platform, and therefore its community of amateur reviewers, play in the contemporary publishing industry and the power of word-of-mouth recommendations. At surface level the commercial benefits of Goodreads to publishers, authors and booksellers are clear. However, exploring below the surface reveals a more complex and more complicated structure of beneficence that is dependent on the unpaid affective labour of Goodreads reviewers. In this essay I investigate the ways in which the Goodreads platform and Goodreads reviewers have in some ways unsettled the role of the professional book review, and how the very nature of the post-digital, platformized publishing sector contributes to and perpetuates this unsettling. Drawing on research around digital and affective labour practices, I argue that the work performed by the community of Goodreads reviewers is a form of affective fan labour with roots in both professional reviewing and informal book clubs.

Book reviewing has long occupied a contested space in the literary field. Debates around the function of and audience for book reviews are a constant presence in literary journals[2] and among participants in what is colloquially known as 'book Twitter'.[3] Upon surveying a number of authors, critics and editors in the Australian publishing field for an essay published in *Australian Book Review*, Kerryn Goldsworthy uncovered a diversity of responses to the question of to whom a reviewer or critic has a responsibility.[4] Answers ranged from the author of the title being reviewed, the broader cultural ecology, the work itself, to the reader of the review and the reading public at large. Goldsworthy's research indicates that among book reviewers and literary editors, the importance of the book review in contemporary literary life is rarely underplayed. Scholarly considerations of the role and positionality of the book review commonly arrive at similar conclusions. Claire Squires' exploration of reviewing and reviews in the contemporary Anglophone book market acknowledges the fundamental dual function of the book review, observing that 'the reviewer sits both in literary judgement, but also as a buyer's guide'.[5] Emmett Stinson similarly observes this duality – 'Book reviews straddle a divide between the economic and the "literary" notions of value'[6] – highlighting the role of the reviewer as both an agent of consecration and a cultural intermediary.[7] In both explicit and tacit ways, book reviewers contribute to the establishment and circulation of capital in the contemporary literary field. Prior to the advent of Web 2.0 and the introduction of bibliocentric social media platforms such as Goodreads, reviewing books was almost exclusively a vocational labour practice with clear structures of benefit, value acquisition and remuneration by all associated parties. However, the rise of participatory cultural practice and amateur 'prosumption'[8] has – like in many other cultural sectors – complicated this clear remunerative labour structure.

Following its launch in 2007, Goodreads has grown to become 'the largest site for readers and book recommendations'.[9] Goodreads serves many functions to its users, acting as a bibliocentric social networking platform, a place to catalogue one's personal library and a source for reading recommendations.[10] The 'About' section of the Goodreads website helpfully lists the various activities that one can undertake on the platform, informing users that they can, among other things, see what their friends are reading, access a 'personalized' book recommendation or 'find out if a book is a good fit for you from our community's reviews'.[11] These descriptions signal the 'bookish' space that Goodreads seeks to occupy in the post-digital literary field,[12] projecting the sense that this is an online community where the pleasure of reading is centred. A major part of the Goodreads platform is the community of readers who write reviews of the books they have read. As of the time of writing this essay, the platform claims that there are more than 90 million book reviews on the site.[13] Sustaining this kind of user interaction for more than a decade is no small achievement, especially when considering the work involved in writing a book review.

Scholars have considered potential benefits of the Goodreads platform for users, citing 'The allure of self-quantification, of curating one's reading life for a global audience of bibliophiles',[14] the 'egocentric' nature of 'public reading performance'[15] and possibility of symbolic and cultural capital signalling.[16] It is not, however, simply the community of readers who benefit from the platform. Amazon.com (the parent company of Goodreads since 2013), along with a number of other publishing industry stakeholders, benefit from the work that the amateur Goodreads reviewers perform. And while publishers, authors and booksellers have long benefited from the labour of book reviewers, traditionally book reviewers have been paid – albeit in arguably small amounts – for their work. When we consider the potential circuit of value for book reviews written by professional reviewers in the contemporary literary sphere, one could argue that each node in the circuit both acquires and transmits tangible, and often economic, benefits: the reviewing publication (such as a cultural magazine or newspaper) has marketable content for its reader; authors, publishers and booksellers are the recipients of publicity and promotion; readers are entertained and/or guided in their purchasing decisions; and, the reviewers are paid and attract the cultural and symbolic capital associated with this work. The Goodreads platform, with its far-reaching community of amateur book reviewers, is now part of this circuit. The major difference between Goodreads reviewers and professional reviewers is that on the whole[17] Goodreads reviewers are not financially compensated for their labour. Essentially, the structure of the circuit remains but there is an adjustment in the value exchange for the reviewer.

Situating the Goodreads reviews and the Goodreads reviewers in this contemporary publishing circuit gives rise to questions about their role and influence, and what form their contribution to the circuit takes. Is this contribution purely economic, do the reviewers have what Beth Driscoll describes as 'readerly capital' and perform a tastemaking function,[18] or, like professional book reviewers and critics, is this contribution complex and multifaceted? Ann Steiner's research into reader reviews on Amazon considers the direct financial relationship between the platform and reviewers, observing that the single purpose of the reviews is to 'sell more books' and that reviews are a 'cheap and efficient way to provide information on its products'.[19] In light of the structural relationship between Amazon and Goodreads, Steiner's observation of reader reviews is worth including in our understanding of the benefit that Goodreads reviewers transmit; however, the arms-length nature of Amazon and Goodreads's relationship suggests a similar distance between a review on the platform and the economic gains for Amazon: the flow of capital appears more indirect between Goodreads and Amazon. Turning, then, to the question of taste production, Driscoll's exploration of the tastemaking function of book blogs considers the ways in which book bloggers are explicitly 'integrated into the commerce of the publishing industry' and the ways in which the public nature of book blog posts function as a guide for what to read.[20] Goodreads reviews, which in a way straddle the gap between Amazon reader reviews and reviews on book blogs, can be understood similarly as contributing in both economic and cultural ways to both the contemporary publishing industry and the contemporary literary sphere.

For the community of amateur book reviewers on the platform, it is important for us to consider the context within which they are participating in contemporary, post-digital literary culture. Goodreads reviewers are part of a much larger group of amateur cultural participants who use socially networked platforms to contribute to the production and circulation of cultural products.[21] Reviewing books on Goodreads can be understood as a kind of fan labour. Using the frame of fan labour to understand the motivations of the reviewers illuminates the way that their work benefits Amazon specifically and the literary field more broadly. An essential characteristic of online fandom and contemporary fan labour is the notion that it is seen as being rooted in self-expression and creativity rather than in 'work'.[22] Structuring the discourse and rhetoric around fandom so that creativity/creative expression are distinct and separate from work/labour disguises the tangible financial benefits of fan labour for professional stakeholders.[23] This is not to say that individuals participating in the Goodreads community are ignorant of the corporate structures that enclose their literary expression, rather the mythology of amateur creative expression and the production of fan culture works to obscure the corporate benefits of this unpaid labour. This obfuscation is particularly successful on the Goodreads platform.

Theorising the work of Goodreads reviewers as a form of fan labour gives rise to questions around the nature of fandom in the contemporary literary field and where semi-permeable distinctions can be established between participation and the nature of fan labour. There are aspects of contemporary literary culture – such as fan fiction – where fandom has been explored deeply and articulated in detail,[24] as well as examinations of the ways in which independent literary publishing operates as a 'prosumption' model,[25] but there has been little inquiry into the nature of literary fans that falls outside these structures. I argue that there are no rigid distinctions between participation and fandom in the literary field, rather literary fandom can be understood as a model of four concentric circles. At the centre of the model is the fanfic community and contributors/subscribers to user-generated platforms such as an Archive of One's Own or LibriVox.[26] For individuals that work within this inner-most circle, their labour is performed for the benefit of the community and this fandom is often rooted in particular books, characters and authors. The next circle out encapsulates the individuals who write reviews on bibliocentric social networking platforms like Goodreads, have amateur book blogs, participate in the Bookstagram community and participate in 'book Twitter'.[27] Attending literary events such as writers festivals and author readings are the kinds of literary participation that characterise the next circle in the model, indicating a more-than-casual engagement with the literary field. Being a member of a book club and participating in mass community reading events would also fall into this category. And finally, the outermost circle of the model is where individuals whose engagement with literary culture involves reading books, as well as book reviews and criticism, are situated. While imperfect, this model demonstrates the various levels of engagement and the activities where the classification of participation moves further towards fandom.

What this model fails to articulate, however, is the distinction between a fandom of a particular story world or characters, and a fandom of literary culture and literary production. Writing fan fiction could be classified as part of the former; writing amateur reviews for a platform like Goodreads could be classified as the latter. There are some activities where this distinction is more difficult to discern: for example, individuals contributing recordings to LibriVox or amateur book bloggers could, depending on the nature of their work, be classified in either group. A gap exists in our understanding of fandom and fan labour as it relates to the literary field broadly, as well as the nature of this labour and how it fits within the capitalist ecosystem of the contemporary book publishing sector. This is where the Goodreads community of reviewers is located: their fandom is not defined by a particular text or narrative world, but rather by literary culture and literary production. The act of reviewing on Goodreads is a form fan labour, characterised by the notion of the 'labor of love' and the remuneration structures of the 'gift economy'.[28] And, like many contemporary, post-digital fan communities, this labour intersects with the economics of the industry in multiple ways.

The Goodreads community of reviewers, however, cannot simply be understood as an amateur fan community. Characterising the reviewers on the platform in this fashion without an understanding of the long history of informal literary discussion groups fails to capture an essential element in the continued vibrancy of the Goodreads reviewer community. Book clubs, reading societies and book discussion events have a long-standing presence in the circulation of literary culture.[29] Reviewing the contemporary scholarship of these practices reveals a number of parallels between reading groups or reading events and the way the Goodreads community of reviewers are described. In their research into community reading events, Danielle Fuller and DeNel Rehberg Sedo observe that the 'processes of connection, learning, identification, and affect are all significant factors in determining participation' in a group reading experience.[30] And while this description of determining factors are related to participation in a large organised community reading event, it could also describe the reasons why Goodreads reviewers contribute their reviews to the platform and echo the way that Lisa Nakamura described the community as engaging in a 'public reading performance'.[31] Readers discussing, analysing and critiquing books is not a phenomenon that arrived with the advent of social networking technologies, and there is a rich tradition of group reading dating back over hundreds of years. Literary societies, mechanics' institutes and mutual improvement societies established in the 19th century formed the foundations for what we understand today as the ritualised practice of the contemporary book club,[32] a practice that informs the way books are discussed on Goodreads.

Being a community of readers is not the only similarity between Goodreads reviewers and the contemporary book club or public reading event. The way that books are discussed at these organised in-person events appears similar in nature to the way titles are reviewed on the Goodreads platform. In her research into women's reading groups, Marilyn Poole describes the way books are discussed among group members thus:

> Textual analysis seemed to be almost non-existent. Occasionally, structure and themes are mentioned, but only superficially. Opinions on books are generally based on subjective, rather than literary, criteria. The recorded discussions indicate that the groups really seem to engage with the characters in the books, who are discussed as if they were real people.[33]

A similar observation can be made with the reader reviews on Goodreads. Reviews are commonly grounded within a personal reading experience and readers commonly cite their reasons for choosing the title at the beginning of their review. Like book group discussions, these reviews are generally not scholarly or grounded in literary theory and the actions of characters (and debate around these actions) are the foundation of many of the reader assessments. Importantly, like the book group discussions described by Poole, relationships are established between the actions of the book's characters and the reviewers' personal lives.[34] It is common for the community of reviewers on Goodreads to bring their personal lives into their reviews, comparing their lives with the experiences of characters, something that is not uncommon in the book group discussion setting. This can occur in reviews with both high and low ratings. For example, a 2018 review of Sally Rooney's novel *Normal People* by a user that rated the title with one star:

> Some of my perplexity with Normal People is that I just couldn't relate to the twenty something, highly educated, politically aware and cynical young adults that populate this novel. I am not sure

how reflective these voices are of young Irish making their way in the world, but as presented here I found them exasperating to listen to and not particularly nuanced.[35]

Or a 2012 five-star review of Kate Grenville's novel *The Secret River* where the user cited their 'Anglo-celtic and Northern European background' and their 'family history' as the reason why *The Secret River* 'is a novel which speaks to' the reader.[36] In both of these review excerpts, it is clear that the rationale behind the rating that each user gave the respective title is grounded in their own personal relationship to the text and the characters. In a study of intimacy within Goodreads reviews, Beth Driscoll and DeNel Rehberg Sedo explore the ways in which Goodreads offers reviewers opportunities to connect and to perform the experience of reading on the platform.[37] Driscoll and Rehberg Sedo's research reveals the significant proportion of Goodreads reviews that express an emotional response to the text, and the ways in which Goodreads offers reviewers the opportunity to explore their own identity in relation to that of the characters in the book they are reviewing.[38] These findings are consistent with the observation of reviews of *Normal People* and *The Secret River* where identity and emotion form the foundation of the analysis.

The context from which Goodreads emerges, as a bibliocentric social networking platform, is informed by a rich history of amateur book groups, public reading events and literary societies. This history has a long-standing attachment to community enjoyment and has in many ways operated outside the field of cultural production and the circulation of symbolic capital. The appearance of community and of sharing the pleasure of reading is essential to the continued success of the Goodreads platform, a success that is expressed in an engaged and lively community of reviewers. And despite the fact that book groups have long been viewed as potentially lucrative marketing avenues by the publishing industry, this conceptualisation of reading groups as drivers of word-of-mouth publicity maintains the arms-length relationship

between publishing professionals and readers: book groups are being marketed *to*.[39] This is where book groups and reading events are distinct from the community of online reviewers on Goodreads. The platformization of the publishing industry and the resulting mediated digital literary enclosure has relocated amateur book reviewers, by virtue of spaces like the Goodreads platform, from beyond to within the field of cultural production.

Goodreads's position within the Amazon suite of literary platforms and activities is essential not only to their survival but also to the continued relevance of the platform to the global literary ecosystem and, therefore, to readers. Mark McGurl argues that the acquisition of Goodreads by Amazon, along with the development of a number of literary productions and publishing platforms and tools, indicates a desire on the part of the corporate giant to 'being literary'.[40] The result of these acquisitions and developments is the dominance of Amazon within almost all facets of the contemporary publishing industry, a position that is not only supported by their ubiquity but also by the masses of user data that user operations on the various parts of the platform elicits. Mark Davis refers to the platformization of the contemporary publishing industry and contemporary literary culture as 'a proprietary alternative literary field based on user data',[41] evoking a platformized reimagining of Bourdieu's field of cultural production where positions that were once established through an exchange of symbolic goods are now dependent on the continued cultivation and analysis of user data.[42]

Davis continues his analysis of the hallmarks of the contemporary publishing industry's platformization by exploring the ways in which Amazon has established a proprietary public sphere that is often disguised as an actual public sphere.[43] He writes: '[Amazon] encloses public culture by moving public exchanges into a privatised domain where all interactions, including those freely made as part of the 'sharing economy', happen within the platform and are part of its business model'.[44] The desire to 'enclose' readers' literary discourse within the Amazon ecosystem, establishing a 'pseudo-public sphere', [45] is evident in the way Goodreads describes itself. Goodreads's 'About' page features a brief description of the kinds of activities that the platform supports, along with a 'message' from the co-founder.[46] There are two key rhetorical signals employed on this page that draw on long-established ideals around the moral dimensions of book reading that, I argue, work to establish the sense that Goodreads is simply a forum for the public discussion of books, ideas and nothing else. First, the rotating banner image at the top of the page is adorned with the phrase, 'The right book in the right hands at the right time can change the world'.[47] The second, in the message from the platform's co-founder, is: 'knowledge is power, and power is best shared among readers'.[48] This veil of public spiritedness is used to obscure the ways in which the platform, as part of the Amazon network, is less about the power of knowledgeable readers and more about the power of knowledgeable platforms.

Maintenance of the powerful position that Amazon occupies in the literary field is dependent on the extraction of user data from multiple proprietary online spaces, including Goodreads. Every time a member of the Goodreads community adds a title to one of their virtual bookshelves or rates and reviews a book they have read, they are increasing the commercial power of this conglomerate.[49] Earlier in this essay I likened the writing of reviews by amateur reviewers on Goodreads to a kind of fan labour, where the reviewers are not only fans of particular books and authors but appear to be fans of literary culture more broadly. There is, however, an added dimension to this unpaid fan labour that, I argue, is an essential and particular element to the continued popularity of the Goodreads platform. Similar to the often deeply personal connections and conversations that happen around books and reading within a social book club, many amateur book reviews draw upon personal experiences and personal relationships to texts in their reviews on the site.[50] And, like in a personal book club, it is these personal connections and contributions that establish and maintain the sense of community on Goodreads. Considering the reviewers and their reviews in this light, it is inadequate to characterise their contributions to the platform as simply fan labour and perhaps more appropriate to characterise them as *affective* fan labour.

Affective labour is a generative but largely invisible capital characterised by the 'creation and manipulation of affects' in the pursuit of 'a sense of connectedness or community'.[51] The commercial benefits of this kind of labour have long been explored by researchers interrogating labour practices in the domestic sphere,[52] the service industries staffed largely by women and people of colour,[53] and the contemporary creative industries.[54] What binds these research streams is the value of managed affect or emotion, a value that results in an immediate sense of comfort within a group or community, and an eventual economic return for those in power. Take, for example, the affective labour of a book publicist working for an independent publishing house. This publicist, whose job it is to represent both the publisher and individual authors, will work to ensure a convivial and connected publicity environment for the author that they are working with, and the media and publicity events they facilitate. This work may include an unacknowledged manipulation of their emotions in order to fulfil the goals of their work. The immediate beneficiary of this labour is the author and the media/events that constitute the community they have established, and the eventual financial beneficiary is, ultimately, the publishing house.[55] There is a radiating economic value to the sense of ease, friendliness and collegiality that they have established. Applying this understanding to the community of amateur Goodreads reviewers reveals similar radiating benefits, from the community of readers in the immediate to the eventual economic return for the platform. The sense of community among the Goodreads reviewers and users is established through the affective labour of reviewers, and the ultimate beneficiary of the ongoing work of the community is the Amazon shareholders.

The desire to cultivate a digital community through reviewing and criticism is a theme explored by Ann Steiner in their work on Amazon book reviews.[56] Steiner is critical of the Amazon enclosure/owned public sphere, highlighting the juxtaposition between the opportunities for seemingly free expression and community that public amateur reviewing affords readers, and the capitalist structures that directly benefit from the reviewers' labour. The Goodreads reviews, now a part of the Amazon conglomerate structure, operate in a similar way and for the reviewers, the community is established not to benefit Amazon but to exist as a space for expression, creativity and connection. However, as Steiner observes, the labour performed by this community benefits Amazon in myriad ways.

The nature of affective fan labour is evident in the language and content of the amateur reviewers' reviews on Goodreads, for example the reviews of Tayari Jones' prize-winning novel *An American Marriage*.[57] Exploring the themes of race in contemporary America, the commitment of marriage and the inequalities inherent in the US justice system, the book's blurb describes *An American Marriage* as a 'stirring love story [that] is a profoundly insightful look into the hearts and minds of three people who are at once bound and separated by forces beyond their control'.[58] In the Goodreads reader reviews (of which there are 20,483 at the time of writing this essay), these themes are explored and linked explicitly to the lives and experiences of many of the reviewers. For example, one reviewer writes:

> I knew Georgia and Louisiana and the depths of love and the reach of heartbreak and the grandstanding of the men in this book and the soft corners of the women in this novel like they were flesh and bone because I could sense them in my personal history.[59]

Another reviewer, citing their personal experience with romantic relationships, writes:

> Roy is the type of man who thinks he's a good and honest modern
> man, but in actuality is a lying, cheating, insecure, man-boy. I
> know Roys. I've dated Roys. Tayari's writing is so honest in that
> way, that despite my dislike for Roy never once did I question his
> innocence. She allowed me to not like Roy the man and still be
> furious at the injustice he and everyone around him had suffered.[60]

While these two excerpts from reader reviews are deeply personal,
they are also publicly available on the Goodreads platform and form
just a small part of the significant amount of discussion about this
book. These reviews, and those they sit alongside, offer a compelling
picture of *An American Marriage*'s reception among readers and are a
great source of information for readers considering the title. However,
beyond an insight into reader reception, these amateur reviewers are
drawing upon their emotional lives and experiences in the spirit of
discussion, discourse and reader community.

It is not, however, just fiction that attracts this kind of affective
writing from Goodreads reviewers. Lisa Taddeo's non-fiction title
Three Women appears to elicit a similar emotional and personal response
in many reviewers.[61] *Three Women*'s publisher, Avid Reader Press,
describes the title thus:

> Three Women is both a feat of journalism and a triumph of
> storytelling, brimming with .nuance and empathy...Three Women
> introduces us to three unforgettable women – and one remarkable
> writer – whose experiences remind us that we are not alone.[62]

The reader reviews of *Three Women* on Goodreads (of which there are
6034 at the time of writing this essay) are often as equally emphatic
as the publisher. For example, the way that this review grapples with
why they enjoyed the book:

> I suppose what hit so hard for me was that I saw aspects of
> myself in all of these women. I found myself identifying with
> each, understanding their circumstances and how they play out

in various ways. I can blame them and empathize with them. They were heroes and villains, madonnas [sic] and whores and still weren't any of these tropes.[63]

Or this reviewer justifying their one-star review:

I was just angry. Angry that this book claims to be the next great feminist read. Angry that only Maggie was given some type of justice through writing. Angry that Lina's traumatic experience as a teen was completely glanced over.[64]

Whether readers loved or loathed the book, reading the reviews of *Three Women* on the Goodreads platform served to reinforce a sense of community – and the feeling of enjoyment, entertainment and empathy that being part of a community elicits – and the role that emotional connections and affective responses to reading plays in the maintenance of the popularity of the site. Amazon directly benefits financially from the manipulation of affect and emotion that serves the reviewer community as the more reviews and readers are using the Goodreads platform, the more sophisticated and valuable their marketable user data and insights.[65]

Amazon and their stakeholders are not, however, the only beneficiaries of this affective fan labour. While there is a direct link between user activity on the Goodreads platform and the sophistication of Amazon's proprietary user data, various actors in the publishing ecosystem similarly benefit from this community. Considering once again the circuit of value that encompasses book reviewing culture – and the addition of Goodreads reviewers in this circuit – publishers, authors and booksellers also benefit. The most explicit benefit to publishers, authors and booksellers is in the promotion and increased visibility of books to new readers.[66] Beyond this baseline function that characterises both professional reviewers in broadsheet newspapers and amateur reviewers on Goodreads, the visible public discourse en masse between readers is a valuable marketing insight for publishers.[67] Moreover, analysis of these reviews illustrates to publishers, booksellers and other essential actors in the contemporary publishing industry broad public reception for a particular title, for publishers especially they can contribute to editorial and acquisition practice. In her exploration of the role of user data in post-digital editorial practice, Claire Squires observed the way that editors working in book publishing houses conceptualise their role and their expertise in the contemporary publishing industry.[68] Squires's research uncovered a resistance on the part of editors to the notion that contemporary editorial and acquisition practice was influenced by reader insights garnered from digital platforms, while at the same time acknowledging that the curatorial expertise of editors was based on experience and immersion within the literary culture.[69] I argue that immersion in the literary culture will increasingly be informed by user data and reader insights established from users of bibliocentric social networking platforms, and that the position of Goodreads reviews will only become more entrenched as a tool for editorial forecasting.

In myriad ways the affective fan labour of book reviewers on Goodreads translates into economic benefits for the contemporary publishing industry. These benefits are rooted in the lively and continuing nature of the community of amateur reviewers on the platform, the success of which is tied to the particularities of the reviews themselves. Goodreads, as a bibliocentric social networking platform, and the platform's reviewers represent a convergence of professional practice and the long-standing tradition of book clubs and informal reading groups that have long had a presence in literary culture. The result of this convergence is a new kind of literary practice that is simultaneously amateur and increasingly an influential node in the post-digital, platformized publishing value circuit. The continued success of this dual function relies on the sense of community among the reviewers on Goodreads and the unpaid affective nature of their labour.

Endnotes

1   'About Goodreads,' Goodreads, n.d., https://www.goodreads.com/about/us.

2   See, for example, Kerryn Goldsworthy, 'Everyone's a Critic,' *Australian Book Review*, 351 (2013); Gideon Haigh, 'Feeding the Hand that Bites: The Demise of Australian Literary Reviewing,' *Kill Your Darlings,* March 1, 2010, https://www.killyourdarlings.com.au/article/feeding-the-hand-that-bites-the-demise-of-australian-literary-reviewing-by-gideon-haigh/; Emmett Stinson, 'Whose Byline is it Anyway? On Pseudonymous Book Reviews,' *Kill Your Darlings*, January 31, 2019, 14-17.

3   See, for example, @mxcreant, '1) is hard or soft criticism the way to go forward; 2) do you need to be monied to be a writer; 3) is the personal essay dead or not......over and over and over again until the end of time,' twitter.com, April 25, 2020, https://twitter.com/mxcreant/status/1253926831738228736.; @EmmettStinson, 'When a reviewer tags the authors under review via social media, tells me everything I need to know about the review', twitter.com, April 3, 2020, https://twitter.com/EmmettStinson/status/1245889008577601536.

4   Goldsworthy, 'Everyone's a Critic'.

5   Claire Squire, 'The Review and the Reviewer,' in *Contemporary Publishing and the Culture of Books*, eds. Alison Baverstock & Richard Bradford (Abingdon: Routledge, 2020), 121.

6   Emmett Stinson, 'How Nice is Too Nice? Australian Book Reviews and the "Compliment Sandwich",' *Australian Humanities Reviews* 60 (2016): 122.

7   Alexandra Dane, *Gender and Prestige in Literature: Contemporary Australian Book Culture* (London, New York: Palgrave Macmillan, 2020), 14.

8   Emmett Stinson, 'Small Publishers and the Emerging Network of Australian Literary Prosumption,' *Australian Humanities Review* 59 (2016).

9   Goodreads, 'About Goodreads'.

10 Lisa Nakamura '"Words with Friends"': Socially Networked Reading on *Goodreads,*' *Modern Language Association of America* 128, no. 1 (2013); Simone Murray, 'Secret Agents: Algorithmic Culture, Goodreads and Datafication of the Contemporary Book World,' *European Journal of Cultural Studies* (2019).

11 Goodreads, 'About Goodreads'.

12 Murray, 'Secret Agents,' 12.

13 Goodreads, 'About Goodreads'.

14 Murray, 'Secret Agents,' 8.

15 Nakamura '"Words with Friends",' 240.

16   Mike Thelwall and Kayvan Kousha, 'Goodreads: A Social Network Site for Book Readers,' *Journal for the Association for Information Science and Technology* 68, no. 4 (2017): 974.

17   The Goodreads Giveaways Program gives Goodreads reviewers in Canada and the United States the opportunity to win books, with the aim of eliciting reviews on the platform. Books are provided to Goodreads for the Giveaways by publishers and authors (Goodreads 2020b).

18   Beth Driscoll, 'Book Blogs as Tastemakers,' *Participations* 16, no. 1 (2019): 286, 301.

19   Ann Steiner, 'Private Criticism in the Public Space: Personal Writing on Literature in Readers' Reviews on Amazon,' *Particip@tions* 5, no. 2 (2008), https://www.participations.org/Volume%205/Issue%202/5_02_steiner.htm.

20   Driscoll, 'Book Blogs as Tastemakers'.

21   Mel Stanfill and Megan Condis, 'Fandom and/as Labor,' *Transformative Works and Cultures*, no. 15 (2014), 3, https://journal.transformativeworks.org/index.php/twc/article/view/593/421.

22   Kristina Busse, 'Fan Labor and Feminism: Capitalizing on the Fannish Labor of Love,' *Cinema Journal* 52, no. 5 (2015): 112; Eran Fisher, 'How Less Alienation Creates More Exploitation: Audience Labour on Social Networking Sites,' *triple – Cognition, Communication, Co-operation* 10, no. 2 (2012): 173; Stanfil and Condis, 'Fandom and/as Labor,' 3.

23   Bethan Jones, 'Fifty Shades of Exploration: Fan Labor and "Fifty Shades of Grey",' *Transformative Works and Cultures* 15 (2014): n.p., https://journal.transformativeworks.org/index.php/twc/article/view/501/422.

24   See, for example, Julia Bullard, 'Motivating Invisible Contributions: Framing Volunteer Classification Design in a Fanfiction Repository,' *Proceedings of the 19th International Conference on Supporting Group Work* (November 2016); Jones, 'Fifty Shades of Exploration'.

25   Stinson, 'Small Publishers and the Emerging Network of Australian Literary Prosumption'.

26   Millicent Weber, 'On Audiobooks and Literature in the Post-Digital Age,' *Overland*, October 3, 2019, n.p., https://overland.org.au/2019/10/on-audiobooks-and-literature-in-the-post-digital-age/.

27   See Kenna MacTavish's contribution to this volume.

28   Busse, 'Fan Labor and Feminism,' 112.

29   Beth Driscoll, *The New Literary Middlebrow: Tastemakers and Reading in the Twenty-First Century* (New York, London: Palgrave Macmillan, 2014), 49; Marilyn Poole, 'The Women's Chapter: Women's Reading Groups in Victoria,' *Feminist Media Studies* 3, no.3 (2003): 263.

30 Danielle Fuller and DeNel Rehberg Sedo, *Reading Beyond the Book: The Social Practices of Contemporary Literary Culture* (Palgrave Macmillan, 2013).

31 Nakamura '"Words with Friends",' 240.

32 Driscoll, *The New Literary Middlebrow*, 50.

33 Poole, 'The Women's Chapter,' 273.

34 Ibid.

35 GR Reviewer 1.

36 GR Reviewer 2.

37 Beth Driscoll and DeNel Rehberg Sedo, 'Faraway, So Close: Seeing the Intimacy in Goodreads Reviews.' *Qualitative Inquiry* 25, no. 3 (2019).

38 Ibid, 252, 256.

39 Danielle Fuller, DeNel Rehberg Sedo, Claire Squires, 'Marionettes and Puppeteers? The Relationship Between Book Club Readers and Publishers,' in *Reading Communities from Salons to Cyberspace*, ed. DeNel Rehberg Sedo (Palgrave Macmillan, 2011).

40 Mark McGurl, 'Everything and Less: Fiction in the Age of Amazon,' *Modern Language Quarterly* 77, no. 3 (2016): 449.

41 Mark Davis, 'Five Processes in the Platformisation of Cultural Production: Amazon and its Publishing Ecosystem,' *Australian Humanities Reviews* 66 (2020): 91.

42 Pierre Bourdieu, *The Field of Cultural Production: Essays on Art and Literature* (Columbia University Press,1993).

43 Davis, 'Five Processes in the Platformisation of Cultural Production,' 93.

44 Ibid.

45 Ibid.

46 Goodreads, 'About Goodreads.'

47 Ibid.

48 Ibid.

49 Ted Striphas, 'The Abuses of Literacy: Amazon Kindle and the Right to Read,' *Communications and Critical/Cultural Studies* 7, no.3 (2010): 305; Joachim Vlieghe, Jaël Muls, and Kris Rutten, 'Everybody Reads: Reader Engagement with Literature in Social Media Environments,' *Poetics* 54 (2016): 27.

50 Driscoll and Rehberg Sedo, 'Faraway, So Close.'

51 Michael Hardt, 'Affective Labour,' *Boundary 2* 26, no. 2 (1999): 96.

52 See, for example, Hardt, 'Affective Labour.'

53 Arlie Hochschild, *The Managed Heart: Commercialization of Human Feeling* (Berkeley, Los Angeles: University of California Press, 1983).

54 Angela McRobbie, *Be Creative: Making a Living in the New Culture Industries* (Cambridge: Polity Press, 2016).

55 Claire Parnell, Alexandra Dane and Millicent Weber, 'Author Care and the Invisibility of Affective Labour: Publicists' Role in Book Publishing,' *Publishing Research Quarterly* 36 (2020): 648–659.
56 Steiner, 'Private Criticism in the Public Space.'
57 Tayari Jones, *An American Marriage* (Chapel Hill: Algonquin Books, 2018).
58 Ibid.
59 GR Reviewer 3.
60 GR Reviewer 4.
61 'About the Book,' Avid Reader Press, https://www.simonandschuster.com/books/Three-Women/Lisa-Taddeo/9781451642292.
62 Ibid.
63 GR Reviewer 5.
64 GR Reviewer 6.
65 Lexi Pandell, 'Goodreads is Finally Cashing in on its Devoted Community,' *Wired*, May 19, 2016, n.p., https://www.wired.com/2016/05/goodreads-selling-books/.
66 Claire Squires, 'Taste and/or Big Data? Post-Digital Editorial Selection,' *Critical Quarterly* 59, no. 3 (2017): 26.
67 Sybil Nolan and Alexandra Dane, 'A Sharper Conversation: Book Publishers' Use of Social Media Marketing in the Age of the Algorithm,' *Media International Australia* 168, no. 1 (2018): 160.
68 Squires, 'Taste and/or Big Data?'.
69 Ibid, 28, 36.

Bibliography

Avid Reader Press. 'About the Book,' https://www.simonandschuster.com/books/Three-Women/Lisa-Taddeo/9781451642292.
Bourdieu, Pierre. *The Field of Cultural Production: Essays on Art and Literature.* New York: Columbia University Press, 1993.
Bullard, Julia. 'Motivating Invisible Contributions: Framing Volunteer Classification Design in a Fanfiction Repository,' *Proceedings of the 19th International Conference on Supporting Group Work* (November 2016): 181–193.
Busse, Kristina. 'Fan Labor and Feminism: Capitalizing on the Fannish Labor of Love,' *Cinema Journal* 54, no.5 (2015): 110–115.
Dane, Alexandra. *Gender and Prestige in Literature: Contemporary Australian Book Culture.* London, New York: Palgrave Macmillan, 2020.

Davis, Mark. 'Five Processes in the Platformisation of Cultural Production: Amazon and its Publishing Ecosystem,' *Australian Humanities Review* 66 (2020): 83–103.

Driscoll, Beth. *The New Literary Middlebrow: Tastemakers and Reading in the Twenty-First Century*. New York, London: Palgrave Macmillan, 2014.

Driscoll, Beth. 'Book Blogs as Tastemakers,' *Participations* 16, no.1 (2019): 280–305.

Driscoll, Beth., and Rehberg Sedo, DeNel. 'Faraway, So Close: Seeing the Intimacy in Goodreads Reviews,' *Qualitative Inquiry* 25, no.3 (2019): 248–259.

Fisher, Eran. 'How Less Alienation Creates More Exploitation: Audience Labour on Social Networking Sites,' *tripleC - Cognition, Communication, Co-operation* 10, no.2 (2012): 171–183.

Fuller, Danielle, Rehberg Sedo,DeNel and Squires, Claire. 'Marionettes and Puppeteers? The Relationship Between Book Club Readers and Publishers,' in *Reading Communities from Salons to Cyberspace*. Edited by DeNel Rehberg Sedo, 181–199. Palgrave Macmillan, 2011.

Fuller, Danielle, Rehberg Sedo,DeNel. *Reading Beyond the Book: The Social Practices of Contemporary Literary Culture*. Palgrave Macmillan, 2013.

Goodreads. 'About Goodreads,' https://www.goodreads.com/about/us.

Goodreads. 'Giveaways,' https://www.goodreads.com/giveaway.

Goldsworthy, Kerryn. 'Everyone's a Critic,' *Australian Book Review* 351 (2013).

Haigh, Gideon. 'Feeding the hand that Bites: The Demise of Australian Literary Reviewing,' *Kill Your Darlings,* 1 March, 2010, https://www.killyourdarlings.com.au/article/feeding-the-hand-that-bites-the-demise-of-australian-literary-reviewing-by-gideon-haigh/.

Hardt, Michael. 'Affective Labour,' *boundary 2* 26, no.2 (Summer 1999): 89–100.

Hochschild, Arlie. *The Managed Heart: Commercialization of Human Feeling*. Berkeley, Los Angeles: University of California Press, 1983.

Jones, Bethan. 'Fifty Shades of Exploitation: Fan Labor and 'Fifty Shades of Grey',' *Transformative Works and Cultures* 15 (2014), https://journal.transformativeworks.org/index.php/twc/article/view/501/422.

Jones, Tayari. *An American Marriage*. Chapel Hill: Algonquin Books, 2018.

MacTavish, Kenna. 'The Emerging Power of the Booksagrammer: Reading #bookstagram as a Post-Digital Site of Book Culture,' in *Post-Digital Book Cultures: Australian Perspectives*, edited by Alexandra Dane and Millicent Weber. Melbourne: Monash University Publishing, 2021.

McGurl, Mark. 'Everything and Less: Fiction in the Age of Amazon,' *Modern Language Quarterly* 77, no. 3 (2016): 447–471.

McRobbie, Angela. *Be Creative: Making a Living in the New Culture Industries*. Cambridge: Polity Press, 2016.

Murray, Simone. 'Secret Agents: Algorithmic Culture, Goodreads and Datafication of the Contemporary Book World,' *European Journal of Cultural Studies* (2019): 1–20.

@mxcreant. '1) is hard or soft criticism the way to go forward; 2) do you need to be monied to be a writer; 3) is the personal essay dead or not……over and over and over again until the end of time.' Twitter, April 25, 2020, https://twitter.com/mxcreant/status/1253926831738228736.

Nakamura, Lisa. '"Words With Friends"': Socially Networked Reading on Goodreads,' *PMLA* 128, no.1 (2013): 238–243.

Nolan, Sybil and Dane, Alexandra. 'A sharper conversation: book publishers' use of social media marketing in the age of the algorithm,' *Media International Australia* 168, no. 1 (2018): 153–166.

Pandell, Lexi. 'Goodreads is Finally Cashing in on its Devoted Community,' *Wired*, May 19, 2016, https://www.wired.com/2016/05/goodreads-selling-books/.

Parnell, Claire., Dane, Alexandra and Weber, Millicent. 'Author Care and the Invisibility of Affective Labour: Publicists' Role in Book Publishing,' *Publishing Research Quarterly* 36 (2020): 648–659.

Poole Marilyn. 'The Women's Chapter: Women's Reading Groups in Victoria,' *Feminist Media Studies* 3, no. 3 (2003): 263–281.

Squires, Claire. 'Taste and/or Big Data? Post-Digital Editorial Selection,' *Critical Quarterly* 59, no. 3 (2017): 24–38.

Squires, Claire. 'The Review and the Reviewer,' in *Contemporary Publishing and the Culture of Books*, edited by Alison Baverstock & Richard Bradford. Abingdon: Routledge. pp. 117–132.

Stanfill, Mel., and Condis, Megan. 'Fandom and/as Labor,' *Transformative Works and Cultures,* no. 15 (2014), https://journal.transformativeworks.org/index.php/twc/article/view/593/421.

Steiner, Ann. 'Private Criticism in the Public Space: Personal Writing on Literature in Readers' Reviews on Amazon,' *Particip@tions* 5, no.2 (2008), https://www.participations.org/Volume%205/Issue%202/5_02_steiner.htm.

Stinson, Emmett. 'How Nice is Too Nice? Australian Book Reviews and the 'Compliment Sandwich',' *Australian Humanities Review* 60 (2016): 108–126.

Stinson, Emmett. 'Publishers and the Emerging Network of Australian Literary Prosumption,' *Australian Humanities Review* 59 (2016): 23–43.

Stinson, Emmett. 'Whose Byline Is It Anyway? On Pseudonymous Book Reviews,' *Kill Your Darlings*, January 31, 2019, 14–17.

@EmmettStinson. 'When a reviewer tags the authors under review via social media, tells me everything I need to know about the review.' Twitter, April 3, 2020, https://twitter.com/EmmettStinson/status/1245889008577601536.

Striphas, Ted. 'The Abuses of Literacy: Amazon Kindle and the Right to Read,' *Communications and Critical/Cultural Studies* 7, no. 3 (2010): 297–317.

Thelwall, Mike., and Kousha, Kayvan. 'Goodreads: A social Network Site for Book Readers,' *Journal for the Association for Information Science and Technology* 68, no. 4 (2017): 972–983.

Vlieghe, Joachim., Muls, Jaël and Rutten, Kris. 'Everybody Reads: Reader Engagement with Literature in Social Media Environments,' *Poetics* 54 (2016): 25–37.

Weber, Millicent. 'On Audiobooks and Literature in the Post-Digital Age,' *Overland*, October 3, 2019, https://overland.org.au/2019/10/on-audiobooks-and-literature-in-the-post-digital-age/.

CHAPTER 4

The Emerging Power
of the Bookstagrammer

Reading #bookstagram as a Post-Digital Site of Book Culture

Kenna MacTavish

Bookstagram is the name for the hashtag-led community on the user-generated-content (UGC) platform, Instagram. The bookish community is a well-established home for carefully curated content where the 'book has pride of place' within the frame.[1] At the time of writing, the bookstagram community had amassed over 40 million public posts tagged with hashtag '#bookstagram'.[2] At the UK Book Blog awards as part of the London Book Fair, the award for Bookstagrammer of the Year is bestowed upon a bookstagrammer who features UK-published books on their account and is judged to be the best in their field.[3] Despite this mass of content and prevalence within the book industry, the bookstagram community is an under-examined sector within 21st century book studies. Recent research into digital reading communities has focused on book blogs,[4] televised or online book clubs,[5] or other bookish platforms including self-publishing platforms,[6] Goodreads[7] and Pinterest.[8] While Instagram and bookstagram often receive a passing reference, they are rarely given the same consideration as other platforms and bookish communities that have helped shape the digital literary landscape. I make a case for bookstagram as a significant post-digital site of cultural and readerly expression in the contemporary book world. I aim to provide an overview of Instagram as a site of post-digital publishing beyond the affordances set out by the platform and explore how reader-users are negotiating their cultural and readerly position within the bookstagram community. I ask, what is bookstagram and what is bookstagram's role in signifying the emerging power of readers as cultural intermediaries in contemporary book culture? Alongside this research question, I also ask why is Instagram an architecturally significant platform for bookish cultural work?

This chapter begins by situating Instagram and bookstagram within a post-digital book world. It then conceptualises the term 'bookstagrammer' and offers an introduction to the cultural network in which a bookstagram user operates within. The theoretical component of this chapter then moves to position the bookstagrammer as a cultural mediator; a role that I argue is elevated by distinct social and visual affordances of the Instagram platform. This chapter then proceeds to outline the different stages of data collection and analysis of its empirical focus, and introduces a situated methodology of an intimate examination of bookstagram posts within their platform context. The final section of this chapter turns to an empirical study of a small but representative bookstagram account. Through an intimate deconstruction of caption-led reviewing practices, bookish props and objects, and visualised prize predictions, I argue that individualised content creation on bookstagram reveals a potentiality for the book-stagrammer to emerge as a culturally significant intermediary in a post-digital book world.

Defining Bookstagram in a Post-Digital Book World

Instagram is a visual-based user-generated-content (UGC) platform. Since its debut in the Apple App Store in 2010, it has transformed the way we communicate online. It is currently available as an app for a handheld device or tablet, or as a desktop website. However, only the app lets users publish new content to the platform. Instagram is a platform designed specifically to frame content in an accessible, shareable and visually appealing way; it allows users to place 'strong emphasis on the visual and on the aesthetics of the ways in which the content is framed'.[9] This means that its interface and perceived affordances are already constructed to optimise the types of content that are generated by users on the platform.[10] In 21st century book studies, Instagram is an under-examined site of bookish cultural production. At the end of 2018, bookstagram included 26 million posts tagged with the hashtag #bookstagram[11] and in September 2020 there were over 50 million posts. This growth only represents two recent years of the hashtag's use, but it also signifies the continued prominence of an online community. At a structural level, bookstagram is a community of users organised by this '#bookstagram' hashtag. This hashtag is searchable within Instagram's global search function, which will show every post tagged with #bookstagram shared by a publicly accessible account. Private accounts may also use the hashtag associated with the community; however, their content will not be searchable by users who have not been approved to follow them.

At its core, bookstagram is a community for Instagram users to create and share content about books and reading. These users are therefore considered what media scholar Axel Bruns defines as 'produsers': the producer-user who simultaneously uses and creates content within particular platforms and online environments.[12] The concept of the produser has often been adopted and extended by book studies scholars who research digital and post-digital bookish environments, as there are many different ways of experiencing and talking about books online. Simon Murray's recent work[13] on the digital literary sphere has opened up additional avenues on research into the systems and conduct of a digital book world. In her 2016 article exploring the cultivation of book buzz within the digital literary sphere, Murray notes in her introduction that 'the internet hosts a plethora of widely trafficked, avidly collaborative, and fiercely disputatious literary communities'.[14] These communities are made up of mediators and contributors within the book world, from publishers and authors, to critics and bookshops, to readers as emerging intermediaries in the value chain. These online communities occupy a post-digital space that promotes what Ted Striphas calls 'an ethos of bookishness', which is used as a catch-all phrase for the promotion of book culture online.[15] I note 'post-digital space' because 21st century book studies, as outlined in a state of the discipline overview by Rachel Noorda and Stevie Marsden,[16] brings with it a push to critically examine both digital and non-digital practices, objects, and architectures in the contemporary book world. With this in mind, this chapter works to further examine online bookish communities through a post-digital lens.

The concept of post-digital is defined by the confluence of digital and non-digital practices in a move to acknowledge the resilience of material culture.[17] In the context of a post-digital book world, this refers to a continuation of the material practices and affordances in the production, distribution, dissemination, and reception of books. Bookstagram is a site of the book industry that operates within all four of those processes. First, it is a digital platform and architecture that enables and promotes the production of books. Second, bookstagram is a site of book culture involved in book distribution through processes of acquiring, purchasing, and gifting books. Third, through the affordances of Instagram, bookstagram offers its community a large platform to disseminate information about books. And last, the individual users within the bookstagram community engage in processes of book reception through the content they create and engage with on the platform. Each process stated above considers the material resilience of books as both objects and practices through their representation on Instagram's visual, shareable, searchable affordances.

Who and What is a Bookstagrammer?

A bookstagrammer is a produser who self-identifies as being a bookstagrammer, who actively participates within the bookstagram community through creating and sharing bookish content, who communicates with other reader-users through comments, tags, reposts, and stories and runs an account that communicates an overwhelmingly bookish aesthetic. While the #bookstagram hashtag and other affiliated hashtags can be used to tag any image of bookish practice or behaviour, it is its ongoing use as an identifier that defines the bookstagrammer. For example, if a barista at a café posted an image of a new book purchase on their personal Instagram account and only tagged #bookstagram in the caption, the barista would not be considered a bookstagrammer by the above definition. They are, rather, demonstrating an awareness of the community and its association with photos of books but not intentionally engaging within the community as a whole. However, if the barista self-identified as a bookstagrammer, if their Instagram handle was '@dabookishbarista', if they included additional relevant hashtags on their post such as, '#bookish', #newbookbuy', #booklover', and '#TBR2020', and their account grid displayed many images of books, bookshelves, acts of reading and cups of coffee they make alongside books they purchase, then the barista would be considered a bookstagrammer by the above definition.

There are, however, different tiers of produsers within the bookstagram community structure. Bookstagram user tiers can be understood in a few networked ways within this collective community structure. Firstly, there are accounts run by produsers with professional affiliations that situate them in an elevated position within this sector of book culture. Any users with professional access to and knowledge of the publishing industry – literary agents, publishing assistants, editors, librarians and booksellers – are afforded a signifier that many everyday reader-users cannot claim. Similarly, authors often run bookstagram accounts to document their reading and writing practices, but their status as 'author' signals a type of professional readerly capital that can only be gained by engaging with the book industry in that way. These personal accounts with professional affiliations blur the lines between who is considered a professional reader and who may be identified then as an everyday or amateur reader. These signals of a tiered hierarchy – which are often written into an Instagram account bio – are significant in deciphering the degree of cultural power and influence that individual bookstagrammers hold. An analogy can be drawn here with Alexandra Dane's work on tote bags as capital signifiers at literary festivals; the paid-for tote bag signals a kind of cultural capital that a tote bag gifted for free does not.[18] However, the networked hashtag-led organisational system on Instagram – in this case '#bookstagram' – can flatten this hierarchy across searchable platform affordances, such as an image-only grid view in the global search page, for example.

Another way the bookstagram community is tiered is within the platform affordances. Users with higher numbers of followers can be considered more influential than those users with fewer numbers, however, I argue that the power of influence within bookstagram is not solely dependent on follower count. Bookstagram users who have been on the platform for a long time (see @lifeandliterature and @bookbaristas) have consequently amassed large followings (over 15,000 followers). This means that the engagement on their individual posts is generally higher than that of a smaller (0–5000 followers) or middling tier (5000–15,000 followers) bookstagram account. However, due to networked shareability via hashtags, stories, reposts and the algorithmic affordances of Instagram stated above, smaller accounts can generate consistent user engagement as well. This networked, tiered system, which is often led by metrics, is similar to that of small independent publishers, middling publishers and The Big Five publishers competing for space within national and international book markets. In the same way that an independent small press publisher may amass higher degrees of symbolic capital through their publication of prize winners versus bestsellers,[19] a small tier bookstagram account has the potential to emerge as a leading cultural mediator through niche content creation and a supportive community of supportive followers who engage frequently and in-depth. Although there is still a significant amount of research to be done into the networked community of bookstagram and other emerging sites of book culture, these smaller, niche-focused bookstagram accounts are what this chapter will focus on.

Bookstagram as a Post-Digital Site for Cultural Mediation

A bookstagram produser has the capacity to take on the role of a cultural intermediary. In the book world, critics, booksellers, book bloggers and book clubs are all considered cultural intermediaries. As defined by Jennifer Smith Maguire and Julian Matthews, cultural intermediaries construct value through how they frame particular goods (such as material products, services and ideas) for end consumers and additional market actors.[20] They negotiate their own location within the commodity chain between the differing actors and stages of cultural production by making 'explicit claims to professional expertise in taste and value within specific cultural fields'.[21] In their examination of the Zoella Book Club headed by vlogger and author Zoe Sugg, Maxine Branagh-Miscampbell and Stevie Marsden draw upon Smith Maguire and Matthew's definition of a cultural intermediary and note that:

> Sugg is a new kind of cultural intermediary: one who has the potential to 'defin[e] what counts as good taste and cool culture in today's marketplace' but being perceived, by some as not being able to 'perform critical operations in the production and promotion of consumption' and 'construc[t] legitimacy and ad[d] value through the qualification of goods' (Smith Maguire and Matthews, 2014, 1).[22]

Cultural intermediaries use a range of devices, each with their own accrued degrees of credibility,[23] to frame particular cultural products (books) as valuable and/or tasteful – or not, in some cases. While Sugg is granted her own 'accrued degrees of credibility' through her position as an author and as a vlogger with a strong appeal to young women, Sugg's taste-making role within the Zoella Book Club was often questioned.[24] Branagh-Miscampbell and Marsden's analysis highlights that there is also 'potentiality' in defining who or what counts as a cultural intermediary, especially in a platformised social media ecology. The discourse around the Zoella Book Club and Sugg's credibility as a bookish cultural intermediary is representative of questions that arise when social media influencers use their 'devices' to cultivate taste-making spaces for cultural objects. In other words, social media remains a 'potential' space for cultural intermediaries because qualifications are more difficult to measure and therefore are often questioned rather than taken as matter of fact.

Instagram's perceived platform affordances make is easier for users to navigate their way through the various ways of framing products through visual and text-based content on their device, and in the case of books, the contours of contemporary reading practices are outlined by bookstagrammers. Much like traditional book bloggers, one way a bookstagrammer can act as a cultural intermediary is using their qualifications to produce book reviews. Reviews can be seen as summaries and valuations of a cultural product or performance,[25] in this case a book or media text. A review is therefore a 'device', written with the aim of constructing value through a knowledgeable or credible opinion. Booksellers will often write short-form shelf-talkers to assist browsers in making purchasing choices based on their opinion as a professional reader, while literary critics offer institutionalised valuations of a particular books and are often published by reputable publications such as *The New York Times* or the *Sydney Review of Books*. The spatial context of the shelf-talker in the bookstore and the critic review in the newspaper add to the credibility of the intermediary, because they situate the exchange within a trusted site of book culture. Whether the consumer is aware of this or not, they will more likely rely on a book recommendation from a professional bookseller than their mechanic, even if the book that is being recommended is the same. The context of the bookstore adds a further level of qualification for the review. As Claire Squires notes, the book reviewer, 'sits both in literary judgement, but also as a buyer's guide, particularly in an age of proliferating numbers of titles available'.[26] Bookstagram offers an organised, searchable platform for users to engage with reviews that can act as a buyer's guide within a saturated global book market, much like the affordances of other social cataloguing and reader review sites such as Goodreads. Unlike Goodreads, the default engagement affordance of a scrollable home page on Instagram prioritises the content creator-turned-reviewer rather than a specific book. While consumers who wish to be guided by judgments of booksellers or Goodreads reviews generally have to be in front of the book in question (either in a bookstore, on an ecommerce site or on a book's dedicated Goodreads page), bookstagram reviews on Instagram offer consumers visual, searchable and recommendation-led modes of engagement. This allows Instagram users to engage more freely with the opinions and judgments of individual bookish actors, and thus suggests one way by which bookstagrammers can emerge as credible purveyors of cultural goods.

Before Instagram, web-based book blogs were a place for dedicated readers to construct value around particular books through long-form written reviews from their own individualised point of view. While book blogs have not disappeared by any means, many bloggers have capitalised on the platformised structure of social media and have often cultivated a burgeoning bookstagram account into their content offerings or have even developed a long-form book blog alongside their bookstagram account. Resh Susan of The Book Satchel began their book blog in 2015 before migrating after the fact to bookstagram under the handle @thebooksatchel (58,300 followers).[27] In some cases, bookstagrammers like Farouhk Naseem of @theguywiththebook (60,300 followers)[28] – who began their book chat journey on Instagram and won the London Book Fair's Bookstagrammer of the Year in 2018[29]

– have instead incorporated a long-form book blog into their content offerings. Whether a book blogger begins on bookstagram or incorporates bookstagram into their model at a later date, Susan and Naseem's follower counts on Instagram reveal that there is no definitive process to platformise bookish content between bookstagram and book blogs in order to build a community of followers on Instagram.

In researching book blogs as tastemakers, Beth Driscoll highlights that blogs are a form of digital self-representation and textual representation, which make blogs 'a particularly synergistic site for engagement with books'.[30] Book blogs, as representative of digital bookish cultural expression, 'play a role in shaping the contours of contemporary reading practices'.[31] Book blogs can be optimised to work with a user's Goodreads account and include affiliate links for other online users to purchase books and/or engage in additional bookish activity. This platformised structure of the book blog is something the bookstagram community have incorporated into their model. As stated previously, Instagram holds perceived affordances that include text, image and rapid, short form shareability.[32] These affordances therefore allow reader-users within the bookstagram community to either use their Instagram account as the main community base or use it as a tool to drive traffic to the long-form book blog they continue to maintain. However, as dedicated bloggers increasingly migrate between long-form blog posts to short snippets captured within a framed image and caption limit on Instagram, cultural expression across the digital book world is becoming more accessible and democratised, thus making a strong claim to the provocation of, 'are we all cultural intermediaries now?'[33]

In documenting the evolving nature of reader-reviews in the 21st century, Squires makes distinctions between book bloggers, Booktubers, and readers who use Instagram to post reviews of books and tag #bookstagram, stating that the 'latter are more likely to be thought of as visual performances of bookishness than "reviews"'.[34] This distinction, one between a review and a visual performance of bookishness, neglects to take into account the platform affordances of Instagram compared to book blogs and Booktube. Book blogs include many affordances that Instagram does not, but both have their strengths. Similarly, while BookTube's home is YouTube – another visual-based UGC platform – Booktubers rely on self-presence within the video frame, and thus their reviews are spoken, watched and listened to. I argue that the presence of the bookstagram produser is just as critical, even if their bodily presence does not always appear in the frame. In their analysis of the #zoellabookclub hashtag on Instagram, Branagh-Miscampbell and Marsden note that 'very few of these images focus on the reader themselves, instead the emphasis is on the book as an object and how it is situated within a staged domestic setting.'[35] While the bookstagram community's 'visual performances' of bookishness are notorious, the visual image in an Instagram post is just one element of an assemblage of cultural intermediation. The image, caption, comments section, content creator and any affiliated bio links (to a book blog, for example) operate as a network to communicate qualifying information to the end-user. This chapter intimately examines how these affordances operate as one whole to engage bookish consumers and demonstrate the cultural work that many professional, amateur and avid readers do to construct value for an audience of end-consumers and market actors on Instagram.

Methods: A Question of Scope

The data for this chapter was collected using my research Instagram account @publishingstudies. It is an account dedicated to researching Instagram's affordances within the bookstagram community and allows for both a manual and automated mode of collection of Instagram posts situated in their original platform layout. This situatedness allows for an examination of the front-facing view of the accounts, algorithms and global search pages while also helping develop a sense of how the bookstagram community evolves over a real-time engagement with the community. I follow a number of bookstagram accounts on the @publishingstudies account, and these accounts have been discovered organically by engaging with bookish Instagram content on the platform. In other words, I did not set out to find specific accounts by searching for their names and handles. Qualitative observations were manually recorded over the course of a three-month period in 2019 in the lead up to the Booker Prize announcement that year, and I then went back and took screenshots of representative posts that demonstrate the three common types of bookstagram posts I have identified.

In 'The Epistemology of Ullapoolism', Driscoll and Squires call for playful, middling and situated methodological approaches in book studies. On the question of scale in multidisciplinary studies, they argue 'mid-level thinking' – that is, combining intimate examination with larger knowledge bases – can offer studies of book culture a way out of merely collecting, counting and modelling.[36] Driscoll and Squires also make a strong case for 'operating *within* the context' of the study, citing their autoethnographic research of the Frankfurt Book Fair as an example of this.[37] In its topic of study, methods and analysis, this chapter implements a methodological approach that looks to what Driscoll and Squires term 'Ullapoolism' for its championing of alternate viewpoints. As argued above, intimate examinations of specific bookstagram posts within their platform context are vital if we are to gain a deeper understanding of such an expansive online bookish community. However, the scope of this chapter purposefully leaves room for more mid-level thinking and 'disruptive possibilities' within the post-digital convergence of book, platform and media studies.

@BookCase1 was selected as a representative account that repeatedly featured the three types of bookstagram posts I wanted to examine more extensively for this chapter. Due to the extensive size of the bookstagram community, there were challenges in justifying the scope of study for this chapter. While #bookhauls, #shelfies and #bookporn are also common hashtags and post types created by bookstagrammers,[38]

I wanted to refine the scope for this chapter and focus on the props signalling post, the review post and the prize prediction post because they are particularly demonstrative of how bookstagrammers are harnessing an emerging literary and cultural power within a bookish community that is too often ridiculed for its focus on visual affordances.

I chose to operationalise a couple of my research questions with the concept of 'props' because props and objects within an Instagram post serve as tools to signal reading and taste-making practices in similar way, for example, to carrying a branded or free tote bag to a writers festival.[39] I argue that bookish props are culturally significant features of visual reading practices, an element of social reading performance that almost exclusively features on Instagram. While the use of props as representative of online bookish behaviour is beginning to be examined to some extent,[40] I argue that the platform affordances of Instagram must be taken into account when examining bookstagram posts and props as powerful devices for cultural mediation. Dynamic visual platforms such as Instagram and, as it emerges in 2020 as a site of bookishness, TikTok, are best understood when examined within their own platform architectures. In other words, consuming media reports and listicles of collated bookstagram posts in *Vulture*, *The Guardian* or *HuffPost*[41] does little to represent the extent of how the nuances of bookstagram posts operate within their own digital community.

Testing the Waters: @BookCase1 as Representative

For the purpose of anonymising the account, I will call this Instagram user @BookCase1. @BookCase1 is a bookstagram produser who runs an account that posts bookish content about literary fiction and prize culture, and who identifies as a German-Japanese bibliophile. @BookCase1 was selected as a representative case study for this chapter because they create content across many common types of bookstagram posts. The posts of well-established bookstagram accounts such as @thebooksatchel, @theguywiththebook, @lifeandliterature and @bookbaristas – all of whom have been mentioned earlier as higher-tier accounts within a networked bookstagram hierarchy – often follow repeated patterns of colour, framing or type of post based on the call to action. @BookCase1 also adheres to a distinct visual aesthetic and is therefore a typical account, however, their account is demonstrative of many common types of bookstagram posts in one place, thus making it an atypical site of study within the structure of the bookstagram community. Another reason for selecting @BookCase1 as a representative case study was for their focus on prize prediction posts, as this is a phenomenon that is of interest to existing scholarship on literary prize culture within the field of contemporary book studies, but, like bookstagram as a whole, is under-examined. @BookCase1 does not host an affiliated book blog of their own, thus making their bookstagram account a primary site for their cultural work. This chapter will now deconstruct and present its analysis of three representative posts from @BookCase1's bookstagram account. The first is a 'caption review post' featuring Margaret Atwood's 2019 release, *The Testaments*.

The 'Caption Review' Post

In the lead up to 2019 Booker Prize announcement, @BookCase1 aimed to read, review and create content for all of the shortlisted titles in what I argue was an effort to consecrate their potential as an emerging cultural intermediary within the bookstagram community. On September 19th 2019, @BookCase1 shared their post for Atwood's long-awaited sequel to *The Handmaid's Tale* (1985).

The image's backdrop is a dark-stained wooden table and features a printed codex of *The Testaments* at its centre with equal distance between the edges of the book and the framed ratio of the image. The image also features a vintage paper map to the book's left, and to its right, a fountain pen, two tea-stained handwritten letters and a cup of black tea. In the top left-hand corner of the image there are two plants. The greenery emphasises the distinct acid green colour featured on the cover of *The Testaments*, and thus elicits an eye-catching visual cue.[42] A majority of @BookCase1's bookstagram posts feature outward facing books, and this positioning mirrors that of a bookstore shelving practice that places certain titles face out on the shelf as a result of paid publisher marketing or a bookstore's independent shelving decision. This outward-facing position focuses a browser's attention to the book more so than that of just the spine facing outwards. By making *The Testaments* the primary focus of this image, @BookCase1 is attempting to focus the attention of users that have an interest in Atwood or this specific book while they are scrolling through their personal or public search feed. Just as the book cover design was created to stand out in an over-saturated market, so too is a bookstagram image that is framed to highlight the cover of the book object in question. While the *The Testaments* image has been constructed using a single book and a collection of additional objects to signal a focus, it forms only one part of an assemblage of the caption review post, and thus it cannot remain as the only object of analysis.

The caption review that accompanies the above image is formulated in two parts: a 'my hope and expectations for this book' and a 'my actual experience of this book.' This structure is used across a majority of @BookCase1's caption review posts. In part one of the review, @BookCase1 voices their expectations for the long-awaited sequel and does the cultural work of constructing an expected value of the book object at hand, they suggest the book 'is going to be quietly brilliant, shedding new light on the power structures of totalitarian regimes and the psychology of oppression'.[43] This readerly expectation of *The Testaments* is shrouded in signalling behaviour and also actively plays into the hype about this book within the 2019 book market more broadly. However, in part two of the review, @BookCase1 describes the book as '[a] flashy, action-adventure thriller written to tie up the loose ends of its predecessor'.[44] While this may mirror the reading experience of many readers after reading Atwood's newest release, @BookCase1 has used their available 'devices' as a literary fiction and prize culture amateur commentator to deconstruct the expectations and reality of their reading experience. This review structure highlights some of the features of many traditionally published book reviews. While outside the scope of this particular chapter, I also wish to raise questions here about bookstagram's capacity – as a unique social reviewing platform with a structure reminiscent of book clubs and democratised social cataloguing practices[45] – to problematise the historical gendered whiteness of traditional book reviewing.[46] As Kristin L. Matthews notes, '[e]mpowerment, authenticity, diversity, and change: these elements seemingly unique to social media are what enable not just women in general, but women of color [sic] in particular to find their voice as writers, readers, and thinkers'.[47]

Towards the end of the caption review, @BookCase1 suggests that their opinion may just be personal bias, but the comments thread on the Atwood post reveals that many members of the bookstagram community share the sentiment of @BookCase1's opinion. The post, which in March 2020 had garnered 694 likes, has attracted comments such as, 'Compelling review. I always look forward to your thoughts', 'Couldn't agree more' and 'You voiced exactly what I felt when I read it, felt very let down by it'.[48] This attentive level of engagement points to the potential for small tier accounts to cultivate a community that both supports and views individual bookstagrammers as arbiters of taste. The power that comes with being able to engage hundreds of users on a bookstagram post featuring a curated image and an individualised opinion arises out of the cultural work that @BookCase1 is doing to construct value for an audience of end-consumers within the affordances of Instagram. The affordances that Instagram offer on the platform – in this case comments threads positioned directly below the original post for users to engage with alongside the image and caption – mean that bookstagrammers can establish and access a dedicated space for validation of opinion within moments of sharing an idea.

The 'Props Signalling' Post

The 'props signalling' post is a common type of bookstagram post that operates as a qualifier for demonstrating different levels of familiarity with a book's content. Props perform the role of accessories while the book object remains the central element of a piece of framed content for Instagram. As Bronwen Thomas states in *Literature and Social Media,* bookstagram posts are 'the photographic equivalent of a still life in which the book has pride of place'.[49] The use of props in bookstagram posts can signal specific visual cues pertaining to the social and cultural capital of reader-users within the community. In the same way that being able to recall the full names and positions of players on your favourite sports team seemingly demonstrates that your support is justified, certain kinds of props within the frame of a bookstagram post take on the role of a device to communicate to other users that you do, in fact, hold a deeper familiarity with the book in centre of the image. The next image I want to focus on here is a still life created featuring a cover-facing printed codex of Lucy Ellman's *Ducks, Newburyport* (2019) surrounded by two eggs and their cracked shells, a single lemon, a slab of butter, wooden mixing utensils, a whisk and a tray of baked cinnamon buns. The backdrop is blue and textured and there are also piles and dustings of loose flour on top of the backdrop.[50] As with the post featuring *The Testaments,* @BookCase1 has centred the book within the frame.

Without any readerly knowledge of the book, the choice to frame the book alongside eggs, butter, a lemon, flour and freshly baked cinnamon buns seem out of place at first. When I inserted this image into a Word document as a reference point for writing this chapter, Word automatically generated an alt-text description of the above image that appeared on the image as I text-wrapped it: 'A picture containing table, food, book, small items.' However, if a fellow book-stagrammer had also read *Ducks*, they would complete the circuit of signalling behaviour and assume @BookCase1 has some knowledge of the book's content. Much like the effort to pay for and carry a branded tote bag,[51] the effort of assembling the above objects on a countertop in order to demonstrate a credible reading act is an example of why props of this kind operate as expressions of cultural capital. As a book of considerable length in the running for the 2019 Booker Prize, many other bookstagrammers signalled their attempts to tackle *Ducks* in its entirety leading up to the announcement of prize winner (see #ducksnewburyport). As users navigate their way through book reviews and guidance on how to approach *Ducks* across the hashtag and user accounts, a user viewing @BookCase1's image in their Instagram feed would assumably acquire knowledge that @BookCase1's opinions of *Ducks, Newburyport* are qualified because the props signalling post demonstrates, at the very least, a credible level of familiarity with the book's content. However, as I have out-lined previously in this chapter, a visual performance of reading on Instagram cannot be examined by itself; it must be examined as part of the Instagram post assemblage of at least the image and caption and by extension, the comments and hashtags.

The first half of the caption that accompanies the *Ducks* image is written as a list of content similar to that of the process of writing a machine learning tool or code frame:

> Take banal reflections on everyday life, add in free-association word lists, throw in plot points on children's books and vintage movies, fret about the state of the environment, insert viral news headlines, insert diner lingo, bemoan the state of US gun laws, insert anxieties about motherhood, enclose a few cleaning tips, throw in memories of bizarre dream sequences – rinse, repeat! There you have it. The algorithm to Ducks, Newburyport.[52]

The decision to call this written list, 'the algorithm to *Ducks, Newburyport*' utilises a kind of humour that both highlights the algorithmic affordances of the platform on which the post has been published, and an individualised readerly experience. But because of this humour, other users who have engaged with the book can share the sentiment of the individual review because perhaps that is how they read the novel as well. However, as is the format of @BookCase1's review captions, there is a second part to the textual signalling. The second part of the caption for *Ducks, Newburyport* reveals that they did not enjoy the book. When reading through the comments thread on this post, most commenters thanked @BookCase1 for this two-part review and said that they are glad they didn't set out on the reading journey, while others commented with their reading progress of *Ducks*. These two comments from two different users summarise the thread well: one user states, 'The fact that you've finished the whole thing despite having had mixed feelings in the first 300 pages is a testament to your stoicism and strength of courage' and another says, 'You finished it! 😵 I have to admit I'm still somewhere between 600 and 700. Not sure if your review has given me the strength to continue'.[53] The word 'strength' in each comment points to the book's considerable length and therefore the time it takes to engage with the reading experience of *Ducks*; a strenuous experience that up until reading @BookCase1's review was already being questioned by each commenter. By deconstructing the entirety of the *Ducks* bookstagram post assemblage, I determined that the visual signalling did not, in fact, align with the sentiment outlined in the caption review, and the comments thread worked to uphold and sometimes challenge the literary capital signalling work that @BookCase1 constructed by creating bookstagram content for their reading experience of *Ducks, Newburyport*. This is significant because the visual signals of @BookCase1's aesthetically pleasing image – one that assumably took a great deal of time and effort to construct – suggest that the book was an enjoyable reading experience, and raises the question of why would someone take the time to construct an intricate and unique bookish image if they did not enjoy the book? Bookstagram offers a communal space for creative and constructive criticism. And this means that just as a traditional book reviewer will review books and often include catchy (often clickable) titles, bookstagrammers can juxtapose positive visual signals of readerly performance with textual criticism within the same bookstagram post assemblage in order to generate engagement.

When is a Prop not a (Literary Capital) Prop?

There are, however, bookstagram posts that do not engage in textual criticism in the same way as @BookCase1 does in the above example. As Thomas notes, 'using photographs or other visual material to share one's reading also predates social media'.[54] Thomas references Jasper Fforde's 2005–2010 photo competition where readers were asked to capture photos of their 'extreme reading' practices to share on Fforde's website at the time.[55] Branagh-Miscampbell and Marsden's critical analysis of posts compiled within '#zoellabookclub' revealed that 'many of these who interacted with the ZBC presented their engagement through images of non-reading' due to the fact that many contributors to the hashtag 'prioritised a performance of the procurement and display of the books [featured in the Zoella Book Club] rather than the reading experience'.[56] Images depicting non-reading are often assumed to be synonymous with a practice of non-reading. This speaks to the long tradition of books used as objects for display to signal cultural and intellectual capital.[57] Consequently, Branagh-Miscampbell and Marsden argue that the Zoella Book Club fostered an 'aesthetic' and 'rhetoric' that 'propagated, commodified, and ultimately perpetuated historical notions of highly feminised and domesticated reading, to construct an image of young women readers online in the twenty-first century'.[58] The 'props signalling' post differs from a bookstagram post featuring non-literary props because of the type of cultural signalling work it is undertaking. Bookstagram posts with a minimalist caption featuring domestic props such as a cup of coffee, tea, plants, candles, socks and cereal are visual performances of reading and are often captured within intimate locations in a household such as a bedroom or reading nook, and the props they choose to feature can create a continuity for an account's overall aesthetic. These kinds of bookstagram posts create a representation of 'highly feminised and homely' readerly experiences and actively signal that a bookstagram user is 'not aspiring to be seen just as [a reader], but [is] aspiring to a specific image of domestic and cosy femininity'.[59] While this argument holds true for many types of bookstagram accounts, it also works to exclude any potentiality for bookstagrammers who choose not to create content that fits the traditional aspirational aesthetic of the community to emerge as subjective, mediating individuals within the platform.

This domestic and aesthetically pleasing side of bookstagram also raises questions more broadly about the types of non-literary objects that appear in bookstagram posts of this nature. Why is it that when associated with social media, the words 'bookish' and 'bookishness' materialise mental images of inherently modernist and aspirational, often gendered and overwhelmingly white, middle-class domestic objects? Again, this question is outside the scope of this chapter, however, I do believe it is an area of study that requires a much deeper level of examination within book studies.

Ultimately, using individual and often personal locations and objects as props to create continuity in an image provides a signifier for bookstagram users to recognise who this account belongs to in a saturated visual media ecology. While this type of content uses props to create readerly experiences in an aesthetically driven digital environment, when examined only as images, the images do not always signal that the bookstagrammer has actually read the book/s featured in the image. However, the role of 'aspirational' bookstagram posts within the community is not made any less significant because of this. It remains a matter of taste as to what kind of bookstagram props signalling post a user prefers to engage with (and this preference may or may not be a conscious preference), but without the mass of visual representations of aspirational performances of readerly experience, the bookstagram community would not exist.

The 'Prize Prediction' Post

Literary prizes have become increasingly visible features of national and global book cultures in the last fifty years.[60] Recent scholarship on the relationship between social media, literary prizes and book culture more broadly examines Twitter as a social media platform with affordances for the circulation of cultural and literary capital.[61] Book Twitter, as it is commonly known, comes together annually for short bursts of time during the lead up to and announcement of literary prize winners. In observations of bookstagram accounts in the lead up to the 2019 Booker Prize, I noted that for the first time, many bookstagram accounts were creating posts outlining their own predictions for the longlist, shortlist and possible winner. The posts often included a photo of a stack of books – much like the media release photos from the Booker Prize each year – and a caption outlining why the user thought their picks were worthy of being in the running for the prize. At the beginning of her chapter titled, 'The Man Booker Prize: Money, Glory and Media Spectacle', Driscoll provides an anecdote about placing a bet on the Booker Prize at a betting shop:

> 'I'd like to place a bet on the Booker Prize.'
> She blinked.
> 'The what?'
> 'It's a prize. For books.'[62]

Placing a bet on a literary prize at a betting shop is a private behaviour; it is an interaction between two individuals either side of a Perspex counter. The act of placing a bet in a betting shop will not influence a jury. Bookstagrammers who post their predictions for literary prize lists and winners are also not trying to influence a jury. However, they are engaging in signalling behaviour in quite a different way to the betting shop example because the 'prize prediction' post is a social performance of literary taste-making.

In her work on tote bags as coded objects, Dane argues that carrying a literary-branded tote bag at a literary festival is a 'conscious act of performance' that can 'act as a surrogate for one's accumulated cultural capital'.[63] Posting a captioned, curated photo of books you own with the signal that you predict these nine books will make the Booker shortlist is much like the carrying of a tote bag at a literary festival; it is a public performance of cultural capital. Therefore, Instagram offers bookish users affordances to publicly engage in the circulation of cultural capital through individual subjective opinions. The act of posting a prize prediction on Instagram is thus signalling more about the person posting than the prize itself. This next section examines what I have identified as the 'prize prediction' bookstagram post. @BookCase1 is representative of this kind of post because not only do they post within the Booker Prize season, but there are other examples of prize predictions featured on their account as well. In other words, a 'prize prediction' offers @BookCase1 a key device to demonstrate potential as a new kind of cultural intermediary.

The 'prize prediction' post is often constructed as a flat lay image or 'bookstack' featuring titles the user tips to possibly make up the longlist for a particular prize that year, or titles that they think ought to make the longlist. This type of post is specific to a small number of users within the bookstagram community; however, the common visual format of the image is visible across the entirety of the community. The third and final image I wish to analyse from @BookCase1 is constructed as a flat lay image with a dark wood-stained backdrop featuring the full covers or fragments of covers of seven books published in 2019 including Valeria Luiselli's *Lost Children Archive*, Ocean Vuong's *On*

Earth We're Briefly Gorgeous, Marlon James's *Black Leopard Red Wolf*, Robbie Arnott's *Flames* (2018), Damian Barr's *You Will Be Safe Here*, Max Porter's *Lanny* and Ali Smith's *Spring*.[64] These seven covers are a visual display of the books @BookCase1 hoped would make the Booker longlist for 2019. Of those seven photographed books, two of them ended up being featured on the Booker Dozen for 2019 – the list of 13 titles longlisted for the award. Unlike the previous types of bookstagram posts this chapter has analysed, this visual assemblage of a prize prediction does not immediately signal what the purpose of the post is from the view of the Instagram grid (that is, the account grid and the global search grid). Within the parameters of common types of posts set out by the bookstagram community, this could be a collection of books that @BookCase1 has on their to-be-read (#TBR) list, or it could be a selection of books that they have just purchased and classified as a #bookhaul. The ambiguity of what this image is signalling works to promote bookishness in a way that attracts a higher degree of engagement with the post. It is not until a user reads the accompanying caption that the signal changes and that @BookCase1's aesthetically-pleasing flat lay is actually a hopeful prediction of books tipped for the Booker Dozen.

Of the additional titles mentioned in the caption on this post as possible contenders, an additional four (Chigozie Obioma's *An Orchestra of Minorities*, Deborah Levy's *The Man Who Saw Everything*, Bernadine Evaristo's *Girl, Woman, Other* and Margaret Atwood's *The Testaments*) were featured on the Booker 2019 longlist. As a result, @BookCase1 had correctly tipped six books out of a possible thirteen and included the eventual joint winners of the 2019 prize (Evaristo and Atwood) in this bookstagram post, keeping in mind that the bookstagrammer's role here is not to influence a jury. However, it raises a question of could anyone who reads widely across new fiction releases predict the outcome of a literary prize longlist? It is possible; but how many of those readers would choose to share their predictions in a public display of opinion and accountability? In the context of the prize prediction post, the difference between an avid reader and a bookstagrammer is a process of mediation through performance. Instagram functions as a mediating force between the reading experience and the sharing of that reading experience. Bookstagram hosts individual reading experiences that other users within the community can scrutinise, affirm or 'like' as an act of admiration or indifference. Just as authors eagerly await a known critic's *New York Times* review, bookstagrammers await the thoughts of other, more influential or top tier bookstagrammers on new releases, almost releases, backlisted titles they never got around to reading or just individualised opinions about book culture more broadly.

Much like a well-trafficked book blog or YouTube channel, an influential bookstagram account operates as a cultural intermediary, constructing the value of products through words, images and opinion. Unlike the book blog or Booktube account, an influential bookstagram account does not always need a large following of subscribers to gain traction with readers and other market actors. However, just as the wider book world operates as a field of small, middling and big scale players, so too does bookstagram. As of September 2019, @BookCase1 had 4723 followers, which would be considered a small account in the bookstagram landscape I outlined previously in this chapter. But in light of this, @BookCase1 has developed a large potential 'following' based on their aesthetic and subjective opinion and are therefore positioned as a significant cultural intermediary within the community they have nurtured. Parallels can be drawn through the way @BookCase1 uses Instagram to frame their literary prize predictions, commentary, valuations, the affirmation and challenges they receive in the comments thread and how other traditional literary cultural intermediaries participate in literary prize culture and book chat on Twitter. @BookCase1 utilises the perceived platform afford-ances that Instagram offers and shares a visual, textual and affirming representation of their opinion. The emergence of the prize prediction post as a form of visual communication of a material and cultural practice, or the broader act of using a bookstagram platform as a way of signalling your literary capital, demonstrates an emerging power of bookstagrammers as significant cultural intermediaries within a post-digital literary landscape.

Conclusion

The power that comes with being able to engage bookish consumers and generate hundreds of likes and comments on a bookstagram post featuring an individualised opinion arises out of the cultural work that many professional, amateur and avid readers do to construct value for an audience of end-consumers and market actors within their chosen platform and/or device. This is an emerging power, and the caption review post, the props signalling post and the prize prediction post are just three devices bookstagrammers like @BookCase1 are utilising as cultural intermediaries in post-digital book culture. Further work within this field could build upon theorising the post-digital landscape of visual-based platforms in order to explore the inner workings of burgeoning online communities that up until now have been under-examined. As more frameworks and methodologies emerge as a result of studies into a post-digital book world, there has never been a better time to explore the intertwining of sociality, material practices and cultural influence.

Endnotes

1   Bronwen Thomas. *Literature and Social Media*. (Oxon: Routledge, 2020) 73.
2   '#bookstagram' Instagram (March 2020).
3   'Bookstagrammer of the Year - The London Book Fair,' https://www. londonbookfair.co.uk/Forms/Forms-2019/Book-Blogger-of-the-Year3/.
4   Ann Steiner. 'Personal Readings and Public Texts: Book Blogs and Online Writing about Literature,' *Culture Unbound: Journal of Current Cultural Research* 2 (2010) 471–494; Simone Murray. '"Selling" Literature: The Cultivation of Book Buzz in the Digital Literary Sphere,' *Logos* 27,

no. 1 (7 June, 2016) 11–21; Beth Driscoll. 'Book Blogs as Tastemakers,' *Participations*. 16, no. 1 (2019) 280–305.

5 Danielle Fuller and DeNel Rehberg Sedo. *Reading Beyond the Book: The Social Practices of Contemporary Literary Culture.* (London: Routledge. 2013); Stevie Marsden. '"I Didn't Know You Could Read": Questioning the Legitimacy of Kim Kardashian-West's Status as a Cultural and Literary Intermediary,' *Logos* 29, no. -3 (17 November, 2018) 64–79; Maxine Branagh-Miscampbell and Stevie Marsden. '"Eating, Sleeping, Breathing, Reading": The Zoella Book Club and the Young Woman Reader in the 21st Century,' *Participations* 16. No. 1 (2019) 412–440; Melanie Ramdarshan Bold. 'Is "Everyone Welcome"? Intersectionality, Inclusion, and the Extension of Cultural Hierarchies on Emma Watson's Feminist Book Club, 'Our Shared Shelf',' *Participations* 16, no. 1 (2019) 441–472; Kristin L. Matthews. '"Woke" and Reading: Social Media, Reception, and Contemporary Black Feminism,' *Participations*. 16, no. 1 (2020) 390–411.

6 Claire Parnell. 'Models of Publishing and Opportunities for Change: Representations in Harlequin, Montlake and Self-Published Romance Novels,' *Australian Literary Studies* 33, no. 4 (2018).

7 Murray 'Selling Literature'; Simone Murray. *The Digital Literary Sphere: Reading, Writing, and Selling Books in the Internet Era.* (John Hopkins University Press, 2018).

8 Nicola Rodger. 'From Bookshelf Porn and Shelfies to #bookfacefriday: How Readers Use Pinterest to Promote Their Bookishness,' *Participations*. 16, no. 1 (2019) 473–495.

9 Bronwen Thomas. *Literature and Social Media*, 69.

10 Maarit Jaakkola. 'From Re-Viewers to Me-Viewers: The #Bookstagram Review Sphere on Instagram and the Uses of the Perceived Platform and Genre Affordances,' *Interactions: Studies in Communication & Culture* 10, no. 1 (2019): 91–110.

11 Maarit Jaakkola. 'From Re-Viewers to Me-Viewers.'

12 Axel Bruns. *Blogs, Wikipedia, Second Life and Beyond: From Production to Produsage.* (New York: Peter Lang, 2008).

13 Murray 'Selling Literature'; Murray 'Digital Literary Sphere.'

14 Murray 'Selling Literature' 12.

15 Ted Striphas. *The Late Age of Print: Everyday Book Culture from Consumerism to Control.* (New York: Columbia University Press, 2009) 101.

16 Rachel Noorda and Stevie Marsden. 'Twenty-First Century Book Studies: The State of the Discipline,' *Book History* 22, no. 1 (2019): 370–97.

17   Christian Ulrik Andersen and Søren Bro Pold. 'Aesthetics of the Banal
      – "New Aesthetics" in an Era of Diverted Digital Revolutions,' in
      Postdigital Aesthetics, ed. David M. Berry and Michael Dieter. (Palgrave
      Macmillan, 2015) 271–88.; Florian Cramer. 'What Is 'Post-Digital'?' In
      Postdigital Aesthetics, eds. David M. Berry and Michael Dieter. (Palgrave
      Macmillan, 2015) 12–26.
18   Alexandra Dane. 'Cultural Capital as Performance: Tote Bags and
      Contemporary Literary Festivals,' *Mémoires Du Livre* 11, no. 2 (2020),
      https://doi.org/10.7202/1070270ar.
19   Stinson, Emmett. 'Small Publishers and the Emerging Network of
      Australian Literary Prosumption,' *Australian Humanities Review* 59
      (April 2016) 23–43.; Stinson, Emmett. 'Small Publishers and the Miles
      Franklin,' in *The Return of Print? Contemporary Australian Publishing* eds.
      Emmett Stinson and Aaron Mannion (Melbourne: Monash University
      Publishing, 2016), 132–42.
20   Jennifer Smith Maguire and Julian Matthews, 'Are We All Cultural
      Intermediaries Now? An Introduction to Cultural Intermediaries in
      Context,' *European Journal of Cultural Studies* 15, no. 5 (2012) 552,
      https://doi.org/10.1177/1367549412445762.
21   Smith Maguire and Matthews, 'Are We All Cultural Intermediaries
      Now?' 552.
22   Branagh-Miscampbell and Marsden. '"Eating, Sleeping, Breathing,
      Reading",' 29.
23   Smith Maguire and Matthews, 'Are We All Cultural Intermediaries
      Now?' 552.
24   Branagh-Miscampbell and Marsden. '"Eating, Sleeping, Breathing,
      Reading",' 419.
25   Grant Black. *Critics, Ratings, and Society: The Sociology of Reviews*.
      (Lanham, MD: Rowman & Littlefield Publishers, 2006).
26   Claire Squires. 'The Review and the Reviewer,' in Baverstock, Alison,
      Richard Bradford and Madelena Gonzalez eds. *Contemporary Publishing
      and the Culture of Books*. (Oxford: Routledge, 2020) 121.
27   @thebooksatchel. Instagram (November 2020).
28   @theguywiththebook. Instagram (November 2020).
29   theguywiththebook. 'Bookstagram for Beginners!' *Theguywiththebook*
      (blog), May 17, 2018. https://theguywiththebook.com/2018/05/17/
      bookstagram-for-beginners/.
30   Driscoll. 'Book blogs as tastemakers,' 281.
31   Driscoll. 'Book blogs as tastemakers,' 302.
32   Jaakkola 'From re-viewers to me-viewers.'

33   Smith Maguire and Matthews. 'Are We All Cultural Intermediaries Now?' 552.
34   Squires 'The Review and the Reviewer,' 130.
35   Branagh-Miscampbell and Marsden. '"Eating, Sleeping, Breathing, Reading",' 431.
36   Driscoll, Beth, and Claire Squires. 'The Epistemology of Ullapoolism: *Making Mischief from within Contemporary Book Cultures,*' *Angelaki* 25, no. 5 (2020): 137–55. https://doi.org/10.1080/0969725X.2020.1807147.
37   Driscoll and Squires. 'The Epistemology of Ullapoolism,' 143.
38   Thomas. *Literature and Social Media.* 74–75.
39   Dane. 'Cultural Capital as Performance.'
40   Rodger. 'From Bookshelf Porn and Shelfies to #bookfacefriday'; Branagh-Miscampbell and Marsden. '"Eating, Sleeping, Breathing, Reading".'
41   Holly Connolly. 'Is Social Media Influencing Book Cover Design?' *The Guardian*, 28 August, 2018, https://www.theguardian.com/books/2018/aug/28/is-social-media-influencing-book-cover-design.; Hillary Kelly. 'Here's an Annoying Instagram Trend: Throwing Yourself on a Pile of Open Books,' Vulture, 29 October, 2018. https://www.vulture.com/2018/10/the-terrible-instagram-trend-of-piles-of-open-books.html.' Shelby Pope. 'Why Instagram's Biggest Book Accounts Aren't Your Usual Influencers,' *The Guardian*, 27 September, 2019, sec. Life and style.
42   @BookCase1. 'September 19, 2019.' instagram.com, https://www.instagram.com/p/B2l2p6JAri9/.
43   @BookCase1 Post, September 19, 2019 instagram.com, https://www.instagram.com/p/B2l2p6JAri9/.
44   @BookCase1 Post, September 19, 2019.
45   Fuller and Rehberg Sedo. *Reading Beyond the Book;* Murray, Simone. *The Digital Literary Sphere*; Driscoll, Beth. *The New Literary Middlebrow: Tastemakers and Reading in the Twenty-First Century* (Palgrave Macmillan, 2014); Bold 'Is "Everyone Welcome"?'.
46   Squires 'The Review and the Reviewer'; Dane, Alexandra. *Gender and Prestige in Literature: Contemporary Australian Book Culture.* (London, New York: Palgrave Macmillan, 2020).
47   Matthews '"Woke" and Reading,' 396.
48   Comments Thread. @BookCase1 Post, September 19, 2019.
49   Thomas. *Literature and Social Media,* 73.
50   @BookCase1. September 26, 2019, instagram.com, https://www.instagram.com/p/B23rQ-cgJJV/.
51   Dane 'Cultural Capital as Performance,' 13.
52   @BookCase1, Post – September 26th, 2019.

53 @BookCase1, Post – September 26th, 2019.
54 Thomas. *Literature and Social Media*, 73.
55 Thomas. *Literature and Social Media*, 73.
56 Branagh-Miscampbell and Marsden. "'Eating, Sleeping, Breathing, Reading".'
57 Stephen Colclough. 'Representing Reading Spaces,' *The History of Reading, Volume 3, e*ds. Crone R. and Towheed, Shafquat (London, New York: Palgrave Macmillan. 2011) 99–114; Pyne, Lydia. *Bookshelf. (London:* Bloomsbury 2016).
58 Branagh-Miscampbell and Marsden. "'Eating, Sleeping, Breathing, Reading",' 415.
59 Branagh-Miscampbell and Marsden. "'Eating, Sleeping, Breathing, Reading",' 430.
60 Dane. *Gender and Prestige in Literature*; Beth Driscoll. 'The Man Booker Prize: Money, Glory and Media Spectacle,' In *The New Literary Middlebrow*. (London, New York: Palgrave Macmillan 2014) 119–51.
61 Beth Driscoll. 'Twitter, Literary Prizes and the Circulation of Capital,' in *By the Book? Contemporary Publishing in Australia*, eds. Emmett Stinson and Nick Trakakis. (Melbourne: Monash University Publishing, 2013); Driscoll, 'The Man Booker Prize: Money, Glory and Media Spectacle'; Millicent Weber and Beth Driscoll. 'Playful Twitter Accounts and the Socialisation of Literary Institutions.' First Monday 24, no. 3 (March 1, 2019). https://doi.org/10.5210/fm.v24i3.9486.
62 Driscoll. 'The Man Booker Prize: Money, Glory and Media Spectacle,' 119.
63 Dane. 'Cultural Capital as Performance,' 8.
64 @BookCase1. 'July 5, 2019.' instagram.com, https://www.instagram.com/p/BziNGIbg9h_/.

Bibliography

@BookCase1. 'My hope and expectations for this book:,' Instagram post with an image of Margaret Attwood's *The Testaments* and a review in the caption, 19 September, 2019, https://www.instagram.com/p/B2l2p6JAri9/.
@BookCase1. 'Take banal reflections on everyday life, add in free-association word lists, throw in plot points…,' Instagram post of an image of Lucy Ellmann's *Ducks, Newburyport* and a review in the caption, 26 September, 2019, https://www.instagram.com/p/B23rQ-cgJJV/.
@BookCase1. 'July means booker longlist month,' Instagram post of an image of various book covers and Booker Prize longlist predictions, 5 July, 2019, https://www.instagram.com/p/BziNGIbg9h_/.

@thebooksatchel. https://www.instagram.com/thebooksatchel/.

@theguywiththebook. https://www.instagram.com/theguywiththebook/.

Andersen, Christian Ulrik, and Bro Pold, Søren. 'Aesthetics of the Banal –
   "New Aesthetics" in an Era of Diverted Digital Revolutions,' in *Postdigital
   Aesthetics*, edited by David M. Berry and Michael Dieter, 271–88. London:
   Palgrave Macmillan UK, 2015.

Blank, Grant. *Critics, Ratings, and Society: The Sociology of Reviews*. Lanham,
   MD: Rowman & Littlefield Publishers, 2006.

'Bookstagrammer of the Year,' *The London Book Fair*, January 9, 2019. https://
   www.londonbookfair.co.uk/Forms/Forms-2019/Book-Blogger-of-the-Year3/.

Branagh-Miscampbell, Maxine, and Marsden, Stevie. '"Eating, Sleeping,
   Breathing, Reading": The Zoella Book Club and the Young Woman Reader
   in the 21st Century,' *Participations*. 16, no. 1 (2019): 64–79.

Bruns, Axel. *Blogs, Wikipedia, Second Life and Beyond: From Production to
   Produsage*. New York: Peter Lang, 2008.

Cramer, Florian. 'What Is 'Post-Digital'?' In *Postdigital Aesthetics*, edited by
   David M. Berry and Michael Dieter, 12–26. London: Palgrave Macmillan,
   2015.

Colclough, Stephen. 'Representing Reading Spaces,' *The History of Reading,
   Volume 3*. edited by Crone Rosalind. and Towheed, Shafquat, 99–114.
   London, New York: Palgrave Macmillan, 2011.

Connolly, Holly. 'Is Social Media Influencing Book Cover Design?' *The
   Guardian*, 28 August, 2018, https://www.theguardian.com/books/2018/
   aug/28/is-social-media-influencing-book-cover-design.

Dane, Alexandra. 'Cultural Capital as Performance: Tote Bags and
   Contemporary Literary Festivals,' *Mémoires Du Livre* 11, no. 2 (2020) :
   1-29, https://doi.org/10.7202/1070270ar. 1–29.

Dane, Alexandra. *Gender and Prestige in Literature*. London, New York: Palgrave
   Macmillan, 2020.

Driscoll, Beth. 2019. 'Book Blogs as Tastemakers,' *Participations*. 16, no. 1
   (2019): 280–305.

Driscoll, Beth. *The New Literary Middlebrow*. London, New York: Palgrave
   Macmillan, 2014.

Driscoll, Beth. 'Twitter, Literary Prizes and the Circulation of Capital,' in *By
   the Book? Contemporary Publishing in Australia*, edited by Emmett Stinson.
   Melbourne: Monash University Publishing, 2013.

Driscoll, Beth, and Squires, Claire. 'The Epistemology of Ullapoolism:
   Making Mischief from within Contemporary Book Cultures,' *Angelaki*
   25, no. 5 (September, 2020): 137–55. https://doi.org/10.1080/096972
   5X.2020.1807147.

Fuller, Danielle, and Rehberg Sedo, DeNel. *Reading Beyond the Book: The Social Practices of Contemporary Literary Culture.* London: Routledge, 2013.

Jaakkola, Maarit. 'From Re-Viewers to Me-Viewers: The #Bookstagram Review Sphere on Instagram and the Uses of the Perceived Platform and Genre Affordances,' *Interactions: Studies in Communication & Culture* 10, no. 1 (July, 2019): 91–110. https://doi.org/10.1386/iscc.10.1-2.91_1.

Kelly, Hillary. 'Here's an Annoying Instagram Trend: Throwing Yourself on a Pile of Open Books,' *Vulture*, October 29, 2018. https://www.vulture.com/2018/10/the-terrible-instagram-trend-of-piles-of-open-books.html.

Ludovico, Alessandro. *Post-Digital Print: The Mutation of Publishing Since 1894.* Onomatopee 77. Eindhoven: Onomatopee, 2012.

Matthews, Kristin L. '"Woke" and Reading: Social Media, Reception, and Contemporary Black Feminism,' *Participations.* 16, 1 (2019): 390–411.

Murray, Simone. '"Selling" Literature: The Cultivation of Book Buzz in the Digital Literary Sphere,' *Logos* 27, no. 1 (June , 2016): 11–21. https://doi.org/10.1163/1878-4712-11112094.

Murray, Simone. *The Digital Literary Sphere: Reading, Writing, and Selling Books in the Internet Era.* Baltimore, USA: John Hopkins University Press, 2018.

Noorda, Rachel, and Marsden, Stevie. 'Twenty-First Century Book Studies: The State of the Discipline,' *Book History* 22, no. 1 (2019): 370–97. https://doi.org/10.1353/bh.2019.0013.

Parnell, Claire. 'Models of Publishing and Opportunities for Change: Representations in Harlequin, Montlake and Self-Published Romance Novels,' *Australian Literary Studies* (December 2018), https://doi.org/10.20314/als.1cd73e2f68.

Pope, Shelby. 'Why Instagram's Biggest Book Accounts Aren't Your Usual Influencers,' *The Guardian*, 27 September, 2019. https://www.theguardian.com/lifeandstyle/2019/sep/26/bookstagram-books-instagram-influencers-reading.

Pyne, Lydia. *Bookshelf.* London: Bloomsbury, 2016.

Ramdarshan Bold, Melanie. 'Is "Everyone Welcome"? Intersectionality, Inclusion, and the Extension of Cultural Hierarchies on Emma Watson's Feminist Book Club, "Our Shared Shelf",' *Participations.* 16, 1 (2019): 441–472.

Rodger, Nicola. 'From Bookshelf Porn and Shelfies to #bookfacefriday: How Readers Use Pinterest to Promote Their Bookishness,' *Participations.* 16, 1 (2019): 473–495.

Smith Maguire, Jennifer, and Julian Matthews. 'Are We All Cultural Intermediaries Now? An Introduction to Cultural Intermediaries in Context,' *European Journal of Cultural Studies* 15, no. 5 (October 1, 2012): 551–62. https://doi.org/10.1177/1367549412445762.

Squires, Claire. 'The Review and the Reviewer,' in *Contemporary Publishing and the Culture of Books*, 117–132, edited by Baverstock, Alison, Bradford, Richard and Gonzalez, Madelena. Oxford: Routledge, 2020.

Steiner, Ann. 'Personal Readings and Public Texts: Book Blogs and Online Writing about Literature,' *Culture Unbound: Journal of Current Cultural Research* 2 (2010): 471–494.

Stinson, Emmett. 'Small Publishers and the Emerging Network of Australian Literary Prosumption,' *Australian Humanities Review* 59 (April 2016): 23–43.

Stinson, Emmett. 'Small Publishers and the Miles Franklin,' in *The Return of Print? Contemporary Australian Publishing,* 132-42, edited by Emmett Stinson and Aaron Manion, Melbourne: Monash University Publishing, 2016.

Striphas, Ted. *The Late Age of Print: Everyday Book Culture from Consumerism to Control.* New York: Columbia University Press, 2009.

theguywiththebook. 'Bookstagram for Beginners!' *Theguywiththebook* , 17 May, 2018. https://theguywiththebook.com/2018/05/17/bookstagram-for-beginners/.

Thomas, Bronwen. *Literature and Social Media.* Oxford: Routledge, 2020.

Weber, Millicent, and Driscoll, Beth. 'Playful Twitter Accounts and the Socialisation of Literary Institutions,' *First Monday* 24, no. 3 (2019). https://doi.org/10.5210/fm.v24i3.9486.

White, Mara, '#Bookstagram: How Readers Changed the Way We Use Instagram,' *HuffPost*, 26 October, 2017. https://www.huffpost.com/entry/bookstagram-how-readers-changed-the-way-we-use-instagram_b_59f0aaa2e4b01ecaf1a3e867.

Part 2:

Exploring
Post-Digital Literary Worlds

CHAPTER 5

The Australian Digital Publishing Bubble, 2012–2016

An Insider Perspective

KATE CUTHBERT

This essay is an autoethnographic discussion of Australian digital-first publishing from 2012–2016. With particular emphasis on Escape Publishing (Escape), the imprint I founded and oversaw from 2012–2018, I will look at how the parallel industries of genre romance, self-publishing, and digital-rights management led to a genre-friendly bubble of digital publishing in Australia in 2012 that eventually deflated by 2016.

The year 2012 saw the launch of four separate digital imprints of established Big Six (later Big Five) publishers within the Australian market. Pan Macmillan Australia announced the Momentum imprint in August 2011, which officially launched on February 1st 2012 with a range of backlist titles and a handful of new releases.[1] In August 2012, Penguin Australia and Harlequin Australia announced new digital imprints at the Romance Writers of Australia conference on the Gold Coast: Destiny and Escape respectively.[2] In December 2012, Random House Australia also announced that they would be introducing a romance-focused digital imprint entitled Random Romance.[3] Momentum announced an expansion in 2013, Momentum Moonlight, a dedicated romance imprint and HarperCollins created Harper Impulse a 'direct to digital' imprint in 2014.

Context: A Selective History of Romance Publishing and Selling in Australia

Although globally genre romance is the most profitable popular fiction genre, historically Australia has not supported a romance publishing ecosystem.[4] Prior to the 21st century, most Australian writers who pursued a romance writing career did so overseas.[5] Many Australian authors began and maintained very successful careers: single-title authors found publishers in New York or London and category romance writers published through Harlequin Mills & Boon in Toronto, London, and New York.[6]

Practically, the industry in Australia was not considered to be set-up to support a romance readership; publishers did not acquire romance genre novels locally; the closest acquisitions were commercial women's fiction or occasional chick lit titles like Anita Heiss's *Not Meeting Mr Right*. Further, there was only a very limited use of parallel importation laws to publish Australian editions of internationally published romances. Historically, the only frontlist romance titles across all subgenres and sensuality levels available on bookstore shelves were in dedicated romance book stores like Rosemary's Romance Books in Brisbane or Ever After, the Romance Book Specialists in Wollongong, which also offered knowledgeable, romance-friendly staff. However, their pricing, more in line with Australia than the US price of less than $10, was not necessarily sustainable for readers who read several books a week and actively purchased new releases regularly. In discount department stores like Kmart or Big W, readers could access category romances and overseas reprints from Harlequin Mills & Boon in a specific branded area within the book sections, and some independent and chain bookstores carried backlist titles of very popular writers, but rarely were romances locally acquired for local audiences.

As a result, romance readers learned to shop outside of the retail market in Australia, becoming early adopters of both online book shopping via Amazon and Book Depository, and digital reading like the Kindle and other ereading platforms. Booktopia, an online Australian-based book retailer, began in 2004 and made a dedicated push to fill the gap in romance bookselling in Australia. They attended the first Australian Romance Readers Association (ARRA) conference, held in Melbourne in 2009, and hired a romance consultant to help curate their list, write a romance dedicated newsletter, and improve their metadata for searchability.[7] Since then, Booktopia has been a major sponsor of the ARRA conferences and awards, debuting the Favourite Australian Romance Author award (to complement Booktopia's annual Favourite Australian Author award) and sponsoring it regularly. They continue to pursue romance sales with a dedicated newsletter and a strong romance presence on their website. However, as will be shown, they were not a strong consideration for the digital-first imprints, which sought to foster partnerships with international booksellers to access as broad a readership as possible.

Context: Self-Publishing from 1999 to 2012

In the late 1990s, when Tina Engler could not find interest from commercial publishers for her romance novels with highly erotic content, she started writing them anyway, creating PDFs to sell online. Engler distributed her books by sending the files via email to people who paid into her paypal account. In 2000, she launched Ellora's Cave and continued to publish her own and then other writers' work, focusing on what she dubbed and then trademarked Romantica. Ellora's Cave's Romantica novels maintained genre romance frameworks, but included more and more explicit sensual content.[8] At a time when ebooks did not officially exist, Engler was on her way to earning $1 million a year.[9]

As Jane Litte points out in an article for which she was subsequently sued by Engler for defamation, the success of Ellora's Cave had an enormous effect not only on romance publishing, but on publishing in general and women in particular in the publishing ecosystem.[10]

It also set the stage for changes in publishing moving into the 21st Century, and in digital publishing and ebooks in general. Ellora's Cave and the publishers that followed like Samhain Publishing, Loose Id, and Imajin Books, were all making money by publishing books that the commercial publishing industry was saying nobody wanted, and creating a community of empowerment and erotic writing.[11] However, peer recognition was not as forthcoming. The Romance Writers of America, arguably the largest writing organisation in the world until January 2020, actively debated whether writers whose work was only available digitally could be considered published authors. In 2009 digital authors seeking professional development from the organisation had to attend a 'rogue workshop' run by the Samhain Publishing editor (and later Carina Press Managing Editor) Angela James; Sarah Wendell of Smart Bitches, Trashy Books; and Jane Litte of Dear Author.[12] Writers who published through small, online presses like Ellora's Cave, and then later, as the creation of centralised distribution channels made self-publishing a financially viable option, self-published writers have had to fight their more traditionally published peers very hard for their rights to be recognised as not only writers, but published, professional writers.

In 2007 Amazon released the first Kindle and in 2010 Apple released both the iPad and Apple Books, a full decade after Ellora's Cave began selling digital books.[13] More alarmingly for digital publishers, Amazon created Digital Text Publishing, now Kindle Direct Publishing, a platform that allows writers to upload their documents to sell directly through the Amazon Kindle Store. Suddenly, self-published authors had similar resources to commercial publishers for both publishing and managing their distribution. While these early titles failed to compete in terms of production value in editorial, formatting, and cover design, it did not take long for self-published writers to access professional level service to lessen this divide. Professional organisations eventually followed, with the Romance Writers of Australia implementing a new definition of 'published' in 2014 to include those who had published independently. The organisation also altered the previous categorisation of 'published/unpublished' to 'aspiring/emerging/established' to focus on stages of the publication journey and provide a framework that was more inclusive of the different pathways to publication.[14] The Romance Writers of America ostensibly recognised digital publishing earlier, inducting Ellora's Cave as a recognised publisher in 2003, and in 2007 changing the eligibility for their Professional Author Network so that it could be achieved by both advance and income.[15] Peer acceptance, however, was not forthcoming and the RWA and its representatives introduced barriers more likely to affect self-published writers.[16] These included prohibiting selling or signing of books with graphic cover imagery at the National Conference, awards only open to books that have been 'mass-produced', and polling to determine if romance can only be defined as between one man and one woman.[17]

While there is a strong argument that equal professional recognition does not yet exist between self-published and commercially published authors, the world of self-publishing remains a lucrative opportunity for writers seeking control, particularly writers who write into genre spaces, and particularly genre writers writing into romance fiction.

Context: Digital Publishing from a Retail Perspective

Although Escape and the other digital imprints did ensure that their books would be available via Booktopia as a local retailer, they prioritised partnerships and promotions with multinational digital booksellers to maximise their market reach. The absence of a local Amazon bookstore made Apple iBooks, which launched in 2010, the local major online bookseller. Destiny, Escape, Random Romance, Harper Impulse, and Momentum books were (and some remain) available via international Amazon stores; international iBook stores; Nook stores; smaller, more niche booksellers like All Romance Ebooks (before its collapse in late 2016); and digital distribution sites like OverDrive.[18] Distributing and selling ebook files internationally meant that the imprints faced challenges previously unimportant to their larger parent companies: the relationship between Digital Rights Management (DRM) and readers.

In 1998, the US Congress introduced and passed the Digital Millennium Copyright Act (DCMA), which inserted new laws into previously existing copyright laws that discouraged copying copyrighted material and included new provisions for companies protecting their copyright. DCMA transformed DRM (which officially means any mechanism, either hardware or software, that attempts to control the use and distribution of intellectual property in digital form) and empowered rights holders to pursue sites hosting pirated files and not just individual pirates themselves. DRM regularly in use in publishing includes data encryption, digital watermarks, and user plug-ins.

The legislation of DRM was crucial for the commercialisation of ebooks in the publishing ecosystem. The extension of DCMA meant that the copying of ebooks could be either limited or disallowed completely, as could be the transfer of an ebook from one device to another. Further, DCMA and the expansion of what digital rights meant legitimised Amazon and Apple, as prime examples, to create proprietary formats that limited readers to their platform and their bookstores. These actions illuminated a fact about ebooks that remains true to this day, but is often either misunderstood or ignored altogether: ebooks are not sold; they are licensed to a reader.

DRM and what a purchase meant in a digital environment was of major concern to consumers in 2012. Only three years earlier, the Amazon Kindle store had removed George Orwell's *1984* from Kindle devices, demonstrating the control Amazon maintained over purchases made by consumers and their ability to manipulate those purchases post-transaction. In September of 2012, the story that Bruce Willis was suing Apple iTunes over the contents of his digital music library was being widely reported by major newspapers all over the world. Later disproved, the story detailed Willis's desire to will his extensive music collection, purchased and held via Apple iTunes, to his children. However, due to Apple's proprietary control over purchases through their iTunes platform, he would not be able to as he did not actually 'own' the music. These two events invigorated the discussion about ownership of digital files and who held which rights within the digital environment.

As with music files, initially DRM was rampant within the ebook industry, with files saddled with both publisher-created and vendor DRM. However, one of the key differences between self-publishing titles and commercially produced titles was the lack of publisher DRM. Readers who then purchased titles from non-proprietary retailers like All Romance Ebooks were able to move their files between platforms, save them on different devices, and be device agnostic in a way that commercial publishers could never match.

Australia in 2012, Digitally Speaking

In Australia 2012, those seeking to be published in genre romance sought overseas publishers. Commercial digital publishing was in its infancy with front-list titles only sporadically receiving a digital edition (often six to twelve months later); while self-published writers represented an enormously powerful and lucrative subsection of the industry, they were still struggling with peer and industry recognition of their craft and professionalism. It was into this environment that Momentum, Destiny, Escape, Harper Impulse, and Random Romance launched.

Momentum published a wide range of titles, including biography, non-fiction, children's fiction, and literary fiction, but actively sought romance and erotic romance as part of their publishing program. In August of 2012 they acquired a series of erotic romantic short stories branded 'Hot Down Under' from a mixture of established and early writers. Momentum also published Kylie Scott's first book, *Flesh*, in October of that year.[19] Both Destiny and Escape focused exclusively on romance titles; Destiny only accepted romance writers from Australia; Escape was open to international writers. As noted, Random Romance focused exclusively on genre romance. When Harper Impulse launched, their publishing program was more inline with Momentum in that it did not focus exclusively on romance, but sought 'fun, fast-paced reads in all commercial genres', with a specific mention of erotica. While genre romance was not a mainstay of commercial publishing in Australia as it is in other English-speaking markets, it was nonetheless at the core of the publishers' digital imprints.[20]

Additionally, at the core was the tension between the flexibility and freedom associated with self-publishing and the financial and reporting expectations of a commercial publishing house. At launch, both Destiny and Escape released their digital titles with specific messaging that titles would not include DRM in their files, and Momentum altered their files shortly afterwards to also remove and subsequently publish titles without DRM. While no longer of note (indeed, DRM is rarely mentioned at all in the concept of digital sales now), major trade publishers releasing titles without DRM was an astonishing concession to the ebook readership at the time. While the digital titles being released via the imprints of these major publishers were DRM-free, those print titles that also had digital releases were not.

When making decisions at Escape about how to acquire, commission, distribute, and market our titles, we recognised that our largest competition, largest potential readership, and largest potential source of authors all came from the world of romance self-publishing. We had to consider what we could offer writers to publish with us, but also what we could offer the public; a delicate balancing act between the corporate structures and policies within the broader Harlequin organisation and what was happening in the market place. Our biggest selling point was the legitimacy and power of the Harlequin brand, a brand almost synonymous with the romance genre. As discussed above, legitimacy was a concern for many digitally published writers, and being published by the imprint of a major publishing house, be it Harlequin, Penguin, or Pan Macmillan, provided credibility with their peers. The digital imprints also provided a potential pathway into a print program or a broader contract. At Escape, some of our writers were also interested in writing category romance for one of Harlequin Mills & Boon's lines.[21] Others had ambitions to be a Harlequin print author and Escape offered a local opportunity to join the Harlequin stable. Still others were interested in the marketing and editorial support that would be provided with Escape.

As an example of managing the tension and balance, Escape Publishing was originally launched as Harlequin Escape and quickly rebranded, though using the Harlequin name certainly would have aided us in terms of international reader recognition. According to research conducted by Harlequin, the brand has 73% recognition from American women and 86% from Canadian women.[22] Initially, we considered Escape as another category within Harlequin's many categories: Blaze, Medical, Sweet, and so on, however working under a Harlequin label also limited us to work within Harlequin's policies. We would have been restricted in some of the areas crucial to success in a digital environment, especially contentious issues like DRM and royalty rates. Making the change to Escape Publishing, a separate imprint as opposed to a separate category, more in line with imprints like MIRA and HQN, allowed us more freedom to make decisions unique to Escape without having to consider how these decisions would affect the rest of the Harlequin Mills & Boon model.

Structures of Digital Imprints

Loosening DRM is not the only way that digital-first publishing explored alternatives within the Australian publishing industry; they also modelled variations of a traditional publishing structure. Momentum functioned as a completely separate publishing house under the Pan Macmillan umbrella, with separate offices and dedicated staff and oversight of their own sustainability. Momentum, Destiny, and Escape all had dedicated editors running the imprints: Joel Naoum, Sarah Fairhall and Carol George, and me, Kate Cuthbert.[23] Random Romance followed a slightly different format; the Random House Australian fiction editor, Beverley Cousins, oversaw the imprint, supported by other Random House staff.[24] As with Random Romance, Harper Impulse was managed in-house as part of the greater fiction team, rather than through a separate division or with a dedicated editor or team. Destiny and Escape fell somewhere in the range, with Destiny employing a dedicated two-person team within the overarching fiction team (both George and Fairhall had other portfolios) and Escape using a primary Managing Editor working off-site to manage all editorial and author responsibilities, with access to the Harlequin team for production, sales, and marketing. In Escape, Momentum, and Destiny, the traditional publishing structure flattened, with senior editors managing all aspects of the editorial process, including reading the slush pile and early submissions, a task normally reserved for junior editorial staff and editorial assistants. This distinction played out in the visibility of the digital imprint management team as well. The editors with more distinct roles within the digital publishing sphere, notably Joel Naoum, Sarah Fairhall, and I, played a more visible role in the discussion of a digital economy in Australia through attending and speaking at conferences and writers festivals, and through interviews and articles for print and digital media. Further, the social media presence of the different imprints (and those of the visible curators) grew in importance as a means of not only communication, but also brand promotion and recognition.

Public-Facing Editors

This performance of the business of publishing is the most pressured expectation of authors and authors are the most common publishing stakeholders to perform. However, the expectations can extend to others within the publishing ecosystem notably, in my experience, commissioning and managing editors and agents. Both these groups of stakeholders have increasingly public-facing roles and a workplace mandate to attract aspiring and established writers to submit to their imprints, houses, or agencies. Publishers and agents rely on frequent and high-quality submissions to drive their business. Without submissions or with only low-quality or inappropriate submissions, agents have nothing to pitch to publishers, and publishers have nothing to publish, rendering both businesses inert.[25]

This greater visibility and editor-as-brand can also be attributed to the emergence of a viable, independent self-publishing option. Where publishers used to be the only way to reliably reach readers, the publishing ecosystem has changed dramatically. Established commercial publishing houses could continue to rely on their history and the associated weight of reputation and quality, but they could no longer afford to be faceless brands. Instead, as well as an ingrained association with high-quality production values and inherent professionalism, they had to offer a personalised experience and a guarantee of partnership.

While agents and editors attend in-person events like conferences, pitch sessions, or writers' festivals to attract new writers to their businesses, much of the day-to-day aspect of visibility is now digital. As authors perform writing, so too do agents and editors perform tasks from their publishing wheelhouse. While many of these performative tasks are as would be expected: photos of slush piles, identifying marks carefully obscured; contracts; newly printed books; or selfies in various reading poses, many of the tasks are more carefully curated to align the editor or agent with a set of values, paradigms, or principles. 'Submit to me', say the filters, the pictures, the backgrounds, the angles, the carefully composed facial expressions. 'Mine is the best place for your comedic/tragic/contemporary/literary/sly/juicy/pacy/romantic manuscript. No one else will understand your work like I do. Witness the way my digital life reflects your ideals back at you. Your work is more than just a business product to me and ours will be more than a business relationship.'

Quantity and Pricing

The third way that self-publishing influenced digital publishing is in the quantity of titles produced. While prior to the establishment of a digital publishing marketplace, popular fiction authors could expect to publish one book a year (indeed, Nora Roberts, the undisputed Queen of Romance, had to begin writing under a pseudonym as her publisher had built up a backlog of new titles from her),[26] in the self-publishing marketplace quantity was key and authors were pushing out new titles sometimes four or five times a year and many at least once a month. Rather than relying on readers' memories, self-published authors ignored the concept of brand fatigue and built and kept readerships by constantly providing new content. When Escape launched, we knew that we would not be able to compete author-by-author, but that did not mean we could not compete in content. We sought to emulate the reputational success of the Harlequin Mills & Boon model, making Escape a preferred brand, where readers would be able to seek and find a never-ending supply of new titles. When we launched, our mandate was to publish at least 100 titles in the first 12 months, to build up a backlist catalogue as quickly as possible. Even in 2012, it was clear that backlist sales kept a digital market afloat and we needed content to make the imprint financially viable.

While Destiny and Momentum have never made their publishing model public, they too published a number of different titles a month, far more than the print program of their respective houses. Destiny committed to two books a month on launch and by 2014 had published 53 titles.[27] Momentum published far more, as did Escape. To find and retain this content, these digital imprints made another concession to the publishing process: open submissions and very quick turnaround times. Where seeking a publisher in Australia prior to 2012 meant seeking an agent, pitching at festivals or conferences, languishing on a slush pile, or taking advantage of publisher-specific pitching opportunities like Allen & Unwin's Friday Pitch, the digital imprints had open submission portals. Writers had the option to submit frequently and regularly, to several different publishers. Momentum established Momentum Mondays, opening their submission portal from 12am to 11:59pm once a week, but both Destiny and Escape had permanently open submission portals, allowing any writer the opportunity to be considered for publication on a much quicker timeline. Further, with the flattened publishing structure, submissions did not have to go through several layers of consideration before reaching the level of decision. Rather, and particularly in Escape's model, the person making the decision was among the first and often only readers of the slush pile. There were also guaranteed turnaround times. When Destiny launched, they promised a response within three months. Escape launched with a turnaround time of two weeks; this eventually changed to a month in 2016. Momentum also had a two-week turnaround, though they did not respond to all rejections.

The substantial increase in the number of books per month is directly related to another reality of self-publishing, one which altered the landscape for publishing across the industry: price points. Self-publishing in many ways is a numbers game: churning out multiple books very quickly at very low prices to sell a large number of copies, thus making money through quantity. In 2012, the standard price point in digital publishing was $0.99, a price impossible to meet within the commercial publishing ecosystem, particularly when considering the number of areas in which publishers provide expertise and support. But the readers reading self-published novels by the hundreds of thousands had been trained not to pay more than $1 a book, and if a book caught their interest but cost more, there were always thousands of other books that they could turn to instead. When Momentum launched, the language around pricing was vague, but still focused on the idea of digital books being cheaper: 'Momentum's prices will be lower than the ebook edition of print books because of the different overhead structure and the advantages of our production and distribution as opposed to traditional publishing methods' and 'Momentum will also be able to operate on a different royalty structure to Pan Macmillan that reflects the savings in print and distribution costs'.[28] Momentum beefed out its list with very low-cost novels that did not come with as many attendant publishing costs; for example, the low-cost classics took out-of-copyright titles and priced them at $1.99 to 'tie-in with contemporary genre titles we're publishing'.[29] Destiny launched its 'competitively-priced' stories of between 25,000 and 60,000 words at prices between $3.99 and $5.99 to ensure as broad a reach as possible, attractive to those readers who were used to paying very little for a full-length book.[30] Escape's launch titles began at $0.99 for pre-orders and for the first two weeks after the launch. Subsequently, Escape's pricing structure was tied to word-count. Fewer than 10,000 words, the books would remain at a $0.99 price point. A book between 10 and 35,000 words would sell for $2.99. Thirty-five to 60,000 words was priced at $3.99 (by far the largest category of books published by Escape). Sixty to 99,000 words sold for $4.99 and over 100,000 word novels were priced at $5.99.

As alluded to in the Momentum quote, this level of pricing came with changes within the financial structure of the author–publisher partnership, most crucially in the form of advances. None of the digital-first imprints mentioned in this article paid advances for accepted titles. Rather, they offered a much higher royalty rate paid immediately; authors earned money from publication and with every copy sold. This was in line with other digital imprints around the world. Carina Press, Harlequin US's digital imprint, launched in 2010, pays a royalty rate of 40%.[31] (For context, royalty rates in commercial print publishing contracts are normally around 10%.) Destiny paid 25% royalties; Momentum paid 35% rising to 40% after 12 months; and Escape pays 40%.[32]

Hybridity

Finally, this tandem course of digital-first and self-publishing created the mode of publishing now widely known as hybrid publishing, wherein an author writes both for a commercial publisher and for the self-publishing market, choosing with each book which market is best suited for the story. Commercial publishing still carries a level of prestige and legitimacy, where self-publishing has the advantage of control and flexibility. While I am unable to speak for the other presses, both Momentum and Escape supported hybrid writers.[33] At Escape, we leaned on the adage that a high tide floats all boats; that is, an author's success with one book would heighten interest in all of their books, including those books published with Escape.

Digital imprints also expected a lot from authors on their lists. Momentum included social media training as part of the new author package, underscoring how important the author had become in the marketing wheel. In digital publishing, the barriers between writers and fans are largely diminished. Readers expect near constant access to their authors of choice and the instant ability to share their thoughts, positive or negative, and even exert influence within the story in terms of plot or characters. Publishing in the digital age requires more from its creatives than appearances at a literary festival and book signings. Instead publishers seek out authors with an already established platform via social media or encourage and train them to take their author platform online.

Many authors find themselves performatively authoring on social media, from posting Instagram photos of their desks or their pets to plaintively tweeting about misplaced muses to productively organising writing sprints with fellow authors, creating a kind of pantomime where readers can marvel at the mysteries of author friendships while still bearing witness to the fundamental act of authorship.[34] This is especially true within the genre community, where the lines between authors, industry, academia, readers, and fans are blurred in what Fletcher,

Driscoll, and Wilkins refer to as 'Genre Worlds'.[35] Online, readers are able to access their favourite authors and discuss shared favourite books. Readers become blog writers, become respected reviewers, become writers themselves who circle back to readers as they support their community with book recommendations and endorsements.

The Reabsorption and Dissolution of Digital Imprints

This digital publishing bubble in Australia lasted about four years. The merger of Penguin and Random House in 2013, now Penguin Random House, began to make sweeping changes across the business, which eventually led to both Sarah Fairhall and Carol George leaving the company. The Destiny imprint was quietly deactivated beginning in 2015.[36] In early 2016, Momentum had been 'scaled back', Naoum had left the company and the 'significantly smaller' list was taken in-house under a fiction commissioning editor.[37] Harper Impulse Australia quietly shut its doors not long after it launched and Random Romance took some of its most successful writers into its print program and stopped publishing in 2016. In the case of Escape, HarperCollins bought Harlequin in 2014, and I left the role of Managing Editor in late 2018 and was not replaced. The imprint was taken in-house and added to the portfolio of an existing editor and still maintains a presence on the HarperCollins Australia website, though only 23 titles are listed of the more than 300 published between 2012 and 2018.[38] The frenetic rate of acquisitions has slowed considerably, but the price points are still within the initial digital pricing established early in the imprint's history. While I am not across the many reasons that the other imprints were discontinued, it is reasonable to assume that they faced similar issues to Escape. While we were more flexible than the print program, we did not have all the flexibility of self-published authors, particularly in regards to pricing changes and publishing calendars. We also faced barriers to the kinds of self-promotion that worked very well for self-published authors, including print-on-demand for conferences and book signings, and new covers and blurbs to take advantage of trends. We also faced a great deal of misunderstanding as to how the digital market worked. While print markets rely on first month sales, the amount of time that a book will generally appear on bookshelves, digital books do not go 'off the shelf' and thus have a much longer sales life. Where print books are expected to make back their investment in a month, digital books gain their profit via a long tail of sales. Publishing house accounts, however, are not designed to consider a title that may take six months to begin to turn a profit; these titles look like failures, rather than long-term investments. Further, any titles or authors who did meet with success within the imprint were quickly transitioned to the more established print programs, at the behest of both the writers and the publishers. Writers sought the experience of a physical copy of their book appearing on bookstore shelves and the more stable base of an advance and print contract; publishers used the digital format to test authors in a market, thus mitigating some of the risk of taking on a debut writer. Therefore, the opportunities for financial viability of the imprints were often undermined by their own parent companies.

However, I think the biggest issue lay in unrealistic expectations of the digital publishing market. When commercial publishers looked at self-publishing, they saw a number of authors making a great deal of money, but they didn't see the time and work that went into those successes. Much like their author peers, I think that commercial publishing underestimated the professionalism of self-published writers, their understanding of the market, and their savvy in attracting and keeping a readership. Without committing fully, commercial publishers expected to succeed in a market they did not fully understand and in the end they failed.

In legacy terms, it is hard to articulate what the digital publishing bubble brought to Australian publishing, if indeed it brought anything, and perhaps I am too close to the subject to be able to determine it with clarity. Certainly, several Australian best-selling authors had their start in these digital imprints, including Kylie Scott, Sarah Barrie, Jennie Jones, and Alissa Callen. Digital imprints also won several industry awards, including Romantic Book of the Year awards in Australia, suggesting that the quality of the books published competed at the level of internationally published print books. Some publishing practices like hybridity, have become accepted if not strictly endorsed. Nonetheless, it is hard not to assume that this short era of publishing in Australia will be mostly forgotten. Not only was it largely commercially unsuccessful, it dealt mainly in the area of genre fiction, and while there is growing genre awareness in Australia, it is impossible to attribute that solely to the digital-first imprints. Rural romance and rural crime began in the print market, though they were ably supported and developed within the digital publishing sphere, with titles being moved quickly into the market by all five imprints, but genre fiction remains an under-serviced area of publishing in the Australian market. For those working within the bubble, it was a time of enormous optimism, exploration, and risk-taking, with a freedom seldom experienced within a commercial publishing environment. Established authors used the digital imprints to try out new genres and styles and carve out new readerships. Debut authors had a greater chance of being picked up, providing them with skills and experience to leverage into a more permanent contract or a self-publishing career. Perhaps a deeper legacy lies in the experiences of not only these authors but also of the editors involved, a small but significant sample size that experienced the sharp learning curves and participation in the market unique to the Australian industry. From an industry perspective, however, I think the greater legacy is an absence: Australian publishers recognising that their strengths and soundness do not translate to the turmoil and pliability of the self-publishing market and that they can learn and draw from the market, but should not play within.

Endnotes

1   'Harding, Treasure join Momentum; first Momentum titles to be released in February,' *Books and Publishing*, 17 January, 2012.

2   'The New Romantics,' *Books and Publishing*, 23 August, 2012, www. booksandpublishing.com.au/articles/2012/08/23/24782/the-new-romantics/.

3   'Random House Australia to launch digital romance imprint,' *Books and Publishing*, 5 December, 2012.

4   An Goris, 'Hidden Codes of Love: The Materiality of the Category Romance Novel,' *Belphégor* 13, no. 1 (2015): 616, doi: https://doi. org/10.4000/belphegor.

5   Beth Driscoll, Lisa Fletcher and Kim Wilkins. 'Women, Akubras and Ereaders: Romance Fiction and Australian Publishing.' *The Return of Print: Contemporary Australian Publishing*, ed. Aaron Manning and Emmett Stinson (Melbourne: Monash University Publishing, 2016).

6   Stephanie Laurens, Anne Gracie, Emma Darcy, Marion Lennox, Sarah Mayberry, Kelly Hunter, to name a few.

7   Full disclosure: this consultant was the writer of this essay.

8   Note that this trademark is now expired as Engler did not file an acceptable declaration under Section 8 in time to renew.

9   Phoebe Reilly, 'Did Amazon Kill the Queen of Romance?' *Vulture*, 24 February, 2015, www.vulture.com/2015/02/amazon-tina-engler-erotica. html.

10 Jane Litte, 'A letter to the DA Readership,' *Dear Author*, 24 March, 2015, dearauthor.com/misc/a-letter-to-the-da-readership/. In her article, Litte details lawsuits brought against Engler for misuse of funds, tax liens brought against Engler by two different cities, and Engler's portrayal of her lavish lifestyle. Engler sued for defamation and the case was settled confidentially outside of court.

11 Imajin Books is where New York Times Bestselling author Keri Arthur, a resident of rural Victoria, was first published – she moved from ebooks to a print and digital contract with a major imprint with advances worth more than $200,000 a book.

12 Aja Romano, and Constance Grady, 'Romance is publishing's most lucrative genre. Its biggest community of writers is imploding.' *Vox*, 10 January, 2020, www.vox.com/2020/1/10/21055125/rwa-what-happened-resignations-courtney-milan-damon-suede-backstory-2020-ritas-conference. Angela James (@angelajames), 'It was actually me, Sarah, and Jane who organized the rogue digital workshop that year. Epubs weren't

recognized in 2009. In 2010, Carina did do a publisher spotlight at RWA that year so they were a recognized publisher but I think was because it's an imprint of Harlequin,' twitter.com, 24 May, 2020.

13 'A look back at 10 Years of the Amazon Kindle,' *Day One, The Amazon Blog*, 21 November, 2017, https://www.aboutamazon.com/news/devices/a-look-back-at-10-years-of-the-amazon-kindle. Britta O'Boyle, 'The Apple iPad through time: A decade of iPad revisited,' Pocket-lint, 11 April, 2020, www.pocket-lint.com/tablets/news/apple/146888-history-of-the-apple-ipad.

14 Nikki Logan, Facebook message, 27 May, 2020.

15 'How to Join the Romance Writers of America,' *Rainbow Romance Writers*, rainbowromancewriters.com/node/544. Note that the required advance for a commercially published novel is $1000, but the required income for a self-published novel is $5000.

16 Organisational chapters, including those for specific genres and those by geography.

17 Laurie Gold, 'At The Back Fence Issue 202: The Romance Umbrella,' All About Romance, 15 June, 2005, http://allaboutromance.com/at-the-back-fence-issue-202/. Self-published books, freed from publisher and bookseller concerns about graphic imagery on covers in family-friendly stores like Barnes and Noble, Borders, and Walmart, often featured more sexually charged images on the covers. Tessa Dare, 'E-publishing and Romance,' *Tessa Dare*, 21 January, 2009, https://tessadare.com/2009/01/21/e-publishing-and-romance/. Shannon Stacey, 'RWA. Rinse. Repeat,' *Shannon Stacey*, 25 June, 2005, https://shannonstacey.com/2005/06/rwa-rinse-repeat/. As with covers, self-published books were also freed from concerns about 'alternate lifestyles' and often explore variations of romantic relationships outside of heteronormativity.

18 Sarah Wendell, 'All Romance Ebooks.'

19 'The New Romantics.'

20 'HarperCollins Launches.'

21 Pamela Regis, *A Natural History of the Romance Novel* (Pennsylvania: University of Pennsylvania Press, 2007), 155; Category romances are short romances (generally 55 000 words) sold via clearly delineated lines, with a certain number of books published in each line monthly. Many of these romances are numbered sequentially. Harlequin Mills & Boon is the largest publisher of category romance.

22 Harlequin Corporate, 8.

23 Naoum won the 2011 Unwin Trust Fellowship and focused on digital experimentation in the publishing industry.

24 'Random House Australia.'
25 Inappropriate submissions may include submissions outside of the scope of the imprint, in terms of genre, sensuality, word count, or subject matter. It may also include submissions considered too commercially risky in terms of format or content.
26 Nora Roberts, 'Not My Job: Author Nora Roberts (aka JD Robb) Gets Quizzed On J.D. Salinger,' interview by Peter Sagal, *Wait Wait... Don't Tell Me*, NPR, 8 July, 2017, www.npr.org/2017/07/08/536000584/not-my-job-author-nora-roberts-aka-jd-robb-gets-quizzed-on-j-d-salinger.
27 Driscoll, Fletcher and Wilkins 'Women, Akubras and Ereaders.'
28 'Pan Mac scales down Momentum publishing program; Naoum steps down,' *Books and Publishing*, 22 February, 2016, www.booksandpublishing.com.au/articles/2016/02/22/42644/pan-mac-scales-down-momentum-publishing-program-naoum-steps-down/.
29 'Momentum launches $1.99 classics,' *Books and Publishing*, 25 January, 2013, www.booksandpublishing.com.au/articles/2013/01/25/26094/momentum-launches-1-99-classics/.
30 Penguin launches digital romance imprint,' *Books and Publishing*, 16 August, 2012, www.booksandpublishing.com.au/articles/2012/08/16/24677/penguin-launches-digital-romance-imprint/.
31 'Submissions Guidelines: Submissions Tips and FAQ,' *Carina Press Blog*, https://www.carinapress.com/blog/submissions-guidelines-page-4-submissions-tips-and-faqs/#31.
32 Carol George, Facebook message, 26 May, 2020.
33 Joel Naoum, 'Re: Awesome!' message to author, 29 June, 2020.
34 inevitably tagged #editorialassistant. Consider #6amwriters and #writingsprints as examples. Another good example, also from Twitter, is #teamhydr8 where the members periodically remind each other to sit up straight, stretch, and drink more water.
35 Lisa Fletcher, Beth Driscoll and Kim Wilkins 'Genre Worlds and Popular Fiction: The Case of Twenty-First-Century Australian Romance,' *The Journal of Popular Culture* 51, no. 4 (2018): 997-1015.
36 David Carter and Millicent Weber, 'Fiction Publishing in Australia, 2013–2017,' in *Publishing and Culture*, ed. Dallas John Baker, Donna Lee Brien, and Jen Webb (Cambridge; Scholars Publishing, 2019), 354.
37 'Naoum steps down,'
38 'Escape Publishing,' *HarperCollins Australia*, www.harpercollins.com.au/romance/?imprint=escape-publishing.

Bibliography

'A Look Back at 10 years of the Amazon Kindle,' *Day One, The Amazon Blog*, 21 November, 2017. https://www.aboutamazon.com/news/devices/a-look-back-at-10-years-of-the-amazon-kindle.

Carter, David and Weber, Millicent. 'Fiction Publishing in Australia, 2013–2017,' in *Publishing and Culture*, edited by Jen Webb, Donna Lee Brien and Dallas John Baker, 354. Cambridge: Scholars Publishing, 2019.

Cuthbert, Kate. 'Escape Publishing has Launched,' *The Escapades Blog*, 14 November, 2012. https://escapepublishingblog.wordpress.com/2012/11/14/escape-publishing-has-launched/.

Dare, Tessa. 'E-publishing and Romance,' *Tessa Dare*, 21 January, 2009. https://tessadare.com/2009/01/21/e-publishing-and-romance/.

Driscoll, Beth, Fletcher, Lisa and Wilkins, Kim. 'Women, Akubras and Ereaders: Romance Fiction and Australian Publishing,' *The Return of Print: Contemporary Australian Publishing*, edited by Emmett Stinson and Aaron Manion, 67–77. Melbourne: Monash University Publishing, 2016.

Ellora's Cave Publishing, Inc. Romantica. US 78190485. United States Patent and Trademark Office, April 18, 2006. Trademark Status & Document Retrieval. https://tsdr.uspto.gov/#caseNumber=78190485&caseType=SERIAL_NO&searchType=statusSearch.

'Escape Publishing,' HarperCollins Australia, n.d., www.harpercollins.com.au/romance/?imprint=escape-publishing.

Fletcher, Lisa, Driscoll. Beth and Wilkins, Wilkins. 'Genre Worlds and Popular Fiction: The Case of Twenty-First-Century Australian Romance,' *The Journal of Popular Culture* 51, no. 4 (July, 2018): 997-1015.

Gold, Laurie. 'At The Back Fence Issue 202: The Romance Umbrella,' *All About Romance*, 15 June, 2005. http://allaboutromance.com/at-the-back-fence-issue-202/.

Goris, An. 'Hidden Codes of Love: The Materiality of the Category Romance Novel,' *Belphégor* 13, no. 1 (2015): 616. https://doi.org/10.4000/belphegor.

'Harding, Treasure join Momentum; first Momentum titles to be released in February,' *Books and Publishing*, 17 January, 2012. www.booksandpublishing.com.au/articles/2012/01/17/22456/harding-treasure-join-momentum-first-momentum-titles-to-be-released-in-february/.

Harlequin Corporate. '2019 Press Kit,' 16 April, 2019. https://corporate.harlequin.com/wp-content/themes/harlequin-corporate/img/2019_Press_Kit.pdf.

'HarperCollins launches 'direct to digital' Impulse imprint,' *Books and Publishing*, 27 May, 2014. www.booksandpublishing.com.au/articles/2014/05/27/30344/harpercollins-launches-direct-to-digital-impulse-imprint/.

'How to Join the Romance Writers of America.' *Rainbow Romance Writers*, formerly available from rainbowromancewriters.com/node/544.

Litte, Jane. 'A letter to the DA Readership,' *Dear Author*, 24 March, 2015. https://dearauthor.com/misc/a-letter-to-the-da-readership/.

Litte, Jane. 'The Curious Case of Ellora's Cave,' *Dear Author*, 14 September, 2014. https://dearauthor.com/ebooks/the-curious-case-of-elloras-cave/.

'The New Romantics,' *Books and Publishing*, 23 August, 2012. www.booksandpublishing.com.au/articles/2012/08/23/24782/the-new-romantics/.

'Momentum launches $1.99 classics,' *Books and Publishing*, 25 January, 2013. www.booksandpublishing.com.au/articles/2013/01/25/26094/momentum-launches-1-99-classics/.

O'Boyle, Britta. 'The Apple iPad through time: A decade of iPad revisited,' *Pocket-lint*, 11 April, 2020. www.pocket-lint.com/tablets/news/apple/146888-history-of-the-apple-ipad.

'Pan Mac launches digital-only imprint Momentum,' *Books and Publishing*, 23 August, 2011. www.booksandpublishing.com.au/articles/2011/08/23/21104/pan-mac-launches-digital-only-imprint-momentum-2/.

'Pan Mac scales down Momentum publishing program; Naoum steps down,' *Books and Publishing*, 22 February, 2016. www.booksandpublishing.com.au/articles/2016/02/22/42644/pan-mac-scales-down-momentum-publishing-program-naoum-steps-down/.

'Penguin launches digital romance imprint,' *Books and Publishing*, 16 August, 2012. www.booksandpublishing.com.au/articles/2012/08/16/24677/penguin-launches-digital-romance-imprint/.

'Random House Australia to launch digital romance imprint,' *Books and Publishing,* 5 December, 2012. www.booksandpublishing.com.au/articles/2012/12/05/25754/random-house-australia-to-launch-digital-romance-imprint/.

Regis, Pamela. *A Natural History of the Romance Novel*. Pennsylvania: University of Pennsylvania Press, 2007.

Reilly, Phoebe. 'Did Amazon Sink the Queen of Romance?' *Vulture*, 24 February, 2015. www.vulture.com/2015/02/amazon-tina-engler-erotica.html.

Roberts, Nora. 'Not My Job: Author Nora Roberts (aka JD Robb) Gets Quizzed On J.D. Salinger,' Interview by Peter Sagal. *Wait Wait… Don't Tell Me*, NPR, 8 July, 2017. www.npr.org/2017/07/08/536000584/not-my-job-author-nora-roberts-aka-jd-robb-gets-quizzed-on-j-d-salinger.

Romano, Aja and Constance Grady. 'Romance is publishing's most lucrative genre. Its biggest community of writers is imploding,' *Vox*, 10 January, 2020. www.vox.com/2020/1/10/21055125/rwa-what-happened-resignations-courtney-milan-damon-suede-backstory-2020-ritas-conference.

Stacey, Shannon. 'RWA. Rinse. Repeat,' *Shannon Stacey*, 25 June, 2005. https://shannonstacey.com/2005/06/rwa-rinse-repeat/.

'Submissions Guidelines: Submissions Tips and FAQ,' *Carina Press Blog*, https://www.carinapress.com/blog/submissions-guidelines-page-4-submissions-tips-and-faqs/#31.

Wendell, Sarah. 'All Romance is Closing Effectively,' *Smart Bitches, Trashy Books*, 28 December, 2016. https://smartbitchestrashybooks.com/2016/12/romance-closing-effective-12312016/.

CHAPTER 6

Digital Literary Cartography

Not Only a Metaphor and a Model, a Methodology

AIRLIE LAWSON

A few years ago, when I first mentioned I was using digital literary cartography as a research methodology I was asked if it was 'really a thing'. Wasn't it really only a metaphor? To be honest, back then I wasn't entirely sure myself. I didn't admit this. I bought myself some time by taking a bite of my vegan chocolate and banana muffin before answering, with a confidence I didn't have, 'Of course it is'.

I'm now ready to provide some evidence. In industry studies such as the global book market report *BookMap*,[1] literary cartography makes an appropriate metaphor, and in literary studies of global circulation – for example Pascale Casanova's *The World Republic of Letters*[2] – it provides a highly effective conceptual model. In publishing studies, it can have another application.

The essay shows how digital literary cartography might be used as a research methodology. Specifically, it reveals how combining technological developments and interdisciplinary approaches can complicate and advance understandings of book production and the global circulation of books. It draws its examples from materials developed for, and my experience working on, the doctoral research project *Conditions of Access*: it is not intended to be a comprehensive introduction to the subject.

After a short discussion of digital methods, mapping and literature, this essay describes the project and its conceptual frame, before demonstrating how mapping can be used as a conceptual, thinking tool; how it can be employed as an illustrative, descriptive tool; and, building on these two approaches, the way in which it can be an exploratory, explanatory tool. It shows, ultimately, that not only is using digital literary cartography as a research methodology a 'thing', but that when applied to the study of the global circulation and production of books, it can be an extremely useful thing.

Background: Digital Research Methods and Literary Cartography

Increasingly, those studying the production, circulation and also the reception of books have employed digital research methods. These methods are evident in large scale database projects such as *To Be Continued*[3] and *Australian Common Reader*,[4] in analysis of aggregated data from social media platforms – for example, Twitter use and marketing,[5] *Goodreads* and gender preferences[6] – and in the use of algorithms to establish content similarities across bestsellers.[7] Digital literary cartography, which only a few years ago was described by the publisher of the collection of essays *Literary Mapping in the Digital Age*[8] as 'a field whose recent and rapid development has yet to be coherently analysed', has commonalities with other digital research approaches – databases, aggregated data, algorithms – but there is a difference: the centrality of mapping and the map as a tool.

As the publisher's description of another collection of essays, *Literature and Cartography: Theories, Histories, Genres* explains, 'the convergence of digital mapping and globalization has spurred a cartographic turn in literature'.[9] Much of this comprehensive and wide-ranging collection is concerned with 'textual geographies'.[10] This is a common focus, with other scholars discussing how 'literary studies have begun to incorporate maps to reveal the geographic imagination at play in literature',[11] and in *Literary Mapping in the Digital Age*, an informative and practical work, interpreting literary cartography as being 'about the relationship between the practice of mapping, the application of geospatial technologies and the interpretation of literary texts'.[12] In recent years the 'cartographic turn' has even captured the attention of the media, with *New Yorker* readers being told: 'Literary cartography includes not only the literal maps that authors commission or make themselves but also the geographies they describe'.[13] This essay takes another approach to literary cartography and is instead concerned with what has been described as 'the geographies of texts'[14] that is, as Neal Alexander, scholar and editorial board member of the journal *Literary Geographies* explains, the 'materialist study of the geographies of literary production, circulation, and reception'.[15]

An early proponent of what might also be seen as this form of *con*textual literary cartography is Franco Moretti; this is evident even in the title of his influential *Graphs, Maps and Trees*.[16] Digital literary cartography, too, is often associated with the use of 'neogeography services', or 'GIS, Geographic Information Services'[17]: physical geography is not the only focus. As demonstrated on the site *A Literary Atlas of Europe* there are multiple other types of mapping, including networks,[18] while others have examined the literary research value of cognitive mapping.[19] Tania Rossetto, a geographer, has proposed that engaging with post-representational geographic theory offers geographers the opportunity to learn from the way in which literary scholars have employed geographic (and so cartographic) concepts.[20]

Within the humanities, this increased use of digital tools, and digital methods, while initially controversial – giving rise to the so-called 'reading wars', between 'distant' and 'close' – has for some years been accompanied by attention to the considerations necessary when working with data (see, for example, Bode 2012), and visualisations (see Jockers 2013); that is to say, they are not objective, but subjective. Johanna Drucker writes of data-driven visualisations that their 'graphic display conceals the decision and processes on which it was based',[21] while as Kitchin and Dodge argue, maps are always 'mappings'.[22] This does not make them any less effective, but points to the necessity of interpreting them carefully.

This section's brief survey of digital methods and mapping suggests contemporary literary cartography can be seen to be an increasingly used interdisciplinary method, used with an increasing awareness of what it can offer, and how it might be used. For those seeking to understand complex areas – such as the global circulation of books, measured by the international trade in publishing rights – combining approaches, and selecting appropriate digital tools, can offer particular advantages as not only a research method, but a methodology.

Source Material: The *Conditions of Access* Project

As discussed in the introduction, the material used in this essay, the data, the maps (some of which were redrawn) and the findings, comes from *Conditions of Access*, my doctoral research project in which I used maps and mapping throughout, and for multiple different purposes: three of these are examined in the following section. To establish the value of Australian literature in the contemporary global marketspace, the project asks the question: how global is Australian literature – and how does literature become global? It takes a sociological, quantitative approach to challenge the common belief that a book's content is the primary reason it will 'travel', to use the trade terminology. Instead, it argues that the global circulation of books, as measured by the international trade in publishing rights, is context dependent. It uses a combination of rights-related data, digitally generated maps, and a three-part conceptual frame to support this contention.

The indictor used for 'the global' in the project is evidence of a publishing contract, in particular, one that grants international rights: an international rights license, which is measurable, and an indicator of cultural exchange (unlike an export sale). The data used in *Conditions of Access* consists of two sets, which the project describes as 'transaction' and 'influence'. The first, so called, as the contents relate to information about of rights licenses, rights deals or international editions of Australian books: evidence that a rights transaction has taken place; that is, that a license has been, or will be, exchanged. This set combines bibliographic and trading information about novels published in Australia from 2000–2015; trading information might include whether the deal was conducted by a literary agent or rights executive, and the territories granted in a licence. The second, as the name suggests, consists of information about quantifiable events the literature review conducted for the project identified as events that might influence a transaction; prizes, sales and grants, for instance. These two data sets are contained in the *Australian Literature Licensing Database (ALLDB)*, a relational database developed for the project. They are linked through common elements which include, but are not limited to, author name and book title. This data is used to populate the maps discussed in the following section: and the maps are used to create, describe, and explore this data.

The issue of data, maps and subjectivity was managed in the project by using the term 'accounts': the transaction set was an 'account' of what the project describes as 'access'; in that it reflects the composition of the set. Analysis of data-generated maps, or map 'readings', took this aspect of the sets into consideration. Along with asking what the map means, other questions that were considered were: what does this data, and so this map, show? What doesn't it show? How universal is it? How specific? How can it be read and interpreted?

Conceptually, the international rights trade can be seen to be one that operates at an international, national and local level, and influenced by power, consecration (in Casanova's sense of institutional approbation), and networks of people and things: the frame through which to interpret the maps needed to manage this complexity. As a single one did not exist, a modified version of the macro, mezzo, micro model developed by scholars from the sociology of translation school to understand circulation was employed. It combines world-systems, the international licensing field (developed for the project and conceived as a sub-field of the field of literary production, composed of its own linguistic and national sub-fields), and a version of the actor-network which gives humans and things equal standing, positioning these within what the project introduces as the 'global literary marketspace', a conceptual space where the rights to novels are available: novels enter the international licensing field from this space, by offer of a license. It is this license that entitles the publisher to publish a work in a specified language, territory, and under certain conditions.

The project's approach to answering the structuring question – how global is Australian literature and how does literature become global? – therefore involved three main parts: organisation of the data; analysis of the data; and interpretation. Mapping was crucial for each part.

Method: Three Different Maps, Three Different Purposes

To demonstrate how digital literary cartography can be used productively as a research methodology to study the global circulation and production of books, this section examines the roles of maps in each of the three parts of the *Conditions of Access* project: in aiding the research design in the early stages of a project; in presenting the results; and in exploring the data. It does so by considering the design or research question that needed to be answered for that part, and examining the role mapping plays in enabling it to be answered.

Stage One: Mapping as a Conceptual Tool

The literature review on rights trading in Australia established that no single existing source was comprehensive enough to supply the information required to discover, from an empirical perspective, where novels circulated internationally, nor where work novels had 'travelled', nor how they travelled. This review also revealed information was available on both rights 'transactions' and 'influences' and suggested that once selected and collected, the most effective way to organise and analyse this information was to build a database.

Of the potential sources of detailed 'transaction' information, three were chosen for the way in which they could provide, individually, an extensive amount of data about the trade. These sources were, respectively: the trade media; publishing houses responsible for licensing international rights; and scholarly edition information. Combining the information from these three existing sources offered a way to build a new data set, one that combined bibliographic and transactional elements and would provide a different way of understanding how rights worked than either alone. The final rights 'transaction' data set drew on fifteen years of deal announcements from the magazine *Books + Publishing*, manually transcribed; non-commercial licensing information from what were four and became three of the country's largest publishers (HarperCollins, Allen & Unwin, and Penguin Random House) supplied in spreadsheets; and bibliographic published edition details extracted from *AustLit*, the Australian literature database.

Each of these sources – deal, license and edition – offers different details: deal announcements in the media reflect the information supplied by contributors, so generally include the name and title of the work, and the language or country where the rights have been traded as well as the company (and often person) responsible; licensing records record this information and, in addition, the name of the acquiring publisher and any third party involved; published edition records do not include information about the party responsible for trading rights, but do include imprint details, as well as gender, genre and series information. Together these three sources provided a basis from which to establish where, when, and often by whom, and to which publishers the rights to novels in the data set were traded. Each 'transaction' was able to be transformed from textual information into quantifiable data.

The question was, how to organise this data? What fields can be, potentially, in a database? What are the features of a record? A visual thinking tool was needed: the answer was to create a topological map.

A map designed to show only a selected feature, such as the stations on the London Underground. Locations are shown as dots, with straight lines connecting them. Distance, scale, and relative orientation are not important.[23]

Figure 1 describes all the potential components of a 'transaction' record, based on the information in the three types of transactions: deal, license, edition. First it was created by hand, in a rough sketch, and then this sketch was recreated using a tool that was easy to use and available: Microsoft Word, by choosing 'Insert' and 'Shapes'.

As the project also sought to understand what influenced the way books travelled, the second task was to work out how 'influence' might be measured empirically. The literature review suggested awards and domestic sales played a key role, but also other international transactions, the category of a work, and events such as book fairs and networking programs. Consequently, lists covering all of these areas were obtained or developed for the project.

This information, too, needed to be transformed into data; it also needed to be, somehow, linked to 'transaction' data.

The question for these data sets was: What are the key components – and how might they be linked to the 'transaction' set? In other words, it meant asking: What are the common components between the records in this set and the records in the 'transaction' set?

Once again, a topological map of the data was sketched by hand; this included all the elements that could be fields, with those common to both sets highlighted. Figure 2 is this map recreated in Word.

The next question, once the elements had been identified, was: How can these two sets interact with each other, and which connections can be measured and explored, as well as discovered? Or, rather, how can they be used to answer questions about the international rights trade?

Facing page: Figure 1. Potential components of a rights 'transaction' record as a topological map.
Source: Airlie Lawson.

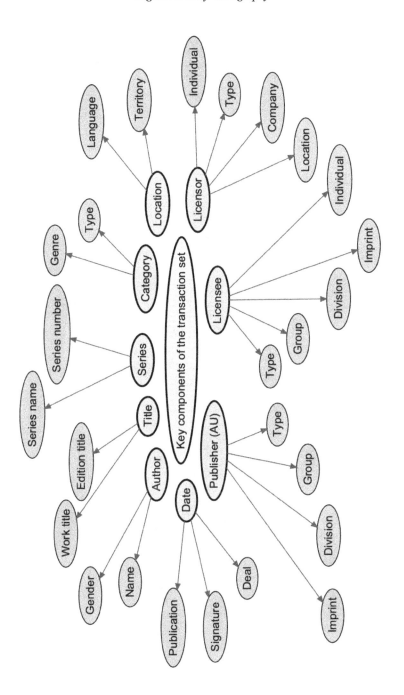

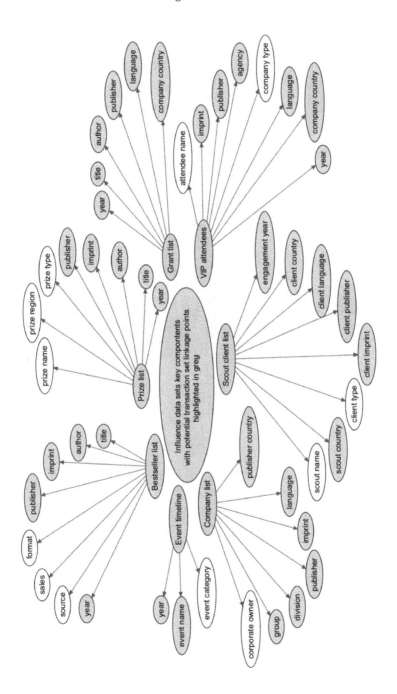

The project understood the trade as a practice and a process. Therefore, it made sense to develop another kind of topological map: a process map. This began with describing in detail how the rights trade worked; that is, understanding the licensing process in terms of the relationship between 'transactions' and (potential) 'influences'. Understanding the rights trade in this way means the map developed for the project had similarities with the well-known book communication circuit,[24] the digital publishing communications circuit,[25] and more specifically, the translation rights-specific *Publishing Trendsetter* infographic.[26]

As with the sets themselves, the first part of the rights trading map was to hand draw all the elements in the sets, and establish how they were connected. The second part was to render this drawing digitally. The complexity of the drawing – not reproduced here because there are too many scribblings and scratchings – indicated that a diagramming application was going to be needed. The main selection criteria were that it did not need programming skills; that it was simple to use immediately (even if all features were not used); and that it was free, stable and fit for purpose. The application chosen, as it fitted all of these was VUE (Visual Understanding Environment), developed by Tufts University, and described on the site as 'a concept and content mapping application'.[27] The map is reproduced in Figure 3.

The process described in Figure 3 is not comprehensive but does include most transaction elements – key people, dates, fairs and programs, for example, shaded by element category – and shows how they might work together. It demonstrates how the data, and data fields might be organised and, subsequently, interrogated.

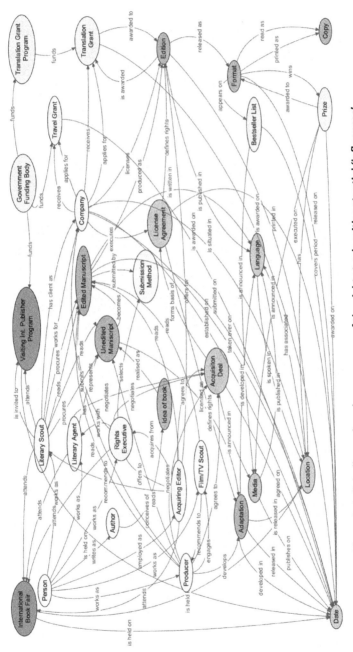

Figure 3. A digitally produced process map of the rights trade with potential 'influences'.

Source: Airlie Lawson.

Together these three topological maps on transaction, influence and process provide a way to describe and conceptualise 'transaction' and 'influence' data and the relationships between them. The maps reveal rights to be a social, global, influenced process and suggest how the data might be organised in a database. These maps can be seen to have been a key part in the first stage of the project, which resulted in the creation of the *ALLDB: the Australian Literature Licensing Database*. The *ALLDB* is a relational database into which the cleaned, raw data were uploaded in CSV format, subsequently to be processed and analysed. At the time of writing, this database spans the period of 2000–2017, includes 2599 primary transaction records from the three subsets (which consist of print novels from mainstream publishers with fiction lists throughout the period), seven influence sets (including prizes, sales, translation grants and scout-client lists), and 71 separate data fields.

The data in the *ALLDB* was analysed statistically and is used in the maps introduced in the following two sections. That is, it provided the basis for constructing the explanatory and exploratory maps used in *Conditions of Access*: it is this data that enabled the international licensing field to be constructed, and subsequently, explored.

Stage Two: Mapping as an Illustrative, Explanatory Tool

As discussed, the international licensing field is modelled in the *Conditions of Access* project as constructed of two sub-fields: linguistic fields and national fields, entered from the 'global literary marketspace'. What the industry calls 'international rights sales', and the project 'transactions', is measured in terms of 'access' to these fields. This 'access' is measured in 'reach', the number of fields where there is evidence of transactions, and 'extent', the number of transactions in those fields. Commonly, these measures are described in the text as figures or percentages, or compared in a table or chart. Yet national fields have a spatial relationship and linguistic and national fields can overlap, complicating how 'access' can be understood.

What is the most effective way to explain the complexities of access? The answer to this question involved three maps: two physical maps to show potential 'reach' and 'extent', and a spatial map to explain the overlap. Used together, these three maps provide a more comprehensive account of how international 'access' works than a single one alone.

A physical map that includes national borders is known as a 'political' map. As with all physical maps, it is based on a representation of the world; it is not the world as such. There are different projections. As it is the most common, and so easily understood, the Robinson projection with UTM Zones[28] was used in *Conditions of Access*. In this projection, Australia is at the bottom right-hand corner: 'down under'. It is a model that describes both the global literary 'marketspace' for novels to be traded, and from which works can be licensed, and gain 'access' to the international licensing field's sub-fields: and where they do gain 'access'.

Overlaying a political map with data points constructs a visual narrative, an 'account'. In the *Conditions of Access* project, this narrative can be seen to be this access to the international licensing field, measured by 'reach' and 'extent'. The choice of mapping tool to create this narrative was, as with the process map, determined by ease of use, cost, and appropriateness for the task. Again, an application not requiring programming skills and developed by a university, this time for a humanities project, was used: Palladio, a data visualization program created by Humanities + Design, Stanford University, originally produced as part of the *Mapping the Republic of Letters* project.[29]

The map in Figure 4 depicts 'reach'. It was created by uploading data from two different *ALLDB* fields: national field (n = 57) and field location (for simplicity, this data set uses the national capital cities as the basis for the co-ordinates – latitude and longitude – rather than publisher address). Figure 5, the companion map, adds another layer: 'extent' (n = 2597, excluding two that reference 'world'). To put it simply, Figures 4 and 5 show where the Australian novels in the data set 'travelled', and in what proportions.

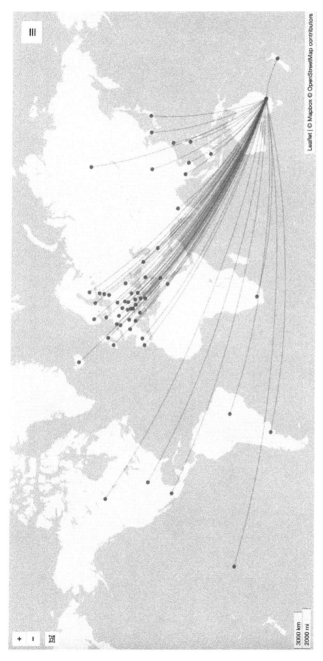

Figure 4. Australian novels in the data set mapped by international 'reach'.
Note: Australian geolocation: Canberra; national fields n = 57. Base map: Copyright: Leaflet. Copyright: Mapbox OpenStreetMap contributors.

Source: Airlie Lawson.

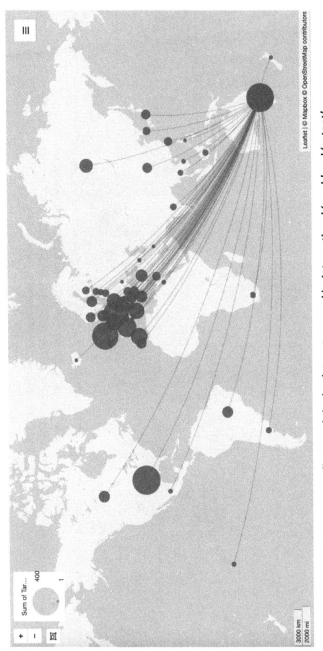

Figure 5. Australian novels in the data set mapped by international 'reach' and 'extent'.

Note: Australian geolocation: Canberra; works n = 779, rights transactions n = 2599. Base map: Copyright: Leaflet. Copyright: Mapbox OpenStreetMap contributors.

Source: Airlie Lawson.

Figure 4 can be seen to show that Australian novels in the data set have achieved wide international access by reach; that they have 'travelled' widely in the sense of national cultural exchange, as measured by rights transactions. Figure 5 shows this to be disproportionate, with a focus on Western Europe and North America, particularly the United States of America. It shows that Australia's key rights trading partners over the period of the data set are not those closest in physical proximity to Australia.

These two physical maps, however, can only provide a partial account of 'reach' and 'extent'. As discussed, there is an overlapping between national and linguistic field: publishers in some national fields acquire the rights for works in multiple languages, for example. In the *Conditions of Access* data set alone North American publishers acquire Spanish rights as well as English language, while (European) Spanish publishers acquire rights for Catalan as well as Castilian and Basque, for example. Using a physical map to describe access to the 'literal' international licensing field is useful but under-represents the reach of the trade, which the project proposes can be measured in three ways: by country or national field; by language or linguistic field; and in terms of 'territory', a concept that make it possible to account for overlapping between the two. Moreover, while Figure 5 provides an indicative proportional representation, without enlarging it, and making clear the borders of the national fields, the larger fields overshadow the smaller.

The limitations of physical maps to describe the rights trade can be overcome by detailed textual explanations. A spatial map, however, makes this clear. Again using the application Palladio, Figure 6 is constructed using two data fields; this time, it only includes languages with editions in multiple national fields, eight languages and 1729 transactions. Like the Robinson projection shown in the maps in Figures 4 and 5, Figure 6 is also a representation. It shows where Australian novels in the set have 'travelled' in a linguistic sense, and in what proportion.

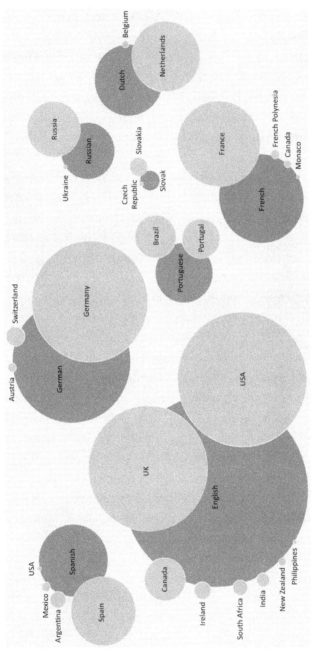

Figure 6. Languages with editions in multiple national fields.
Note: Transactions n = 1729.

Source: Airlie Lawson.

Figure 6 combines the detail of Figure 4 with proportional information from Figure 5 and provides an easily readable map of 'access'. This map is one that simultaneously describes the national and linguistic sub-fields of the international field, and does not represent any kind of physical reality, but instead a conceptual space. It shows the international licensing field is not only constructed of uneven flows – a commonly made observation – but shows just how uneven the flow of rights transactions is within countries and language groups. Additionally, this map makes it clear why adding the term 'territory' to 'language' and 'country' (or national field), the usual measurements of rights activity, provides an important level of precision.

Specifically the maps in Figures 4, 5 and 6 give an account that suggests Australian novels in the data set have 'travelled' widely and extensively, but are more often acquired by English language publishers in the US and the UK – and German publishers acquire Australian novels more often than publishers in other translation territories.

Stage Three: Exploratory Mapping

Physical and spatial maps can be used to describe the 'where' of the rights trade and the 'how much'. The other half of the question asked in *Conditions of Access* is: how? How and why are rights traded? What can the data reveal about rights and the German and English language fields, or the fields in the United States of America, the United Kingdom and Germany or, perhaps, the relationships between publishers – or even the temporal logic of the licensing field?

The growth in data collection and analysis, and the rise of social media, has led to an increase in network analysis: mapping networks is another form of spatial mapping. There are also many network mapping applications: Gephi is used to create the maps in this section. Unlike Vue and Palladio, Gephi was selected because I knew others who used it; I'd seen what it could do; and it does not require programming skills, is free, and is open source. The landing page claims it 'is the leading visualization and exploration software for all kinds of graphs and networks' (gephi.org n.d.). Users can experiment with their data, using the different algorithms that construct the networks, and the networks can be manipulated and reproduced. It can perform statistical analysis of the graphs, and the graphs can be explored using different approaches (choosing, for example, 'modularity' or 'centrality').

To answer the question about those fields which acquire the most rights, a network was created, linking linguistic fields, and national fields ('target'), through Australian novels jointly (or independently) acquired ('source'). In Figure 7, connecting points ('nodes') are the novels and the linguistic fields, and the links ('edges') show how they are connected; in Figure 8, the 'nodes' are national fields.

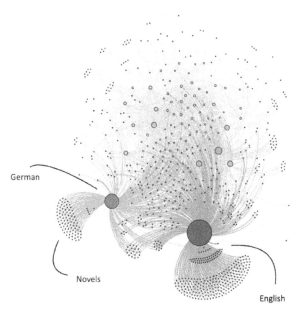

Figure 7. Acquisitions of individual Australian novels by linguistic field.
Note: Data from ALLDB, novels n = 779, transactions n = 2597.
Source: Airlie Lawson.

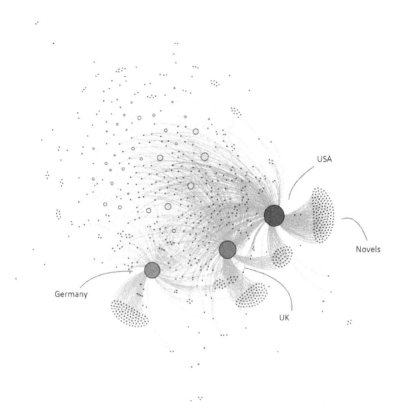

Figure 8. Acquisitions of individual Australian novels by national field.
Note: Data from ALLDB, transactions, n = 2597.
Source: Airlie Lawson.

Creating and visualising fields and novels as data points in the network, as shown in Figure 7, provides another way of understanding rights. Here, German language publishers appear not only to be similar to English language publishers in terms of the number of rights to Australian novels they acquire, but also in their acquisition approach: both German and English language publishers acquire works that no other country acquires, as evidenced in the spray of smaller, unlinked nodes connected to both. Other translation publishers are more likely to acquire novels that others have acquired; this is shown through them being highly connected. (Dutch and French publishers are, it is worth noting, central in this network.) The spatial map in Figure 8 allows a deeper level of analysis. Here English language publishers are shown not to be all the same: the United States shares fewer works with translation publishers (the larger, unnamed nodes) than they do with British publishers. German publishers, meanwhile, have more works in common with European publishers. Using the insights that can be gained from analysis of these two maps provides a basis from which to recontextualise the international rights trade, and the global circulation of books, moving beyond the traditional English language and translation binary, using an approach based on acquisition patterns.

The visual description given by creating a network and mapping it spatially also provides a method by which to interrogate global relationships between companies. In Figure 9, the data used is Australian publisher (and imprint), Australian novels, and international publishers (and imprint). The 'nodes' are Australian publishers and international publishers; they are linked by individual works, the 'edges'. It is created with the same data as the map in Figure 9, but another algorithm, the 'circular layout' algorithm. Using a circular form creates an illusion of 'the global' relationships: and suggests publishers to be highly connected. Figure 10 is the same data, structured with Force Atlas 2.

The maps in Figures 7 and 8 showed how, linguistically and nationally, the international licensing field can be seen to be a highly connected space. The map in Figure 9 shows the extent to which Australian publishers in the data set – 19, with 41 imprints between them – are connected to international publishers, or their associated imprints. The difference between Figures 9 and 10 demonstrates the role of the algorithm in enabling data exploration and interpretation: Figure 9, while interesting, lacks the clarity of Figure 10, which shows a highly connected space as well; albeit with some publishers more connected than others. It also shows certain imprints – HarperCollins' Voyager is marked here – have independent relationships with international companies (the smaller nodes), demonstrating the different ways multinational companies operate. The *Conditions of Access* project distinguishes between 'the global' and 'globalised' (the first designates exchange enabled through a trade of rights, the second circulation through distribution, or issuing). Under this model, those publishers with wider ranges of independent connections, as well as a high volume of transactions, can been seen to be more global.

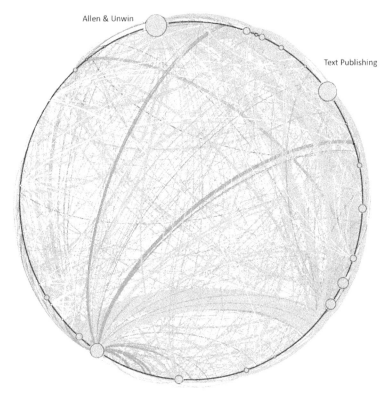

Figure 9. Australian publishers (and imprints) connectioned to international publishers (and imprints) through novels in common. Independent connections not revealed.
Note: Data from ALLDB, international publishers and imprints n = 832; publishers and imprints counter-clockwise.
Source: Airlie Lawson.

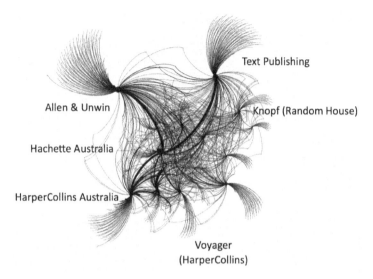

Text Publishing

Allen & Unwin

Knopf (Random House)

Hachette Australia

HarperCollins Australia

Voyager
(HarperCollins)

Figure 10. Australian publishers (and imprints) and connections to international publishers (and imprints) through shared novels, showing independent connections.
Note: Data from ALLDB, international imprints n = 832 structured by common connections, outer edge individual relationships.
Source: Airlie Lawson.

Using diversity of contacts as a measure for 'the global' is not dissimilar to Casanova's argument for France continuing to be the centre of the publishing world, even when London and New York are more commercially active: centrality is positioned as more important than activity, although in Casanova's case, the centrality is associated with consecration.[30] That two independent Australian publishers – in this map, Text and Allen & Unwin – can be seen to have a wider number of international connections, established through books both publish, is therefore significant, if they are responsible for licensing them.

The maps in Figures 9 and 10 do not show who is responsible for licensing the international rights – author, agent or publisher – only connections to international publishers through novels published. This means these maps do not show that Allen & Unwin or Text are more active in selling rights, only that rights to novels published by these two houses have, when aggregated, been licensed more widely internationally than other houses according to the account given by the *ALLDB*'s data set.[31]

Analysis of the maps in Figures 9 and 10 does suggest that using this form of spatial map as an exploratory tool can reveal the complexities of relationships between different publishing houses domestically and internationally – and the value of distinguishing between publishing house and publishing imprint when studying international access.

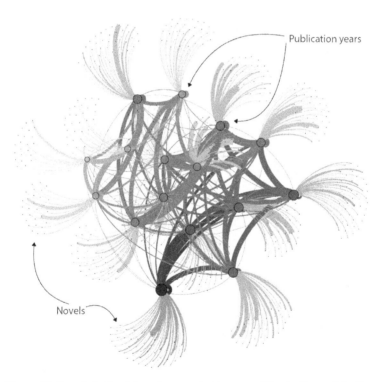

Publication years

Novels

Figure 11. Novels in the data set connected by year of Australian publication and year of international edition publication (2000–2015).
Note: Data from *ALLDB*; Australian editions, n = 779.
Source: Airlie Lawson.

The final map in this essay, Figure 11, is another network. It is constructed using data associated with a novel's publication year in Australia, and the year (or years) it has been published internationally. It covers the period of the *ALLDB*, as it currently stands, so deals conducted between 2000 and 2015. Links and years are sized by number of transactions. It is structured by the Yifan Hu algorithm.

The map in Figure 11 shows that in some years, there are highly successful novels – novels that gain extensive access to the international field, through its many subfields – and that over time, that there is a relatively even number of novels that gain access, if to different extents.

Some years are more strongly connected, which may be the result of multiple trades for successful individual novels or trades for multiple single novels: this is not significant, as the structure of the set is not balanced towards individual rights 'successes'. What this shows is how rights trading is a long-term process, unlike domestic sales. It is often said that rights is as much about backlist as front-list activity: the map in Figure 11 demonstrates the way in which this works, and in a single image illustrates just how much the contemporary rights trade differs from domestic sales on a temporal level.

Three Types of Maps, Three Types of Methods

Taking a broad approach to literary cartography, and using multiple types of maps – here, topological, physical and spatial – can aid in project design, help with data explanation, and enable data exploration. In the examples used in this section taking this approach contributed to building a rights-oriented database, and so providing a new tool for studying circulation; to revealing trading relationships between languages that removes the binary between English and other languages (translations); to showing publishers are highly connected; and to demonstrating graphically the different logic of sales and circulation enabled by licensing the rights to novels.

In a period when trade publishing has a front-list focus, when authors and companies are judged on domestic sales, this finding in particular offers another way to think about literary value: the methodology of the project itself, a way of measuring this value and mapping it.

Conclusion: Using Digital Literary Cartography as a Research Methodology

To conclude, as I claimed to my companion several years ago, digital literary cartography is indeed a 'thing'. It is a contemporary inter-disciplinary approach, most often used to study texts themselves, but can also be used to study the circulation of texts. This essay has illustrated how it might be applied, using just a few static examples, so has only touched on its potential. Much more is possible, using dynamic maps and interactive maps, for instance, to show change over time. It also shows, when combined with other methods, here the digital and quantitative, and combined with an appropriate interpretive framework, literary cartography can be more than a method. This form of cartography can be a useful way of describing where and the extent to which books travel; it can also be used to investigate, from an empirical perspective, in this way, why books travel – along with provoking new ways of thinking about circulation. When understood in its broadest terms and combined with different types of data, it can be a powerful methodology: a very useful thing indeed.

Endnotes

1 Rüdiger Wischenbart, et al. 'How Big Is Global Publishing? A Bird's Eye Perspective,' *BookMap Report*, 2017.
2 Pascale Casanova. *The World Republic of Letters* (Cambridge MA: Harvard University Press, 2004).
3 Katherine Bode. *To Be Continued* (n.d.).
4 Julieanne Lamond. *Australian Common Reader* (n.d.).

5   Sybil Nolan and Alexandra Dane. 'A Sharper Conversation: Book Publishers' Use of Social Media Marketing in the Age of the Algorithm,' *Media International Australia* 168, no. 1 (2018): 153-166.

6   Mike Thelwall. 'Reader and Author Gender and Genre in Goodreads,' *Journal of Librarianship and Information Science* 51, no. 2 (2017): 403–430.

7   Jodie Archer and Matthew L. Jockers. *The Bestseller Code: The Anatomy of a Blockbuster Novel*. (New York: St Marten's Press, 2016).

8   Christopher Donaldson, Patricia Murrieta Flores and David Cooper, *Literary Mapping in the Digital Age*. (Oxford: Routledge, 2016).

9   Anders Engberg-Pendersen (ed). *Literature and Cartography: Theories, Histories, Genres*. (Cambridge MA: The MIT Press, 2017)

10   Miles Ogborn. 'Mapping Worlds,' *New Formations* 57, no. 149 (2005).

11   Leah Thomas. 'Cartographic and Literary Intersections: Digital Literary Cartographies, Digital Humanities, Libraries and Archives,' *Journal of Map & Geography Libraries* 9, no. 3 (2013): 335. 2013.

12   Cooper. *Literary Mapping in the Digital Age*. 1.

13   Casey Cep. *The Allure of the Map*. 2014.

14   Ogborn. 'Mapping Worlds,' 149.

15   Neal Alexander. 'On Literary Geography,' *Literary Geographies* 1, no. 1 (2015): 1.

16   Franco Moretti. *Graphs, Maps, Trees: Abstract Models for Literary History*. (London: Verso, 2005).

17   Petra Mitchell. 'Literary Geography and the Digital: The Emergence of Neogeography,' in: Robert Tally ed *The Routledge Handbook of Literature and Space*. (Oxford: Routledge 2017), 8.

18   Lorenz Hurni and Barbara Piatti. *Mapping and Analysing the Geography of Fiction with Interactive Tools*. (n.d.).

19   Thomas. 'Cartographic and Literary Intersections,' 335.

20   Tania Rosetto. 'Theorizing Maps with Literature,' *Progress in Human Geography* 38, no. 4 (2014): 513–530.

21   Johanna Drucker. *Grapheis: Visual Forms of Knowledge Production*. (Cambridge MA: The MIT Press 2014).

22   Rob Kitchen and Martin Dodge. 'Rethinking Maps,' *Progress in Human Geography* 31, no. 3 (2007): 331.

23   'Topological Map,' Oxford Reference, https://www.oxfordreference.com/view/10.1093/oi/authority.20110803104939207.

24   Robert Darnton. 'What is the History of Books,' *Deadalus* 111, no. 3 (1982): 68.

25   Padmini Ray Murray and Claire Squires. 'The Digital Communications Circuit,' *Book 2.0* 3, no. 1 (2013): 3-24.

26 publishingtrends.com. 'Lifecycle of a Book in Translation,' Publishing Trendsetter 12 May, 2014, http://publishingtrendsetter.com/industryinsight/lifecycle-of-a-book-in-translation-kristin-harmel-author-holly-root-original-rights-holder/.

27 'What is Vue?' Tufts University, 2020, https://vue.tufts.edu/about.

28 '*Commonly Used Map Projections*,' ANXLIC Committee on Surveying and Mapping, 2020, www.icsm.gov.au/education/fundamentals-mapping/projections/commonly-used-map-projections.

29 'Palladio: Visualize Complex Historical Data with Ease,' Stanford University, 2020 https://hdlab.stanford.edu/palladio/.

30 Casanova. *The World Republic of Letters*, 119.

31 The question of responsibility and agency is explored in the project extensively. For more information see *Conditions of Access* (Lawson 2019, 301–360).

Bibliography

Alexander, Neal. 'On Literary Geography,' *Literary Geographies* 1, no. 1 (2015): 3–6.

ANZLIC Committee on Surveying and Mapping. *Commonly Used Map Projections*, n.d. www.icsm.gov.au/education/fundamentals-mapping/projections/commonly-used-map-projections.

Archer, Jodie, and Jockers, Matthew L. 2016. *The Bestseller Code: The Anatomy of a Blockbuster Novel*. New York: St Martin's Press.

Bode, Katherine. 2012. *Reading by Numbers: Recalibrating the Literary Field*. London: Anthem Press.

Bode, Katherine. n.d. *To be Contined*, n.d. https://katherinebode.wordpress.com/projects/to-be-continued/.

Casanova, Pascale. 2004. *The World Republic of Letters*. Translated by Malcolm DeBevoise. Cambridge MA: Harvard University Press.

Cep, Casey. 'The Allure of the Map,' *The New Yorker*, 22, January 22, 2014 https://www.newyorker.com/books/page-turner/the-allure-of-the-map.

Cooper, David, Donaldson, Christopher and Murreita-Flores, Patricia. *Literary Mapping in the Digital Age*. Oxford: Routledge, 2016.

Darnton, Robert. 'What is the History of Books?' *Daedalus* 111, no. 3 (1982): 65–83.

Drucker, Johanna. 2014. *Graphesis: Visual Forms of Knowledge Production*. Cambridge, MA: Harvard University Press.

Engberg-Pedersen, Anders, ed. *Literature and Cartography: Theories, Histories, Genres*. Cambridge: The MIT Press, 2017.

gephi.org. n.d. *Gephi: The Open Graph Viz Platform*. https://gephi.org.

Hurni, Lorenz, and Piatti, Barbara. *Mapping and Analysing the Geography of Fiction with interactive Tools*. Institute of Cartography and Geoinformation, ETH Zurich, n.d. http://www.literaturatlas.eu/en/.

Jockers, Matthew L. *Macroanalysis: Digital Methods and Literary History*. Urbana: University of Illinois, 2013.

Kitchen, Rob, and Dodge, Martin. 'Rethinking Maps,' *Progress in Human Geography* 31, no. 3 (2007): 331–344.

Lamond, Julieanne. *Australian Common Reader*, n.d. www. australiancommonreader.com/spotlight/australian-common-reader/feature/about.

Lawson, Airlie. 'Conditions of Access: Mapping the Value of Contemporary Australian Literature in the Twenty-First Century Global Marketspace.' Ph.D. dissertation, Australian National University, 2019. http://hdl.handle.net/1885/185191.

Mitchell, Petra. 'Literary Geography and the Digital: the Emergence of Neogeography,' in *The Routledge Handbook of Literature and Space*, edited by Robert Tally Jnr, 85–94. Oxford: Routledge, 2017.

Moretti, Franco. *Graphs, Maps, Trees: Abstract Models for Literary History*. London: Verso, 2005.

Nolan, Sybil, and Dane, Alexandra. 'A Sharper Conversation: Book Publishers' Use of Social Media Marketing in the Age of the Algorithm,' *Media International Australia* 168, no. 1 (2018): 153–166.

Ogborn, Miles. 'Mapping Words,' *New Formations* 27 (2005): 145–149.

Oxford University Press. 'Topological Map,' *Oxford Reference*, n.d., https://www.oxfordreference.com/view/10.1093/oi/authority.20110803104939207.

publishingtrends.com. 'Lifecycle of a Book in Translation,' *Publishing Trendsetter*. 12 May, 2014. http://publishingtrendsetter.com/industryinsight/lifecycle-of-a-book-in-translation-kristin-harmel-author-holly-root-original-rights-holder/.

Ray Murray, Padmini and Squires, Claire. 'The Digital Publishing Communications Circuit,' *Book 2.0* 3, no. 1 (2013): 3–24.

Rossetto, Tania. 'Theorizing Maps with Literature,' *Progress in Human Geography* 38, no. 4 (2014): 513–530.

Stanford University. 'Palladio. Visualize Complex Historical Data with Ease,' Stanford Humanities & Design, n.d. https://hdlab.stanford.edu/palladio/.

Thelwall, Mike. 'Reader and Author Gender and Genre in Goodreads,' *Journal of Librarianship and Information Science* 51, no. 2 (2017): 403–430.

Thomas, Leah. 'Cartographic and Literary Intersections: Digital Literary Cartographies, Digital Humanities, and Libraries and Archives,' *Journal of Map & Geography Libraries* 9, no. 3 (2013): 335–349.

Tufts University. What is VUE. n.d. https://vue.tufts.edu/about.

Wischenbart, Rüdiger, Bueno, Robert, Carrenho, Robert and Fleischhacker, Michaela Anna. 'How Big Is Global Publishing? A Bird's Eye Perspective,' *BookMap Report* January, 2017, Rüdiger Wischenbart Content & Consulting.

Part 3:

Understanding a New Paradigm of Literary Production

CHAPTER 7

Crowdfunding Book Publishing through Creativity and Connectivity on Kickstarter

A Case Study of a Small Publisher

CLAIRE PARNELL

With slim financial margins, incredibly competitive support schemes, and a general decline in federal and state government funding for the arts in countries like Australia, some writers and publishers are turning to crowdfunding platforms as a means of financing their creative projects. In December 2019, Galley Beggar Press created a GoFundMe campaign to raise £40,000 or risk going under due to the financial arrangements related to its book *Ducks, Newburyport* being shortlisted for the Booker Prize. Before being picked up by Penguin Books, the children's book *Goodnight Stories for Rebel Girls* raised over US$1 million across Kickstarter and Indiegogo. Microcosm Publishing, a small press in Portland, US, regularly uses Kickstarter to fund and distribute their own-voices books. And OFFICE, a not-for-profit organisation in Melbourne, Australia, funds their quarterly publication *The Politics of Public Space* on Pozible, in conjunction with RMIT University. These examples demonstrate the variety of publishers, from small to large, non-commercial to commercial, using crowdfunding approaches to both finance production and source creative works.

Crowdfunding approaches to arts financing are not wholly an internet phenomenon. Subscription models in book history provide a close match to the reader sponsorship of crowdfunding.[1] However, the centricity of data to digital crowdfunding platforms has introduced important new aspects to these models. Networked communication technologies provide creators access to incredibly large and powerful backer communities online that they can engage with and build their audience. Digital crowdfunding platforms also enable audiences to engage in the direct financing and tastemaking of book publishing by determining where they distribute their funds. For producers, it can also be a valuable space for audience and community building. The data from these users allow platform owners and creators to learn more information about online creative audiences. While digital crowdfunding platforms offer opportunities for multinational and independent publishers alike, it is a particularly viable option for small publishers and literary communities that typically have close ties to their audience, greater creative agency and smaller overheads.

The financial–legal framework in which crowdfunding operates, the behaviour of backers and the purpose and composition of campaigns have been the primary areas of inquiry of crowdfunding scholarship.[2] This chapter extends these research areas by looking holistically at the foundational characteristics of crowdfunding platforms. Specifically, it looks at the technological and socioeconomic characteristics of the Kickstarter platform and campaigns of small publisher Thornwillow Press as a case study. Through its practices, Kickstarter positions itself as part of the contemporary creative industries while the crowdfunding efforts by Thornwillow Press are indicative of the potential for small publishers and literary communities to find success. Kickstarter is becoming a viable alternative for funding creative works in an increasingly abundant marketplace at a time of increasingly competitive top-down funding schemes.

Theorising Crowdfunding Platforms

The scale of crowdfunding platforms is growing worldwide. The European Finance Benchmarking report shows that reward-based crowdfunding, where creators offer gifts and products in exchange for financial donations, grew by 127 per cent in Europe from the previous year, and now represents the second-largest alternative finance model after peer-to-peer lending.[3] Australian crowdfunding platforms raised AU$8.7 million in the first quarter of 2019.[4] This growth is facilitated by the ease of access creators and consumers have to platforms as well as the variable financial commitments required and encouraged by highly publicised success stories like *Goodnight Stories for Rebel Girls*. Unlike equity crowdfunding, which was passed into Australian legislation in 2017 and allows large groups of individuals to invest in early-stage businesses in return for part-ownership, crowdfunding platforms allow individual creators and community organisations to run campaigns in addition to businesses. The connectivity embedded in digital crowdfunding platforms is integral to their functionality and success.

Crowdfunding platforms draw on the collective and connective power of social media communities. Drawing on W Lance Bennett and Alexandra Segerberger's logic of connective action, which shows how communication-based networks operate as large-scale organisational processes for mobilisations, this research theorises crowdfunding platforms as spaces of connective funding.[5] In this theorisation, arts-based crowdfunding is viewed as a practice that is geared towards funding but that prioritises the social connections forged around financing a creative project through mediated communication systems. The extraction and use of data centred on these networks are highly valuable for creators as well as the platform's economic structures.

Crowdfunding platforms are predicated on the structures of digital and platform capitalism. Digital capitalism describes a system wherein the forces of production are transformed by digital technologies. In this system, digital media constitutes the central apparatus of a supranational market system by which workers control productive technologies, and around which the management of work is organised.[6] Platforms increasingly function as circulation infrastructure for the interchange of goods, services and money.[7] This infrastructure includes general ecommerce sites like Amazon, which became the world's largest retailer in 2019, controlling approximately 50 per cent of the ecommerce market.[8] It also includes relatively smaller sites like Etsy, eBay and Craigslist; social networking sites with an ecommerce component, like Facebook Marketplace and Instagram business accounts; as well as intermediary platforms like Uber and AirBnB. As is demonstrated by these platforms, as well as crowdfunding platforms, some aspects of capitalism endure in the digital capitalist structure, including private ownership, wage labour and commodity markets. Types of property, assets and forms of capital, however, are sometimes transformed through internet technologies.[9] The economic structure of crowdfunding platforms provides a primary spoke in the framework for understanding their role and possibilities in the cultural industries.

While crowdfunding platforms seem to be characterised by a democratisation of arts financing, they reflect the familiar workings of the market system. Now, in the early twenty-first century, digital and platform capitalism is centred around extracting and using data.[10] Labour and material are further hidden in the digital sphere behind the seemingly intangible connectivity between people, content and objects, so inequalities persist online. The commercialisation of community networks formed on these platforms are important for both campaign creators and platform owners. Producers can build their audience and community through marketing their funding efforts. Most crowdfunding platforms have an in-built audience of backers and repeat backers – that is, people who donate or pledge money to campaigns. However, these platforms can be productive spaces for content that can be shared across established audience touchpoints, including other social media platforms like Facebook, Instagram and Twitter. These platformed network connections are shaped by the technological, social and economic features of platforms.

The technology, governance structures, ownership, business model, content and users of individual platforms set the context for crowdfunding campaigns.[11] Elements including interface affordances, the multimedia capabilities, the economic structure of platforms, terms of service influence the creation and reception of crowdfunding efforts, and ranking mechanisms through both owner-generated algorithms and user-generated popularity indexes.

This framework is operationalised in this research through a multimethod approach. This chapter draws on a website analysis of Kickstarter, an interview conducted with the Director of Publishing at Kickstarter, and a case study of crowdfunding campaigns run by Thornwillow Press. Kickstarter is a particularly useful case study for researching crowdfunding in the arts due to its strong focus on creative industry projects while Thornwillow represents an innovative and successful project creator on the platform. The website analysis is informed by Johanna Drucker's humanistic approach to interface design, which defines interface as 'not so much a "between" space as it is the mediating environment that makes the experience'.[12] Books, newspaper pages, bathroom faucets and ATM machines, as artefacts of complex processes and protocols, are interfaces by this definition. Importantly, the technical structures of the platforms dictate certain opportunities for users' engagement and organise information in meaningful ways through algorithms.[13] This analysis focuses on Kickstarter's ranking indexes and algorithms, software architecture and interface, as well as human engagement with the platform by its staff and users. While not comprehensive, they provide a starting point to consider the professional, personal and social outputs on crowdfunding sites as well as the conditions for creative possibilities.

Following Drucker's humanistic approach to interface theory, this chapter also draws on primary interview data with Margot Atwell, the Director of Publishing at Kickstarter, which offers further insight into the workings of the platform and its engagement with creative producers. Finally, the use of Kickstarter by contemporary book publishers is explored through a textual analysis of the crowdfunding campaigns of Thornwillow Press as a case study, paying particular attention to the construction of campaigns, their textual and multimedia components, and rewards. As of March 2020, there have been 49,297 campaigns launched in the Publishing category on Kickstarter.[14] While the examples from Thornwillow Press are by no means generalisable, their campaigns have a high success rate and are thus considered exemplary cases.

By applying this framework and these methods, this chapter emphasises the socioeconomic and techno-cultural structures of digital crowdfunding in contemporary book publishing. Beyond the microsystem of the platform, Kickstarter exists within a technological, connective ecosystem and aligns itself within the broader creative industries. These connections, both technological and cultural, influence the direction and possibilities of Kickstarter as an agent for positive change in book publishing.

The Technological and Creative Ecosystem of Kickstarter

Kickstarter is a global reward-based crowdfunding platform based in Brooklyn, New York. It is specifically geared towards creativity and merchandising. Creators who set up campaigns on Kickstarter must sort their projects into one of the platform's fifteen creative categories: Publishing, Music, Games, Food, Crafts, Dance, Film & Video, Design, Fashion, Technology, Journalism, Comics, Photography, Theatre and Art. Its narrowed focus on creative projects positions it as distinct from platforms like GoFundMe, which allows users to raise money for events and challenging circumstances such as illness and accidents, and Indiegogo, which allows users to fundraise for charities alongside ideas or creative works. As part of their creative focus, Kickstarter directly engages with people and organisations in the creative industries through category directors, including Margot Atwell. Atwell works with a range of writers and publishers across the industry but particularly focuses on working with independent publishers, authors from underrepresented communities, and literary communities and organisations to develop successful Kickstarter campaigns. From her perspective, these groups are already doing valuable work, such as nurturing new voices, taking risks and facilitating and advocating for inclusive publishing practices, and would benefit the most from the money and visibility that can come with a successful Kickstarter campaign.

Atwell's focus in the publishing field is in line with Kickstarter's organisational designation as a Public Benefit Corporation (PBC). PBCs are for-profit companies that are required to balance public interest and their impact on society with profitability and the interest of shareholders. In reincorporating as a PBC, Kickstarter outlined further missions, values and commitments in its charter. Some of these include not selling user data to third-parties; attempting to limit its environmental impact by investing in green infrastructure, for example; annually donating five per cent of its after-tax profit towards arts and music education, and to organisations fighting to end systemic inequality; and supporting employees to work on their own creative projects, including providing time off to pursue them.[15] In addition to the values inferred in its charter, the company fought for net-neutrality policies in 2014 and against the anti-trans bathroom law in North Carolina in 2016, and joined the Global Climate Strike in 2019.[16] In February 2020, it became one of the first technology companies to form a union after some pushback from management.[17] Kickstarter is among only a few technology companies, including Change.org, Etsy and Hootsuite, that are designated as a benefit corporation. Rather than a move away from the structures of digital capitalism, the PBC model represents a new, dynamic and conscious form of capitalism that prioritises social responsibility and other forms of capital alongside economic growth. Whether or not this marriage of models prevents the inequalities and exploitation associated with some forms of digital capitalism requires further investigation.

Many of its PBC responsibilities encourage the company to position the platform within the arts and cultural sectors by partnering with companies, holding conferences on issues facing these industries and, as stated in its charter, pledging to always support, serve, and champion artists and creators, especially those working in less commercial areas. Bob Walker at *The New York Times* has referred to Kickstarter as 'the people's NEA' [National Endowment for the Arts].[18] The progressive ethos of Kickstarter is integral to its branding as a crowdfunding social media platform as well as its position within the creative industries ecosystem.

Kickstarter also directly engages in conversations and programs in the broader cultural industries. In 2019, the company held The Next Page: Creating the Future of Publishing conference, where industry and creative professionals discussed issues and opportunities around technology, representation and cultural inclusivity, economic sustainability, and community in the publishing industry. Later in the same year, Kickstarter launched Students of Art, a digital resource for emerging and student artists featuring advice on how to apply for grants, how to work with galleries and collectors, and promotion.[19] In 2018, it ran its first Summer of Poetry, a campaign that combines in-person and online poetry events in New York with a push to launch poetry crowdfunding projects on the platform.[20] Kickstarter has a presence at PAX East, the gaming conference, and the London Design Festival. It will host the Bluestockings Comics Fest for Queer and Trans Creators, and it has partnered with the Rhode Island School of Design and Guanajuato International Film Festival, for example.[21] These active connections to the creative and cultural industries are designed to fulfil Kickstarter's commitments in its charter as a PBC, preserve and reinforce its position as creative-focused crowdfunding platform and develop its creative community.

The platform also exists within a technological, connective ecosystem wherein other social media platforms and software infrastructures are integral to its operations. Between 2012 and 2017, the platform began to expand globally, primarily in Anglophone countries or places where English is widely spoken. Globally, projects were launched in the United Kingdom, Canada, Australia, New Zealand, the Netherlands, Denmark, Ireland, Norway, Sweden, Germany, France, Spain, Austria, Belgium, Italy, Luxembourg, Switzerland, Singapore, Hong Kong, Mexico and Japan. Kickstarter rolled out in these countries in conjunction with its payment processor, Stripe, which is only available in certain countries. Atwell told me that laws, payment and culture are the main factors when they are considering where to roll out. One of the challenges for Kickstarter entering the Chinese market, for instance, is the tendency for people in China to use WePay, a payment process integrated with the popular social networking platform WeChat, and not credit cards for online payments, which Stripe necessitates. In a publishing context, the unrestricted reach of Kickstarter projects within the available countries redraws some lines in an industry that is organised by territorial rights. However, according to data from Similar Web, like the publishing industry, the US represents the largest market for Kickstarter users.[22] The different technological practices of internet users across the world and software affordances undercut the apparent globalised nature of Kickstarter.

While campaigns may be targeted at audiences around the world and rewards shipped worldwide at the creator's bequest, localism is still important to backer communities on Kickstarter. Backers can develop strong ties to campaigns and projects they feel are important to the communities that they belong to or align with.[23] These communities can come in the form of physical and geographic spaces, such as the Australian literary community or in backers' local cities. Sites like Kickstarter may facilitate investment in local businesses and artists.[24] However, technology extends notions of communities beyond geographical manifestations. Publishers' online writing and reading communities can also be leveraged successfully in crowdfunding campaigns. Other social media platforms often used for marketing, such as Instagram and Facebook, often contribute to the success of an organisation's campaign as well. Other social media platforms such as the online gaming platform Steam are positioned within the creative business ecosystem that enables Kickstarter projects to exist in the globalised creative industries.

The platform and business ecosystem in which Kickstarter is embedded is also shaped by services recommended by the platform. On a help resource page on the Kickstarter website, the platform has compiled a list of services that can aid in the completion of creators' campaigns. These service platforms range in categories and functions, from design services, disc and vinyl pressing, fulfilment, merchandising, prototyping, shipping, tax and legal, and so on. For book publishing, the suggestions include services for book printing, self-publishing, and retailing and distribution. Some of these are environmentally-friendly – as indicated by a little green leaf graphic next to their name – and all are independent companies whose business ethoses are similar to the values outlined in Kickstarter's charter. These include Blurb, Lulu and IngramSpark, for self-publishing; and Bookmobile, Make That Thing, and PrintNinja for printing services. While Kickstarter does not earn a referral fee from these services, the list does contribute to the platform's brand associations and is indicative of the creative business ecosystem in which Kickstarter is positioning itself.

Kickstarter's advice for creators extends beyond suggested fulfilment services to cover a range of creative and recommended uses of the platform. While creators are only bound by the terms of service and do not necessarily have to follow advice presented by the platform, it is a useful resource for exploring what Kickstarter deems to be best practice in the creation of campaigns on the platform. Kickstarter's recommendation content typically includes straightforward and helpful information, such as how to create a project video, with tips on lighting, camera angles and orientation, and scripting.[25] Their resources are also sourced from creators who have used Kickstarter, demonstrating the direct engagement the platform invests in with creative professionals across the world to connect to the global cultural industries. The construction of campaigns, then, is not only delimited by the interface design of the platform, but also by recommendations for how to create a campaign in the 'handbook' and on their social media accounts, including their YouTube channel, Instagram page and Tumblr blog. Tips and advice centre on the design of campaigns and use of rich media, including video, for creators to tell the story of their projects or businesses.

Kickstarter's multi-modality platform enables creators to tell the story of their creative ventures through a range of textual and rich, communicative media techniques. Digital tools, including high-quality videos, GIFs (graphic interchange format), social media and email are used to do what Atwell describes as an old practice: have people 'subscribe to the book before it exists'. A key feature of Kickstarter is the way in which multimedia can be embedded into the project campaign page. Many successful campaigns use both text and multimedia to convey a narrative around the importance of the campaign as well as the organisation behind it. Atwell says that campaigns with highly produced videos are generally more successful, for example. The emphasis on video content on social media platforms is not unique. Facebook announced that in 2020 its algorithm would favour high-quality video that lasted longer than three minutes.[26] TikTok, a popular short-video platform, gained 30 million new users within three months of launching.[27] Finally, 'stories' – short, ephemeral videos – became a popular feature on all Facebook platforms (Facebook, Instagram, Messenger and WhatsApp) after first being successful on Snapchat.[28] Video content is a popular media format for social media owners in part because it tends to keep users on the platform longer, and user engagement is relatively easy to track based on how long users watch. The expense of producing high-quality videos, however, may be prohibitive for independent and start-up producers and literary organisations. More research is needed to explore the relationship between video content, successful campaigns and the resource capacity of creators.

Elements of textual communication, including voice and language, remain incredibly important. Rewarding textual engagements with backers typically occurs in two ways for book publishers on Kickstarter: through acknowledgements in a published book and through the language used in campaigns. Typically, backers are credited as patrons inside the physical copy of the book, which, as Francesca Tondi notes, 'gives life to a new dynamic between author, reader, and book', creating 'a bond between backers and books which precedes the act of reading'.[29] The language used in campaigns has been shown to have an effect on the likelihood of Kickstarter users backing projects to begin with. In an analysis of language use in over 26,000 Kickstarter projects, successful projects were found to be more emotive, thoughtful and colloquial, including expressions of reciprocity, social relationships, emotional appeal, gratitude and collectivism.[30] This reformation of cultural capital exchange reflects the practices and values of subscription and community-led models of publishing, while the language directly contributes to building communities.

Kickstarter has a robust repeat backer community. Repeat backers are people who pledge money to more than one project, and approximately a third of Kickstarter backers are repeat backers over time. As of mid-March 2020, there were approximately 17.6 million total backers and 5.8 million repeat backers, who have cumulatively contributed around 60.3 million pledges.[31] The community of active users and repeat backers on Kickstarter are likely to be people who are also Kickstarting projects as well as people who are involved in the creative communities and industries that are represented as categories on the platform. Atwell herself is deemed a 'Superbacker', having supported around 476 projects since 2012. She also Kickstarted her own book on roller derby. To date, Thornwillow Press, the case study explored later, has launched 29 projects and backed 14. This trend of community behaviour is similar to the prosumer nature of Australian literary publishing. As Emmett Stinson suggests, 'contemporary literary audiences are increasingly made up of prosumers who are themselves involved in the creation or mediation of literary works … whose investment in reading literary works is bound up with their own creative work'.[32] In cases where concerns over market and genre expectations might prevent publishers from acquiring projects that exist interstitially or outside of known markets, crowdfunding platforms offer a space to test ideas and consumer viability. Books that are not perceived to have a large enough audience, particularly in smaller markets like Australia, can be tested and potentially find readers through sites like Kickstarter.

Repeat backers move between and support multiple categories once they are in the Kickstarter ecosystem. Atwell says, 'We see when a major project comes in, backers of that project will then go and back other projects, sometimes not even in the same category.' This movement is true for creators as well. Creative projects on Kickstarter must fit into one of the fifteen categories on the platform, but they can span more. On Kickstarter, Atwell tells me, 'You can work across category and across genre.' In 2017, Thornwillow Press launched a campaign for a portfolio of prints by German Dada artist Hannah Höch that they tagged in the Publishing category, rather than Design & Tech. The choice of category, then, will likely depend on the audience and community the creator is hoping to tap into for support. The technical architecture of Kickstarter and user behaviours somewhat eliminate the silos around sectors in the creative industries.

There are of course many instances where projects fail to reach their funding goals. One of the risks of running a Kickstarter campaign is that it runs on an all-or-nothing funding mechanism. That is, if creators do not reach their total funding goal set for their project, backers are not charged. For Atwell, this is an in-built safety measure for both creators and backers. However, it does mean that there is a potential for loss for creators who have invested time and money in the setting up and marketing of their campaign. Campaigns may be unsuccessful for a variety of reasons, including lack of awareness around the campaign, creators not leveraging already established communities on other platforms, and what is being offered. Researchers have found that claims of novelty and usefulness can increase project funding by 200 per cent and 1200 per cent, respectively.[33] Pre-existing personal and professional networks are also integral to successful Kickstarter campaigns, while factors like having a high-quality video explaining the project specifications and the presence of special offers for early backers are helpful in creating a successful campaign. Kickstarter offers a project budget calculator for creators to avoid unforeseen costs, with the idea that creators include these in their overall funding goal. Creators are able to estimate manufacturing costs, including those for merchandise, as well as associated marketing costs under either Research and Development or Miscellaneous. Utilising the range of affordances of the platform, including the reward system and multimedia capabilities, as well as creators' already established community channels is thus important for creating a successful Kickstarter campaign.

The technological, economic and social features of Kickstarter shape how campaigns are produced on the site. However, creators are not limited to straightforward uses of these affordances. How creators play with the platform features can impact the success of their campaigns. The crowdfunding campaigns by Thornwillow Press exemplify this well.

Kickstarting Book Publishing: Thornwillow Press

There were 371 live projects under the Publishing category on Kickstarter as of mid-March 2020, and this number is changing every day. Since the platform launched, around US$155 million has been successfully raised for Publishing campaigns and 49,297 projects have been launched. Individual authors, small and large publishers and literary organisations are all tapping into Kickstarter's in-built audience to fund creative works. Among them is Thornwillow Press. Thornwillow Press has a highly innovative and successful Kickstarter presence. The company's multi-modality and gamified approach to designing campaigns has helped their campaigns to be featured on the homepage of Kickstarter by way of the platform algorithm and Kickstarter staff picks.

Thornwillow Press is a small publisher of speciality letterpress printed, hand-bound books, founded by Luke Pontifell in 1985 and based in Newburgh, New York. It has printed and published original works by John Updike, Walter Cronkite and Barack Obama as well as republished works by canonical authors such as Jane Austen, Agatha Christie and Mary Shelley. Their books appear in the permanent collections of the Metropolitan Museum, the Smithsonian Institution, the Vatican and the White House.[34] They also create custom stationery and print artefacts, including engraved calendars, rain paper notebooks and broadside portfolios on topics such as American protest, subversion, and alternative facts. Thornwillow Press joined Kickstarter in 2016 and have since created 29 projects. Their latest completed campaign for *The Book of Genesis* ran for 16 days in late 2019 and raised US$70,732. Thornwillow Press's presence on a digital platform like Kickstarter is not at odds with a company that has a strong reverence for the print book. Rather, this relationship demonstrates the post-digital nature of contemporary book publishing, wherein digital and print media systems intermix in messy ways through the blending, overlapping and coevolution of digital and analogue practices.[35] Thornwillow Press combines strategic digital communications strategies with material rewards to run successful Kickstarter campaigns.

The crowdfunding model of Kickstarter is built on a kind of gamified rewards system. Gamification is the use of 'game design elements in a non-game context to motivate and increase user activity and retention' through rewards systems with points, badges, levels and leader boards.[36] It has been adopted in online and service marketing, education, tourism and health and fitness to encourage engagement and brand satisfaction.[37] On Kickstarter, backers pledge between certain monetary ranges, or levels, to access different rewards rather than donating random amounts of money to campaigns. For example, for Thornwillow Press's letterpress-printed and handbound book of Agatha Christie's *Death on the Nile*, backers can pledge US$10 or more to get a letterpress-printed broadside of Christie quotes. For US$95 or more, backers get a copy of the letterpress edition of *Death on the Nile*, or two copies for US$190. Backers that break US$1000 receive a full leather copy of *Death on the Nile*, stamped in gold and presented in a suede-lined clamshell box along with a paper-wrapped reading copy, and so on.

In their more recent campaigns Thornwillow Press have begun gamifying the reward-based system of Kickstarter further. For *Death on the Nile*, Thornwillow Press set up a mystery puzzle game, incentivised by the promise of a prize. For the mystery puzzle, Thornwillow Press posted clues or questions, and the first or last letter for each would form an anagram that could be unscrambled to reveal the final answer. This gamification is designed to increase engagement by potential backers, which increases the likelihood of engagement from other potential users as well as the campaign gaining visibility on Kickstarter.[38] Higher user engagement and greater visibility of projects contribute to the development and maintenance of Thornwillow's online community as well as the financial success of their campaigns.

The design of the mystery puzzle also increases instances where users return to the campaign. On Kickstarter, the discoverability of projects is mediated by the technological features of the platform. In particular, the interface design of Kickstarter and its algorithm impact who sees projects at key stages of their fundraising campaign. Kickstarter's homepage contains tiles of projects based on different designations. There are 'featured projects', 'recommended' projects, new 'fresh favourites', projects that are 'taking off' and ones that are on their 'home stretch'. How these projects become featured on the home page is a part of the 'secret sauce' of Kickstarter's algorithms. Factors include the number of backers the campaign has per day, the amount of traffic to campaign pages, the amount of funding received as well as the return rate of users to the campaign pages. Page views for *Death on the Nile* as well as time spent on the campaign page contribute to algorithmic data that underpin visibility on Kickstarter. Efforts to generate the kinds of traffic that feed algorithms that determine visibility may extend beyond the platform to social media communities.

The opportunities presented by crowdfunding are not limited to financing projects. Atwell says that while people think about Kickstarter really specifically in the financial realm, 'it's the weird secret of Kickstarter publishing that it's actually an audience-building platform as much as a funding platform'. Crowdfunding can be a space for audience building, marketing and market testing to assess the quality of the creative ideas, a promotional tool for new products, and as a direct sales channel.[39] According to Atwell, it is a platform where publishers can achieve a high level of interaction and relationship building with audiences in a more productive way. The platform provides a channel for creators to build their brand among a highly engaged social media community. While Kickstarter enables creators to market content beyond the standard social media sites like Facebook, Twitter and Instagram, the campaigns also provide productive content to share via these more mainstream social media communities. Colista and Duvall's research into backer behaviour shows that 74 per cent of backers said that they told someone about the project in person and 71 per cent shared projects on their social media pages after backing them.[40] Thornwillow Press encourages this further reach through strategic communications.

Through the gamification for *Death on the Nile*, Thornwillow Press extends the reach and impact of its community. Projects are more likely to be backed by friends, family and close networks at the beginning of a campaign, and are more likely to be backed generally near the end when potential backers can see that they are needed.[41] The mystery game triggers this need earlier in the campaign, creating more steps of lower-level engagement that are likely to lead to higher levels of engagement, including backing. In this way, backers become word-of-mouth advocates for projects, not just a passive purchaser of the book. While social media platforms like Kickstarter enable greater accessibility to media creators and production processes, access does not assure active participation. Historically, data suggests that the majority of users of user-generated content sites are passive spectators or 'inactives'. The broad middle of users may simply join, comment, rate or bookmark (in this case pledge), and only a minority actually produce and upload content, demonstrating that 'participation is a relative term'.[42] By gamifying *Death on the Nile*, Thornwillow Press enhances the community members' engagement and offers new ways of monitoring and analysing the online community.

Conclusion

Connective crowdfunding platforms offer a number of opportunities for publishers in the digital age. First, and most obviously, they provide a direct and relatively low-risk means of financing creative projects. In an epoch of decreased federal and state government funding, and increased precarity in Australia, this is incredibly valuable for smaller companies and organisations as well as sole traders. Crowdfunding also offers creators an avenue for marketing products, testing ideas and building their audience on a dedicated creative platform. As can be seen with Thornwillow Press, independent print publishers are successfully and creatively using these digital platforms to tell the story of what they do and why, and expand marketing and engagement activities with established and new audiences, all while prizing the book as the ultimate end product.

While Kickstarter and other crowdfunding platforms certainly open up new avenues for authors and publishers to compete in a highly saturated contemporary market, these platforms are not neutral entities. The technological, social and economic aspects of Kickstarter shape how projects are communicated on the site. Its recommendation algorithm, determined through user-generated data on user behaviour, impacts the visibility of campaigns and thus their likelihood of success. The discretion of the Kickstarter staff to choose their favourite campaigns to be featured or creators to be mentored also impacts visibility and success on the platform. While it is not explicit which campaigns on the homepage are chosen by staff, most rotating categories on the homepage are filtered by a 'Projects We Love' tag, suggesting that staff have a great deal of power over featured campaigns. An exception to this, for example, is the projects 'Near Me' category, which is based solely on geolocation data. Despite Kickstarter's reincorporation as a PBC, it, and other crowdfunding platforms, are predicated on a form of digital platform capitalism that reproduces market systems and commodifies user-data. These factors influence the life and potential success of campaigns in important and often invisible ways.

Kickstarter deliberately works to position itself as part of, and not just ancillary to, the creative and cultural industries. At a distance, this effort is reminiscent of Flickr's attempts to brand itself as the professional photographer's social media platform, or LiveJournal as the writer's platform. However, through programs, conferences and creative directors, including Margot Atwell, Kickstarter supports and advocates for the success and evolution of the creative industries. Given the perpetually changing nature of the internet and social media platforms, it remains to be seen how this develops.

Endnotes

1   Francesca Tondi, *'Alternative Publishing Models in a Changing Cultural Landscape: The Rise of Crowdfunding,'* Logos 28, no. 4 (2017): 32-37.

2   Kathryn Judge, 'The Future of Direct Finance: The Diverging Paths of Peer-to-Peer Lending and Kickstarter,' Wake Forest Law Review 50, no. 520 (2015).; Rita Colista and Kevin Duvall, 'Show Me the Money: Importance of Crowdfunding Factors on Backers' Decisions to Financially Support Kickstarter Campaigns,' Social Media + Society, 2017, 1–12.; Nihit Desai,Raghav Gupta, and Karen Truong, 'Plead or Pitch? The Role of Language in Kickstarter Project Success., Department of Computer Science, Stanford University, 2015. https://pdfs. semanticscholar.org/c26e/4b8cd5b8f99718e637fa42d1458275bea0a2. pdf?_ga=2.258293258.161696692.1613695101-1363197297.1613695101.

3   Tondi, *Alternative Publishing Models.*

4   Sam Jacobs 'Coming of Age: Australian Crowdfunding Platforms Raised $8.7m in the March Quarter.' Stockhead, 14 April, 2019. https:// stockhead.com.au/private-i/coming-of-age-australian-crowdfunding-platforms-raised-8-7m-in-the-march-quarter/.

5   Lance W Bennett and Alexandra Segerberg, 'The Logic of Connective Action: Digital Media and the Personalization of Contentious Politics,' *Information, Communication and Society* 15, no. 4 (2013): 739–768.

6   Daniel Schiller, *Digital Capitalism.* (Cambridge, MA: MIT Press, 1999).

7   Jonathan Pace, 'The Concept of Digital Capitalism.' *Communication Theory* 28, no. 3 (2018): 254–69.

8   Lauren Debter, 'Amazon Surpasses Walmart As The World's Largest Retailer.' Forbes, 15 May, 2019. https://www.forbes.com/sites/laurendebter/2019/05/15/worlds-largest-retailers-2019-amazon-walmart-alibaba/#d3e3c24171c6.

9   Pace, *The Concept of Digital Capitalism.*

10 Nick Srnicek, *Platform Capitalism.* (Cambridge: Polity Press, 2017).

11 Jose van Dijck, *The Culture of Connectivity: A Critical History of Social Media.* (New York: Oxford University Press, 2013).; Jose van Dijck and Thomas Poell, 'Understanding Social Media Logic.' Media and Communication 1, no. 1 (2013): 2–14.

12 Joanna Drucker, *Graphesis: Visual Forms of Knowledge Production.* (Cambridge, MA: Harvard University Press, 2014).

13 van Dijck and Poell, *Understanding Social Media Logic.*

14 Kickstarter, *Kickstarter Stats, 2020,* https://www.kickstarter.com/help/stats?ref=press.

15   Kickstarter, *Charter*, https://www.kickstarter.com/charter.
16   April Glasser, 'Kickstarter's Tumultuous Journey to Where No Tech
     Company Has Gone Before: Unionization.' Slate Magazine, 13
     September, 2019. https://slate.com/technology/2019/09/kickstarter-
     turmoil-union-drive-historic-tech-industry.html.
17   Kate Conger and Noam Scheiber, . 'Kickstarter Employees Vote to
     Unionize in a Big Step for Tech.' The New York Times, 18 February, 2020,
     https://www.nytimes.com/2020/02/18/technology/kickstarter-union.html.
18   Rob Walker, 'The Trivialities and Transcendence of Kickstarter.' The
     New York Times Magazine, 5 August, 2011. https://www.nytimes.
     com/2011/08/07/magazine/the-trivialities-and-transcendence-of-
     kickstarter.html.
19   Sharp, *Kickstarter Launches New Digital Resource for Emerging and Student
     Artists.*
20   Margot Atwell, 'Join Us for Kickstarter's Summer of Poetry.' Kickstarter
     Blog, 17 May, 2018. https://www.kickstarter.com/blog/join-us-for-
     kickstarters-summer-of-poetry.
21   Burning Wheel, 'Take a Seat, Play Some Games: Come to Kickstarter's
     Couchland at PAX East.' Kickstarter Blog, April 5, 2018. https://www.
     kickstarter.com/blog/take-a-seat-play-some-games-come-to-kickstarters-
     couchland-at-pa.; Nick Yulman, 'Splat! Kickstarter at the 2017 London
     Design Festival.' *Kickstarter Blog*, 14 September, 2017. https://www.
     kickstarter.com/blog/splat-kickstarter-at-the-2017-london-design-festival.;
     Camilla Zhang, 'Kickstarter to Host Bluestockings Comics Fest for Queer
     and Trans Creators.' *Kickstarter Blog*, January 31, 2020. https://www.
     kickstarter.com/blog/kickstarter-to-host-bluestockings-comics-fest-for-
     queer-and-tran; Celia Vermicelli, Kickstarter and Guanajuato International
     Film Festival to Feature 12 Student-Led Film Projects in Mexico.'
     Kickstarter Blog, February 28, 2020. https://www.kickstarter.com/blog/
     kickstarter-and-guanajuato-international-film-festival-to-feature.
22   SimilarWeb. 'Kickstarter.com Analytics - Market Share Stats & Traffic
     Ranking.' SimilarWeb, 2020. https://www.similarweb.com/website/
     kickstarter.com.
23   Colistra and Duvall, *Show Me the Money.*
24   Judge, *The Future of Direct Finance.*
25   Kickstarter. 'Let's Make Your Project Video.' YouTube, April 27, 2016.
     https://www.youtube.com/watch?v=L3h828EtWoA.
26   Paige Cooper, 'How the Facebook Algorithm Works in 2020 and How
     to Work With It.' Hootsuite (blog), 27 January, 2020. https://blog.
     hootsuite.com/facebook-algorithm/.

27   Rebecca Fannin, 'The Strategy Behind TikTok's Global Rise.' Harvard Business Review, 13 September, 2019. https://hbr.org/2019/09/the-strategy-behind-tiktoks-global-rise.

28   Will Oremus, 'How Facebook Beat Snapchat and Won the Teens Back.' Slate Magazine, July 31, 2017. https://slate.com/technology/2017/07/teenage-clicks.html.

29   Tondi, *Alternative Publishing Models.*

30   Desai, Gupta, and Truong, *Plead or Pitch?*

31   Kickstarter, *Kickstarter Stats.*

32   Emmett Stinson, 'Small Publishers and the Emerging Network of Australian Literary Prosumption.' Australian Humanities Review 59 (2016): 23–43.

33   Mukherjee et al., 'Does the Crowd Support Innovation? Innovation Claims and Success on Kickstarter.' SSRN Scholarly Paper. Rochester, NY: Social Science Research Network, 5 September, 2017. https://papers.ssrn.com/abstract=3003283.

34   Thornwillow Press, 'Our Story.' Thornwillow Press, 2020. https://thornwillow.com/about-us.

35   Christian Ulrik Andersen, Geoff Cox and Georgios Papadopolous, 'Postdigital Research – Editorial.' A Peer-Reviewed Journal About Post-Digital Research 3, no. 1 (2014): 4–7; Florien Cramer, 'What Is Post-Digital?' In Postdigital Aesthetics: Art, Computation and Design, edited by Berry, David M. and Dieter, Michael, 12–26. (New York, NY: Palgrave Macmillan, 2015).

36   Sebastian Deterding et al., 'From Game Design Elements to Gamefulness: Defining "Gamification"'. Proceedings of the 15th International Academic MindTrek Conference: Envisioning Future Media Environments., 2011.

37   Daniel Johnson et al., 'Gamification for Health and Wellbeing: A Systematic Review of the Literature.' *Internet Interventions* 6 (November 1, 2016): 89–106.; Kai Huotari and Juho Hamari, 'A Definition for Gamification: Anchoring Gamification in the Service Marketing Literature.' Electronic Markets 27, no. 1 (February 1, 2017): 21–31. https://doi.org/10.1007/s12525-015-0212-z.; Darina Dicheva et al., 'Gamification in Education: A Systematic Mapping Study.' Educational Technology & Society 18, no. 3 (2015).

38   Marianna Sigala, 'Gamification for Crowdsourcing Marketing Practices: Applications and Benefits in Tourism.' In *Advances in Crowdsourcing*, edited by Gil Pechuan, Ignacio, Estelles-Miguel, Sofia and Garrigos-Simon, Fernando J., 129–45. (New York: Springer, 2015); Yang Yang, Yoursa Asaad and Yogesh Dwivedi, 'Examining the Impact of

Gamification on Intention of Engagement and Brand Attitude in the Marketing Context.' Computers in Human Behavior 73 (August 1, 2017): 459–69. https://doi.org/10.1016/j.chb.2017.03.066.

39   Terrence E Brown, Edward Boon, and Leyland F Pitt, 'Seeking Funding in Order to Sell: Crowdfunding as a Marketing Tool.' Business Horizons 60, no. 2 (2017): 189–95.

40   Colistra and Duvall, *Show Me the Money*.

41   Venkat Kuppuswamy and Barry L Bayus, 'Crowdfunding Creative Ideas: The Dynamics of Project Backers.' The Economics of Crowdfunding, 2018, 151–82.

42   Jose van Dijck, 'Users like You? Theorizing Agency in User-Generated Content.' *Media, Culture & Society* 31, no. 1 (2009): 41–58.

Bibliography

Andersen, Christian Ulrik, Cox, Geoff and Papadopolous, Georgio. 'Postdigital Research – Editorial,' *A Peer-Reviewed Journal About Post-Digital Research* 3, no. 1 (2014): 4–7.

Atwell, Margot. 'Join Us for Kickstarter's Summer of Poetry,' *Kickstarter Blog*, May 17, 2018. https://www.kickstarter.com/blog/join-us-for-kickstarters-summer-of-poetry.

Bennett, W. Lance, and Segerberg, Alexandra. 'The Logic of Connective Action: Digital Media and the Personalization of Contentious Politics,' *Information, Communication and Society* 15, no. 4 (2013): 739–768.

Brown, Terrence E., Boon, Edward and Pitt, Leyland F. 'Seeking Funding in Order to Sell: Crowdfunding as a Marketing Tool,' *Business Horizons* 60, no. 2 (2017): 189–95.

Burning Wheel. 'Take a Seat, Play Some Games: Come to Kickstarter's Couchland at PAX East., *Kickstarter Blog*, 5 April, 2018. https://www.kickstarter.com/blog/take-a-seat-play-some-games-come-to-kickstarters-couchland-at-pa.

Colistra, Rita, and Duvall, Kevin. 'Show Me the Money: Importance of Crowdfunding Factors on Backers' Decisions to Financially Support Kickstarter Campaigns,' *Social Media + Society* 3, no. 4 (2017): 1–12.

Conger, Kate, and Scheiber, Noam. 'Kickstarter Employees Vote to Unionize in a Big Step for Tech,' *The New York Times*, 18 February, 2020, https://www.nytimes.com/2020/02/18/technology/kickstarter-union.html.

Cooper, Paige. 'How the Facebook Algorithm Works in 2020 and How to Work With It,' *Hootsuite* (blog), 27 January, 2020. https://blog.hootsuite.com/facebook-algorithm/.

Cramer, Florian. 'What Is Post-Digital?' In *Postdigital Aesthetics: Art, Computation and Design*, edited by David M. Berry and Michael Dieter, New York, NY: Palgrave Macmillan, (2015), 12–26.

Debter, Lauren. 'Amazon Surpasses Walmart As The World's Largest Retailer,' *Forbes*, 15 May, 2019. https://www.forbes.com/sites/laurendebter/2019/05/15/worlds-largest-retailers-2019-amazon-walmart-alibaba/#d3e3c24171c6.

Desai, Nihit, Gupta, Raghav, and Truong, Karen. 'Plead or Pitch? The Role of Language in Kickstarter Project Success,' Department of Computer Science, Stanford University, 2015. https://pdfs.semanticscholar.org/c26e/4b8cd5b8f99718e637fa42d1458275bea0a2.pdf?_ga=2.258293258.161696692.1613695101-1363197297.1613695101.

Deterding, Sebastian, Dixon, Dan, Khaled, Rilla and Nacke, Lennart. 'From Game Design Elements to Gamefulness: Defining "Gamification",' *Proceedings of the 15th International Academic MindTrek Conference: Envisioning Future Media Environments.*, 2011.

Dicheva, Darina, Dichev, Christo, Agre, Gennady, and Angelova, Galia. 'Gamification in Education: A Systematic Mapping Study,' *Educational Technology & Society* 18, no. 3 (2015).

Drucker, Johanna. *Graphesis: Visual Forms of Knowledge Production*. Cambridge, MA: Harvard University Press, 2014.

Drucker, Johanna 'Humanities Approaches to Interface Theory,' *Culture Machine* 12 (2011): 1-20.

Edim, Glory. 'Rhode Island School of Design & Kickstarter Partner to Educate Artists,' *Kickstarter Blog*, 12 October, 2016. https://www.kickstarter.com/blog/rhode-island-school-of-design-and-kickstarter-partner-to-educate.

Etter, Vincent, Grossglauser, Matthias and Thiran, Patrick. 'Launch Hard or Go Home! Predicting the Success of Kickstarter Campaigns,' In *Proceedings of the First ACM Conference on Online Social Networks*, 177–82. Boston, Massachusetts, USA: ACM, 2013.

Fannin, Rebecca. 'The Strategy Behind TikTok's Global Rise,' *Harvard Business Review*, 13 September, 2019. https://hbr.org/2019/09/the-strategy-behind-tiktoks-global-rise.

Fuchs, Christian. *Digital Labour and Karl Marx*. New York: Routledge, 2014.

Glaser, April. 'Kickstarter's Tumultuous Journey to Where No Tech Company Has Gone Before: Unionization,' *Slate Magazine*, 13 September, 2019. https://slate.com/technology/2019/09/kickstarter-turmoil-union-drive-historic-tech-industry.html.

Groshoff, David. 'Kickstarter My Heart: Extraordinary Popular Delusions and the Madness of Crowdfunding Constraints and Bitcoin Bubbles,' *William and Mary Business Law Review* 5, no. 2 (2014): 490.

Huotari, Kai, and Hamari. Juho 'A Definition for Gamification: Anchoring Gamification in the Service Marketing Literature,' *Electronic Markets* 27, no. 1 (February, 2017): 21–31. https://doi.org/10.1007/s12525-015-0212-z.

Jacobs, Sam. 'Coming of Age: Australian Crowdfunding Platforms Raised $8.7m in the March Quarter,' Stockhead, 14 April, 2019. https://stockhead.com.au/private-i/coming-of-age-australian-crowdfunding-platforms-raised-8-7m-in-the-march-quarter/.

Judge, Kathryn. 'The Future of Direct Finance: The Diverging Paths of Peer-to-Peer Lending and Kickstarter,' *Wake Forest Law Review* 50, no. 520 (2015).

Johnson, Daniel, Sebastian Deterding, Kerri-Ann Kuhn, Aleksandra Staneva, Stoyan Stoyanov, and Leanne Hides. 'Gamification for Health and Wellbeing: A Systematic Review of the Literature,' *Internet Interventions* 6 (November 1, 2016): 89–106. https://doi.org/10.1016/j.invent.2016.10.002.

Kickstarter. 'Charter,' https://www.kickstarter.com/charter.

Kickstarter. 'Kickstarter Stats,' 2020, https://www.kickstarter.com/help/stats?ref=press.

Kickstarter. 'Let's Make Your Project Video.' *YouTube*, April 27, 2016. https://www.youtube.com/watch?v=L3h828EtWoA.

Kuppuswamy, Venkat and Bayus, Barry L. 'Crowdfunding Creative Ideas: The Dynamics of Project Backers,' *The Economics of Crowdfunding*, 2018, 151–82.

Li, Jun-Sheng. 'How Amazon Took 50% of the E-Commerce Market and What It Means for the Rest of Us,' TechCrunch. 27 February, 2019. https://techcrunch.com/2019/02/27/how-amazon-took-50-of-the-e-commerce-market-and-what-it-means-for-the-rest-of-us/.

Mukherjee, Anirban, Yang, Cathy L., Xiao, Ping and Chattopadhyay, Amitava. 'Does the Crowd Support Innovation? Innovation Claims and Success on Kickstarter,' SSRN Scholarly Paper. Rochester, NY: Social Science Research Network, 5 September, 2017. https://papers.ssrn.com/abstract=3003283.

Oremus, Will. 'How Facebook Beat Snapchat and Won the Teens Back,' *Slate Magazine*, 31 July, 2017. https://slate.com/technology/2017/07/teenage-clicks.html.

Pace, Jonathan. 'The Concept of Digital Capitalism,' *Communication Theory* 28, no. 3 (August, 2018): 254–69.

Schiller, Daniel. *Digital Capitalism*. Cambridge, MA: MIT Press, 1999.

Sharp, Daniel. 'Kickstarter Launches New Digital Resource for Emerging and Student Artists,' *Kickstarter Blog*, 10 September, 2019. https://www.kickstarter.com/blog/kickstarter-launches-new-digital-resource-for-emerging-and-stude.

Sigala, Marianna. 'Gamification for Crowdsourcing Marketing Practices: Applications and Benefits in Tourism,' in *Advances in Crowdsourcing*, edited by Gil Pechuan, Ignacio, Estelles-Miguel, Sofia and Garrigos-Simon, Fernando J., 129–45. New York: Springer, 2015.

SimilarWeb. 'Kickstarter.com Analytics - Market Share Stats & Traffic Ranking,' SimilarWeb, 2020. https://www.similarweb.com/website/kickstarter.com.

Srnicek, Nick. *Platform Capitalism*. Cambridge: Polity Press, 2017.

Stinson, Emmett. 'Small Publishers and the Emerging Network of Australian Literary Prosumption.' *Australian Humanities Review* 59 (2016): 23–43.

Thornwillow Press. 'Death on the Nile,' Kickstarter, 2019. https://www.kickstarter.com/projects/thornwillow/death-on-the-nile.

Thornwillow Press. 'Our Story,' Thornwillow Press, 2020. https://thornwillow.com/about-us.

Tondi, Francesca. 'Alternative Publishing Models in a Changing Cultural Landscape: The Rise of Crowdfunding,' *Logos* 28, no. 4 (2017): 32–37.

Vermicelli, Célia. 'Kickstarter and Guanajuato International Film Festival to Feature 12 Student-Led Film Projects in Mexico.' *Kickstarter Blog*, February 28, 2020. https://www.kickstarter.com/blog/kickstarter-and-guanajuato-international-film-festival-to-featur.

van Dijck, José. *The Culture of Connectivity: A Critical History of Social Media*. New York: Oxford University Press, 2013.

van Dijck, José. 'Users like You? Theorizing Agency in User-Generated Content,' *Media, Culture & Society* 31, no. 1 (2009): 41–58.

Dijck, José van, and Poell, Thomas. 'Understanding Social Media Logic,' *Media and Communication* 1, no. 1 (2013): 2–14.

Walker, Rob. 'The Trivialities and Transcendence of Kickstarter,' *The New York Times Magazine*, 5 August, 2011. https://www.nytimes.com/2011/08/07/magazine/the-trivialities-and-transcendence-of-kickstarter.html.

Yang, Yang, Asaad, Yousra and Dwivedi, Yogesh. 'Examining the Impact of Gamification on Intention of Engagement and Brand Attitude in the Marketing Context,' *Computers in Human Behavior* 73 (August 1, 2017): 459–69. https://doi.org/10.1016/j.chb.2017.03.066.

Yulman, Nick. 'Splat! Kickstarter at the 2017 London Design Festival,' *Kickstarter Blog*, 14 September, 2017. https://www.kickstarter.com/blog/splat-kickstarter-at-the-2017-london-design-festival.

Zhang, Camilla. 'Kickstarter to Host Bluestockings Comics Fest for Queer and Trans Creators,' *Kickstarter Blog*, 31 January, 2020. https://www.kickstarter.com/blog/kickstarter-to-host-bluestockings-comics-fest-for-queer-and-tran.

CHAPTER 8

Converging Margins

Punk Publishing Beyond the Codex

SARAH LAYTON

Definitions of the book post-Gutenberg have been characterised by an ongoing focus on the book as an object 'immortalized on dead trees'.[1] As scrolls and clay tablets shuffled into the pages of book history, the print codex became the definitive 'book' in literary analysis.

Only in recent years after being 'lulled into somnolence by five hundred years of print' Katherine Hayles argues, 'as the new medium of electronic textuality vibrantly asserts its presence, are these assumptions clearly coming into view.'[2] In the shift from bound codexes to digital books using new media, it is not possible to ignore the definitional questions that have hit publishing academics. The objects we know as books are being constantly fragmented and reconstructed, and the modern book is not a finite object or bound within the frame of print – but what is it? This chapter adds to this conversation by further complicating what a book can be and exploring the transmedial space that post-digital books now inhabit as something 'elastic, capable of being made longer or wider' to encompass new forms across media.[3] When the print codex converges with not only digital media but also with digital spaces and communities, one result is new forms of post-digital books on the fringes of trade publishing – what this essay terms 'combined transmedial books' and USB books.

These combined transmedial books exist as a combined work across Twine games, web platforms, USBs and print, and the small publishers and micro-presses creating them are challenging the unspoken tech norms of the publishing industry around acceptable digital book forms. These books are web-first literature that do not fit neatly into transmedia or Marie-Laure Ryan's concept of the augmented book,[4] and their existence further problematises definitions of the book for scholars. These books represent a punk approach to post-digital publishing that rejects dominant industry conventions around digital book forms, and the dialogic space they create between web and print represents a unique contemporary idea of what post-digital publishing can be for publishers looking to blur the line between codex and Other. Combined transmedial books like these, made using new publishing models, challenge the status quo of what a book can be and experiment with the boundaries of how the book is conceptualised and how other collectable and shareable book forms can mirror some of the codex's attractive features. In this chapter I look at two combined transmedial books that span across web platforms, Twine games, print pages, ePub files and animations. I also examine USB books, which are another book form that does not fit neatly into a print-centric definition of the book. These experimental forms create an opportunity for diverse and niche content that places trade publishing within a more dynamic and innovative digital literary sphere[5]. They also position their publishers as punk publishers on the margins of the traditional, existing in an as-yet-undefined definitional space. In experimenting with these books, publishers place themselves in opposition to some dominant tech norms in the publishing industry, which currently value specific digital book forms such as ebooks and audiobooks and restrictions around shareability, while also finding new ways to experiment with conventions around online community engagement.

This chapter does not engage with debates around the saliency of the paperback, but it does seek to show new ways that books are being conceptualised by publishers experimenting with combined books. In the case of the books I discuss, the idea of the post-digital book is pushed further, with the possibility to encompass multiple forms at once. What I've defined as a combined transmedial book doesn't sit comfortably within the dominant west-coast definition of transmedia proposed by Clark,[6] but it is undeniable that these new book forms are transmedial in many respects. In these titles, different forms and mediums work in combination to create one product that cannot be fully understood through one form discretely. The examples discussed show that storytelling across different media has blurred the line between the codex and Other to the extent that in these cases, the combination of multiple forms consumed simultaneously is essential for a text to have full meaning. Overall, this piece will focus on how combined transmedial books further complicate how we view books definitionally, both within the publishing industry and within academia.

Combined Transmedial Books and the Augmented Book

In a 2012 report prepared for the Book Industry Strategy Group in Australia, key industry actors including publishers, printers, authors and booksellers identified 'the changing format of the book' and 'globalization' as the two key factors likely to determine the future of the publishing industry.[7] While the industry has weathered a global financial crisis and has seen a rise again in paperback sales since 2015, tension around book forms remains as the proverbial digital ground continues to shift beneath publishers' feet.

This tension, created by convergence across media, has been approached in a variety of ways in research – often in the context of converging legacy media forms, but some of the most interesting and dramatic examples of its impact on the book can be seen in publishing connected to digital spaces and technologies. When print books converge with digital media, the print codex form becomes immediately less certain and less central.[8] The alarm first sounded with the rise of ebooks – books without paper – and now publishers have weathered audiobooks, where all elements of print are eschewed in favour of spoken word. In these recent, popular forms, publishers have grappled with the inevitability of catering to new reader demands. Ebook and audiobook publishing is now standard, and they have become conventional forms of digital books. But when print converges with not only digital media, but also with a more actively rebellious model of publishing more defined by fandom and less by profit, the result is something very different to what is largely seen or produced by legacy publishers. In particular, post-digital books that cross the divide between the codex and new digital scrolls.

Exploring the possibilities of a post-digital book forces publishers to think of the 'book (as codex) in terms of contingency rather than permanency'.[9] What these new books achieve is something closer to a book-history conceptualisation of the book than the codex-centric conceptions that have dominated modern publishing and literary studies. The current upheavals in book forms are deeply connected to book history – at the tipping point of the Gutenberg parenthesis, there can only be limited stability in an object that is not inherently stable. Leslie Howsam notes, 'the history of the book is a way of thinking about how people have given material form to knowledge and stories', but with the exception of the common aim of making these stories accessible, there is no determination of what form books must take[10] – a purposeful means of including the many forms that came before the codex in the study of book history. But Howsam's definition can just as easily be applied now; books can be physical objects, intangible code on a computer or something in between, and there is a possibility for the post-digital book to encompass multiple forms at once, with different forms and platforms working in tandem and rendering the forms in combination a more mutable but complete book.

It is important to note about these books that they do not currently sit comfortably anywhere in a definitional sense. While using the term post-digital in Florian Cramer's sense provides a space for them,[11] this is a broad tent which lacks specificity. They are also not the 'narratives that refuse to leave the stage'[12] that Marie-Laure Ryan discusses in her definition of transmedia – summarised as 'the expansion of popular storyworlds beyond their original medium.'[13] The west-coast model of transmedia popularised by Jenkins expects a blockbuster, a broader narrative with new arcs explored and expanded in different mediums,[14] which these texts do not aim to provide. There have also been attempts to define similar books to those discussed as 'augmented books' or a print book with 'additional resources'.[15] [16] Marie-Laure Ryan defines texts like *Night Film* by Marisha Pessl as an 'augmented book', a print book with a digital component you can access, through a QR code or web link, that gives you additional content. This content is not required for the story to make sense but is a repository for 'additional content that could not be printed, or that would be too digressive to include in the book'.[17] This description, while on a surface level appears to apply to combined transmedia books, is not accurate to what makes these texts unique. To apply this title would position them as a print book plus, rather than grappling with what makes these books so different. In Ryan's definition, the codex is central, and it comes from a space of analysis that assumes print first and then the creation of supplemental digital components, but it is a very different text that results from a web-first product transitioning to include a print component.

So, what does a combined transmedial book – or like one text discussed in this chapter that is both a print codex and also a collection of playable Twine games on topics ranging from 'kink to depression to biomechanical horses' – have to say about what a post-digital book is?[18] These books do not fit comfortably into the definition of transmedia, but they are undeniably transmedial in their cross-media storytelling, and they are a form of book that is not only consumed in different formats, but which also spans multiple formats within itself. They enable user participation and contributions to the story in a similar way, either as an ongoing project or in their creation. They are not the augmented book, with the implication being that it is the print codex that is central and being added to like the aforementioned biomechanical horse, but instead have evolved from online authors and content stretching to encompass a print codex. They also exist within an already expansive space of digital literature, from audiobooks to books made from Twitter poetry or written on cell phones. These combined transmedial books, like the books mentioned above, are also moving from web to print forms. But instead of embracing a new holistic print container for their content or using only a digital container, these texts exist unapologetically within that transition, refusing to have any aspect lost in translation. Instead, they create something that can only be understood fully through multiple containers, a combined book form that exists in the dialogic space between digital and print.

There has been previous research on publishers who have worked to blend codex publishing with new forms, creating codexes that interact with other media. *Agrippa* as discussed by Matthew Kirschenbaum is just one example, including a diskette in a hollowed-out cavity inside the print text that when played in a circa 1992 Mac scrolls through a 305-line poem by William Gibson.[19] But as more examples accumulate, there is something interesting that can be said about the changing ecology of book culture. Even publishers can no longer completely dismiss the impact of digital technology on definitions of the book, and while print is king economically, the work of some punk publishers is complicating our ideas about how books are defined within industry and academia.

This chapter will look at two specific examples of combined transmedial books, *Videogames for Humans* by Instar Books and *Homestuck* by Viz Media. It will also look at how the occurrence of USB books raises questions about whether the physical form of a book is only the domain of the paperback and adds to conversations about current shifts in the centrality of the codex. In *Videogames for Humans*, we can look at the Twine medium – a digital tool that can be used to create free, interactive stories in the form of a playable choose-your-own-adventure style narrative – and its connectivity with printed text to create a whole book with a paperback playthrough and analysis. It is also important to note that since its creation in 2009, the Twine medium has been popular among marginalised artists, queer authors and a significant number of acclaimed authors who are trans women. Similarly, in Viz Media's approach to turning the immense multimedia saga Homestuck[20] into a series of hardcover books connected to the original free webcomic we see directly the transition from a digital reading experience to a new print codex that both offers unique story elements but is unable to stand alone. These three examples show the collision point between traditional codex-based publishing and digital mediums to create mutable book forms and indicate that a non-codex centric model is critical in defining the book into the future.

Videogames for Humans and Homestuck: Combined Transmedial Books

The examples of combined transmedial books discussed in this chapter are both in some ways a product of the domestication of Internet technology and consumer devices that has leant normalcy and banality to web usage.[21] They are also, in some ways, examples of ergodic literature, not designed to be easy, complete reads in one medium and requiring some effort from readers to traverse multiple media forms to gain a full understanding. For ease, I will define them as books that have two key attributes: they are made up of a combination of inter-reliant print and digital components where the print component is reliant on the digital component for meaning, and they are web-first texts with a basis in digital authorship, where value is placed on not altering the original digital text to become a print-only book. What a print codex can add to an existing 'other' form is not something that book publishers typically grapple with. But this and how to create a connected dialogue between multiple components to create one whole book are questions that publishers Viz Media and Instar Books grappled with, in their creation of the books discussed. These books are designed to be made up of multiple media forms reliant on each other for meaning, and they challenge the conception of additional media as extra material rather than an integral part of the book itself.

This connectivity and conversation between media can be seen in the combined transmedial book by New York micro-press Instar Books – *Videogames for Humans*. Instar's 2015 book inhabits a converging space between videogames and print in a way that reflects the Twine medium it discusses, a medium that editor Merritt Kopas describes as 'flourishing at the intersections of digital games and fiction'.[22] The book, like all of Instar's books, exists in a transformative state from its inception. On Instar's website the publisher notes that from their inception, 'when one of our brave electronic editions sells 500 copies, it becomes a real-life paper book … Each purchase is a vote for permanent metamorphosis!'[23] The publisher's name 'instar'[24] is also deliberate, with the connotation of an invertebrate animal shedding part of a previous body and growing into something new – an idea the micro-press embodies in their active engagement with deeply mutable book forms and shareable digital content.

Videogames for Humans is highly unconventional in the same manner and is sold to readers in combination: a mailed-out paperback, a downloadable ePub file, and a downloadable Zip file of the Twine games featured in the book that the reader can play on their computer.[25] There is also now the imminent possibility of further metamorphosis for this text; with the goal for 500 sales of the book being reached, Instar has promised a Twine edition of the complete book will be published – currently under construction.[26] Instar currently sells all the *Videogames for Humans* components in combination as a collective book, with at least two of the forms essential to complete the text – either the print codex or ePub file, and the games. This connectivity is something that Kopas and the publisher work to establish. The print component is a means of forcing Twine games 'into conversation with … more established literary communities',[27] a dialogue further deepened between the book's print and digital components by having many of the original Twine game creators become the writers analysing other games in the paperback. This creates not only a connection between the paperback and Twine game forms, but an ongoing dialogue between them, as readers experience the games, read a playthrough analysis, and then have a chance to gain a further understanding of the various games' creators. It also reinforces the role of the codex as one part of a larger whole, forcing it to exist in a space where its full meaning is reliant on readers' ability to play the games themselves. In this, the full meaning of the *Videogames for Humans* codex component is dependent on a reader's access to the games, and the games achieve real discussion and engagement with their themes through the codex or ePub file. Also, as Christine Yao notes in her review of the book, 'the imposition of linearity by the material format', in this case, the inclusion of a codex form, 'is an illusion'.[28] The nature of Twine games is to branch in unexpected directions, interactive and unfolding in new and serendipitous ways with each playthrough, and in the same way, this book is designed not to be read in any specific order. Instead, it exists as a jumble of moments connected together, allowing the reader-player to explore either games or analysis first and make their own way through.

In one of the many Twine games featured in the book, 'Even Cowgirls Bleed' by Christine Love, played and discussed by Leigh Alexander, readers can play through the game by slowly scrolling down and moving their crosshair shaped cursor over red-lettered words and phrases in the story text. 'So much as touch [a] red phrase in your crosshair and you've started shooting, whether you meant to or not'.[29] Alexander's playthrough analysis engages with each of these moments, and meditates on the feelings of readers, somewhat out of control in their own story – 'You are afraid for your safety both practically and on a subtle emotional level' she says.[30] Each moment is one that readers can experience in playing the game themselves, but also with the potential of missing something as they make their way to the conclusion of their cowgirl's big city adventure, which in every attempt to avoid it ends in tragedy with the crosshairs over and over again.

In Tom McHenry's game 'Horse Master', the connectivity between reader, playthrough and game is even closer. In the game the reader-player designs and raises a futuristic biomechanical horse to achieve their vision of glory as a Horse Master. In this game horses are grotesque entities constructed by the player – 'Things to know about horses: they come from a factory. They can be made to specification.'[31] – Their colouration is defined with hexadecimal numbers, much like the colours on a web page, they gestate in egg sacs, and they require you, the down-on-your-luck player, to raise them. Naomi Clark, in her playthrough, obsessively picks apart the source code for the game to understand it and ends with unresolved questions about how to achieve the ending she wants, stating 'As we approach the finale, I have a secret to tell you: I have flayed this game to its bones, I have read the code. I know how the decisions are made … I make games, so this is how I play them … I rip them apart where nobody can see.'[32] She leads readers safely through the game's cul-de-sacs and sometimes dead ends, letting them know where they can safely rest in their horse-raising efforts. In this game, it is increasingly clear that the full meaning of *Videogames for Humans* is dependent on a reader's ability to both play the game and be a part of the dialogue between Clark and the game, picking it apart for themselves. It's this conversation that creates the connection between the codex and Twine components of *Videogames for Humans* – an ongoing dialogue between readers, the playthroughs and the games themselves. It also reinforces the role of the codex in *Videogames for Humans* as a medium additional to Twine, forcing it to exist as just one component of a larger whole.

One of the most interesting facets of this relationship between the Twine games in *Videogames for Humans* and the print component is that as these games rely on text and a choose-your-own-adventure style of play, there could easily have been an assumption by the publishers that the Twine games discussed could just be rendered in print. In *Videogames for Humans*, Instar faces this question and Kopas discusses the deliberative process that was undertaken by both Instar's publishers and themself as the editor of how to render the games in the introduction to the paperback, noting that trying to 'literally reproduce [the Twine games] as physical choose-your-own-adventure books … seemed like a pointless exercise'.[33] Instead, the explanation Kopas gives in *Videogames for Humans* of why her book can only work in combination addresses an informed reader-player and exists as commentary for other publishers on why the book could not have been as true to its source material as a codex alone. This refusal to imitate and conscious decision to instead add speaks to the web-first nature of these texts and the influence of digital authorship on combined transmedial books. Rather than lose anything inherent to the much-beloved games that are played and discussed, readers can continue to interact with them in the form that makes them unique. The codex is a fascinating addition, but an addition all the same, never becoming its own individually consumable product. It is arguable whether this same deference and approach is inherent to all books that combine other playable digital components with print formats or ebooks, but it is core to *Videogames for Humans* and also to the second book discussed in this chapter, *Homestuck*.

In 2017, Viz Media began the process of publishing *Homestuck* in a print format. Spanning over 8000 online 'pages', its genre-defying, hybrid form, which comprised of webcomic pages, chat logs, playable video games, animation and music became, as Viz described it, a 'sprawling saga … immortalized on dead trees'.[34] This tongue-in-cheek description and irreverence immediately spoke to an understanding by Viz of the artistic limitations of print to capture a text like Homestuck – referred to by fans and commentators as 'the *Ulysses* of the internet'.[35] For context, Mordicai Knode from science fiction publisher Tor describes Homestuck as 'the first major piece of literature to really take advantage of the internet in the way it was intended'.[36] With the serial nature of a comic blended with the interactive characteristics of a videogame, the very essence of what Homestuck *is* is an example of what a shift from paper to webpages can allow. Readers move from static panels to cinematic Flash sequences and into playable games. One such page begins only with lights in the sky as a video pans down to reveal a vista over the new world that main character has just found himself in.[37] After a couple of instructions are given, readers are then given free rein to play the comic as a game, using the arrow keys on their keyboard to move the character around and attack enemies who take the form of ghoulish jester-cat monsters. For lovers of the Homestuck webcomic, it's immediately clear that there is no way to encapsulate a webcomic like this in a print codex. Viz's words share this understanding, but there is also a question inherent in their statement that they needed to answer in order to create the *Homestuck* book – what value can dead trees add to an already immense and complex text like Homestuck? The static page is one of the key limitations of the codex as a product.

When Viz acquired Homestuck they completely re-platformed and updated the original webcomic, which was in danger of becoming unreadable. The Flash Player reliant animation was facing the prospect of being lost to rapid internet change, which saw Adobe's Flash software become obsolete at the end of 2020. In Viz's undertaking to rehouse and reanimate all 8000 pages of Homestuck's original content, there was an acknowledgement about the nature of its acquisition. Viz, as a print publisher, knew that its hardcopy *Homestuck* codex could not succeed in the absence of the original online text which had built Homestuck's fanbase and was untranslatable to print. Unlike other successful webcomics that have been acquired and more easily adapted into traditional books, with *Nimona* by Noelle Stevenson one example,[38] the author Andrew Hussie's attempt to create a text that was 'as much a pure expression of its medium as possible' also created a webcomic that could not be removed from public view and encapsulated in a print form.[39] In a similar way to *Videogames for Humans*, the complete *Homestuck* book also shows the power of digital authorship on how web-first works are reimagined and adapted. Homestuck's webcomic would always be central to any print production, and it is clear that Viz's hardcopy book remains reliant on the original webcomic form to have its full meaning.

There is also a question of what a *Homestuck* codex adds to the original text, something that Hussie grappled with as he worked to '[figure] out what to say about it all in order to make the books worth reading'.[40] As a reader-player of Homestuck myself, the thought of it laid out on a static page was initially jarring. With animations on nearly every page and the collaborative nature of it as a game and a piece of writing, I was used to the fluidity and a digital form. Homestuck is also couched in fandom. It owes its success to a significant following of Homestucks, a well-known niche online group of fans with roots in Tumblr who have worked for years to unpack the webcomic and who would need to follow the text over to a print codex in order for it to be successful. In his introduction to the first book, Hussie states 'Homestuck is a story that was made for the internet. It was designed to exist on the internet, crafted to exploit the versatility of the internet … And this thing you are holding – this rigid, rectangular thing in your hands – this is a book'.[41] However, in his detailed commentary on each page of the hardback, Hussie creates a conversation between the two texts, a two-way flow of information where only readers of both can access Homestuck's complete intended meaning. The hardback refers readers back to the webcomic in the top left or right-hand corner of every page by including symbols for content that is animated or interactive and a web address for each panel so that the reader can easily find the webcomic in its full form online.[42] This mirrors similar texts which have used image to URL recognition software or QR codes to connect print to an online continuation of the story, and acts as a bridge which readers can cross back and forth, from print to digital components. In this interaction and inter-reliance between hardcover codex and webcomic, Hussie and Viz create something that can be seen as a much larger transmedia book, a text that becomes complete only in combination.

In looking at *Videogames for Humans* and *Homestuck* it is important to note that these books are not completely unique or new discoveries. There are other books that have included playable online game components with a print codex and that have directed readers from a print codex to additional online material, even if they do not exactly mirror what I have described as a combined transmedial book. But what these specific books do in terms of how they are defined, not only by scholars but by industry, is interesting. It's not uncommon now to see attempts at defining the book in academia begin to stretch to attempt to include the digital, though nothing definitive has been settled upon. As Miriam Johnson argues, 'the definition of a book must capture the essence of content, while remaining fluid enough to encompass existing and future packaging',[43] but this argument is far more complex when it comes to industry. In Claudio Pires Franco's research on classification and reinventing the book, 'a common remark … from the more traditional corners' in speaking to publishers was that 'many of the texts analysed … are not books – they are games, or apps, or something else, but definitely not books.[44] Because of this, it's worth drawing these types of books into the light – books where a conventional print component that is undeniably book-like exists, but which also rely on a digital component for meaning. This draws the digital irrevocably into definitions of the book, because in order for their print components to exist, they require their digital other half. They are also an indication of movement within publishing to classify combined texts like these as books, even if it is on the margins.

USB Books: A Non-Codex Physical Book

Another challenge to the way the book is defined comes in the creation of custom shaped USB books, selling shareable ePub files and PDFs in this uniquely non-print physical form. Like a modern twist on the clay tablet or scroll, in an effort to include the digital in our definitional approach there must also be space for new kinds of physical books beyond print. These books play with much of the experiential and tactile elements that make print books so appealing with their own kind of visual interest, touchability, wide shareability and capacity to act as collectables.

In comparisons between print and digital book forms, as Ryan Leach notes, there are different affordances for each medium that grant them advantages and disadvantages within a reading market. The physicality of the print book is one of these affordances, closely tied to its symbolic capital after 500 years of value-add and to its appeal as a collectable physical art object.[45] With the highly recognisable and loved print book form remaining a strong market force, it is also no wonder that 'e-books and their associated reading devices have come increasingly to resemble paper books in almost every regard: in their shape, size, feel and functionality.'[46] While USB books have ePub files and PDFs which share some of this same ghost of print, their outward form is a deviation from this formula, and enticing in its abject difference from a print book. There is no attempt to imitate a recognisable book-like shape or what it feels like to hold a book in your hands, as is common among e-readers. They have instead their own kind of value as a physical object. George Szirtes suggests in the introduction to the book *The Looking Book: A Pocket History of Circle Press* that 'A book, in short, is something you can play with.'[47] Similarly, in her discussion of the value of print, Lucy Roscoe lovingly describes the print book as a non-static 'artefact of sculpture' that invites you to pick it up and experience it in a tactile way.[48] In short, print books are 'experiential products' that 'while fulfilling functional needs … also elicit hedonic responses'.[49]

In an uncanny mirror, the USB books created by Instar Books have the same high value of visual interest and tactile qualities – an alternate kind of packaging or ornamentation – making them products consumers will value. Instar's *The Black Emerald* USB has a visually arresting green diamond head. Its black base pulls away to reveal the USB inside, but left connected it could easily sit on a shelf display. It has interest as a physical item. When I observed and handled this book in New York, it was easily turned over in a hand. The gem-shaped surface felt angular and inviting. In this way, Instar's USBs utilise some of the same traits that are noted by consumers as desirable in paperback books, appearing as an art object or collectable.[50] It is easy to imagine a greeting-card-style rack of hanging USBs to one side as you walk in the door of an indie bookshop showcasing new experimental local texts for $4.99, or a custom black 3D printed Grecian bust artfully positioned against a stark background on #bookstagram, the USB element tucked away inside a sculptural work. This treatment of an electronic device as equivalent to a printed codex is unique, and while readers' preference for print books is clear in recent studies,[51] [52] Instar's USBs provide an interesting alternative.

In combining a USB medium with digitally adapted book files (ePubs), Instar's USBs also become books with a high degree of share-ability. While attaching extra digital forms such as CDs to print books as an additional resource has been common, especially in educational publishing, Instar's USBs are designed to act as standalone titles, sold independently from a codex form in bookstores. The shareability of Instar's USBs also mimics the social ritual of sharing books available with the codex[53] and the feeling of passing a book on to another friend at school, watching your friendship group devour a text together. In some ways, these USB books mirror that ease in ways that are not achieved by the majority of ebooks and audiobooks, (with the exception of eLibrary books and achive.org), which publishers have largely limited to one user or account only through digital rights management.

Instar's USBs include a PDF text and an ePub file, designed to be shared widely without restriction. In this, while Instar's USBs do not challenge the market value of a paperback book, they do challenge the idea that only print codexes can have the shareable quality that many readers associate with them in a preference over other digital book forms.

Alternate hard copy book forms born from now everyday digital technology merit further research than this chapter allows, particularly as regards collectability and in a comparison of their affordances vs. print books. But more meaningful to this specific study is the reminder they provide that new digital book innovation by publishers is not limited to online code, but can include a wide variety of new physical forms as well – all of which are useful in looking at how the book is defined moving into the future.

Punk Publishing – New Margins

Publishing combined transmedial books is just one part of a broader reaction by the small publishers Viz Media and Instar Books against publishing industry norms around technology use and digital practices. Innovation around combined transmedial books and USB books has also seen publishers like Viz and Instar embrace wider shareability with free content and invest in a community-focused model for selling their books, shown through a different approach to website use and funding techniques. These techniques allow the presses to tap into an existing online community of readers and expand how we define the book.

Instar and Viz both create content that is inherently shareable and, in some cases, free to access. *Videogames for Humans* is based around free-to-play Twine games that readers can look up and play online. The games are downloadable with any purchase of the paperback or ebook, and unlike standard AAA games, are designed to be playable for free online. Instar's approach is focussed on inviting this kind of play with their codex playthrough and analysis, as they attempt to place Twine games within a broader literary conversation – a contrast to the tension between some larger game companies, YouTube and Twitch content creators streaming game playthroughs. *Videogames for Humans'* ePub file and PDF are also unrestricted, allowing readers to share all of the content with other readers. In some ways similar is Viz's approach to the Homestuck webcomic, which remains freely accessible and so tied to their print codex that readers of the *Homestuck* book can easily direct others to the webcomic. Both of these approaches stand in direct contrast to the industry practice of taking down free webcomics that have been published (with Nimona as one example)[54] and restricting the ability of users to download or share ebooks through DRM. While the publishers adopt this technique to varying degrees – Viz with Homestuck and Instar for all of its books – both demonstrate an awareness and adoption of a more digitally-free web convention of shareability.

Another web-based creator trend that is embraced by Instar and Viz is an approach to building community through online spaces. The background to the Instar Books website is a disaster pink and neon green shifting cityscape, fluorescent and deliberately trippy. Other backgrounds are blurred or edited references to underground films – with small demons providing the publisher 'about' page information.[55] The same focus on the experiential that Instar uses to great effect in its USB books is clear here on their website, and when I spoke to Instar's publishers in New York, they said that this was because they wanted their website to be the best 'home' for their books – a space that loyal readers would want to revisit and purchase from. The effort put into creating a website this detailed, not only in its listing of products but in its ability to be a unique experience for readers, creates an overall sense of how important an online community is to Instar's model as a small, experimental publishing house. While this idea is not popular in mainstream publishing, where the author name is key in sales, you can see echoes of the same sentiment of publisher brand first in other small publishers. Melbourne's Subbed In also uses its website to great effect as a community space that encapsulates the grungy feel of the press's experimental fiction.[56] Viz Media, as both a manga publisher and anime distributor, has a fan zone on their website with a section purely for sharing cosplay photos sent in by fans, and they also maintain a 'Community' page with a regular blog.[57] Another small press in New York, O/R Books, also plays with the concept of interactivity, using a Twine game to promote their book *Autopilot*.[58] These efforts are an attempt to build a more meaningful and reciprocal relationship with customers by giving the publisher an attractive identity for booklovers in a similar way to what is attempted by many publishers through social media presences. It is in an invitation to participate where the terms of the participation are clearer and more driven by identity – both that of the readers enjoying the experience and for the publishing house itself.

As consumers increasingly appear to care less about what a 'book' is,[59] audiences have emerged for new book forms, with many readers buying online rather than in-stores and supporting self-published books by their favourite webcomic authors or via Kickstarter. There is already a market for innovative books and publishers who want to tap into an online community of transmedial book readers – shown through the success of *Steampunk Holmes* on Kickstarter[60] and *Mapping Lineage* by Tamara Ashley on Indiegogo,[61] alternately through innumerable webcomics now self-published as hard copies. Publishers, if they are able to adopt similar community-building online publishing norms are also able to publish into these spaces and build a community of backers. In the case of *Videogames for Humans*, there is that same recognisable Kickstarter model with an Instar twist on their website. At 100,000 sales, 'Merritt will legally change her middle name to Twine', at 666,666 sales, 'All contributors will be summoned to the Crystal Cave in Spring Valley, Wisconsin to perform a mystic binding ritual (in the cave, obviously) culminating in a massive public party and festival to celebrate the spirit that has been summoned and harnessed for eternity via Twine (spirit TBD).'[62]

It is worth noting the purpose behind this active rejection of major industry tech norms in favour of web ones, and the non-traditional cultural capital that presses create for themselves by publishing outside of the norm. For a micro-press like Instar, the goal of their books is to create something avant-garde and punk – with beauty in deliberate ugliness, literariness in challenging the literary norm, and value in creating something that pushes the boundaries. It reinforces that despite conflict over the dual nature of publishers as both businesses and tastemakers, publishers can make a choice to create something new, and in doing that build a unique readership. Both Viz and Instar's attempts to break publishing norms and take new steps that position them closer to their readers work to place publishing within an innovative digital space that can take advantage of transmedial book forms and the reader-player as a target audience. They also re-emphasise that publishers do not have to be spectators to emerging self-published digital works or have a codex-centric concept of combining the digital with print, but instead have a role in creating digital-first books that exist in an as-yet-undefined space. Marie-Laure Ryan notes that 'in the entertainment industry, there is no such thing as 'success of esteem', no such thing as transmedia driven by…an artistic vision.'[63] In the case of Instar Books at least, a press focussed far more on an artistic vision than financial success, these books also show that outside of the costly and closed space of the transmedia storyworld, relying on cheaper, widely available technologies rather than blockbuster franchises may be a more achievable digital innovation for other publishers as well.

Ultimately, the book as we've known it is changing. As Lichtenberg argues, 'since Gutenberg, the form factor itself defined both container and content … the internet and digital technologies have broken them apart.'[64] In looking at industry reluctance to categorise new digital products as books, Franco notes that 'one could argue that if some publishers and authors are making these kinds of new forms of digital books, it does not really matter whether they ought to be called books or something else.'[65] But these combined transmedial books avoid this capitulation. By having codex components, enough that they are undeniably books, but also intrinsic digital components that the print text relies on for meaning, the publishers creating these books are tacitly acknowledging a change. Most critically, the work of these publishers shows that even amid reluctance to define them, publishers are already creating books we don't quite understand – collapsing the divide between the physical and digital and the boundaries we had conceived to understand what a book is. In part, it is still unclear the ultimate importance that books like these have in defining the book, but they do further complicate the process. As we move further away from the book as a codex, the book is infinite things in a way that is both challenging and intensely exciting for publishing and book history scholarship.

Endnotes

1   Andrew Hussie, *Homestuck, Book 1: Act 1 & Act 2*, (New York: Simon and Schuster, 2018), https://www.simonandschuster.com.au/books/Homestuck-Book-1-Act-1-Act-2/Andrew-Hussie/Homestuck/9781421599403.
2   Katherine Hayles, 'Print Is Flat, Code Is Deep: The Importance of Media-Specific Analysis,' *Poetics Today* 25, no. 1 (2004): 67–90.
3   Claudio Pires Franco, 'Reinventing the Book : Exploring the Affordances of Digital Media to (Re)Tell Stories and Expand Storyworlds,' PhD Thesis, University of Bedfordshire, 2017: 6.
4   Marie-Laure Ryan, 'Transmedia Narratology and Transmedia Storytelling,' *Artnodes* 18 (2016): 1–10.
5   Simone Murray, 'Charting the Digital Literary Sphere,' *Contemporary Literature* 52, no. 2 (2015): 311–339.
6   Ryan, 'Transmedia Narratology and Transmedia Storytelling,' 3.
7   Oliver Freeman, 'An Australian Perspective on the Future of Book Publishing,' *LOGOS: The Journal of the World Book Community* 23, no. 3 (Oct 2012): 35.

8   Bill Cope and Diana Kalantzis. *Print and electronic text convergence*. C-2-C project. Altona, Victoria: Common Ground Publishing, 2001.

9   Lars Ole Sauerberg, 'The Gutenberg Parenthesis - Print, Book and Cognition,' *Orbis Litterarum* 64, no.2 (2009): 79.

10 Leslie Howsam, 'The study of book history,' in *The Cambridge Companion to the History of the Book*, ed (Cambridge University Press, 2014), 1.

11 Florian Cramer, 'Post-Digital Literary Studies,' *MatLit : Materialidades Da Literatura* 4, no. 1 (2016): 11–27.

12 Marie-Laure Ryan and Thon Jan-Noël, *Storyworlds across Media : Toward a Media-Conscious Narratology*, (Lincoln: University of Nebraska Press, 2014).

13 Ryan, 'Transmedia Narratology and Transmedia Storytelling,' 4.

14 Henry Jenkins, *Convergence Culture : Where Old and New Media Collide*, rev. ed. (New York University Press, 2008).

15 Ryan, 'Transmedia Narratology and Transmedia Storytelling,' 3.

16 Annette Lamb, 'Reading Redefined for a Transmedia Universe,' *Learning and Leading with Technology* 39, no. 3 (Nov 2011): 15.

17 Ryan, 'Transmedia Narratology and Transmedia Storytelling,' 3.

18 Christine Yeo, 'Review of Videogames for Humans: Twine Authors in Conversation, edited by Merritt Kopas (Instar Books),' hastac, 8 June 2015, https://www.hastac.org/blogs/thevorpalblade/2015/06/08/review-videogames-humans-twine-authors-conversation-edited-merritt.

19 Matthew Kirschenbaum, *Mechanisms: New Media and the Forensic Imagination* (Massachusetts: MIT Press, 2008).

20 Hussie, *Homestruck*.

21 Roberta Pearson and Anthony Smith, *Storytelling in the Media Convergence Age: Exploring Screen Narratives* (London, New York: Palgrave Macmillan, 2015), 1.

22 Merritt Kopas, *Videogames for Humans*, (New York: Instar Books, 2015), 10.

23 'About,' Instar Books, http://www.instarbooks.com/help/roach/7.html.

24 Macquarie Dictionary, 'instar,' https://www.macquariedictionary.com.au/. Defines 'instar' as 'an insect in any one of its periods of post-embryonic growth between moults'.

25 Kopas *Videogames for Humans*.

26 Kopas *Videogames for Humans*.

27 Kopas, 12.

28 Yeo, 'Review of Videogames for Humans: Twine Authors in Conversation, edited by Merritt Kopas (Instar Books).'

29 Kopas, 427.

30 Kopas, 427.

31 Kopas, 88.

32 Kopas, 124-125.

33 Kopas, 16.

34 Hussie, *Homestruck*.

35 Lilian Min 'A Story That Could Only Be Told Online,' *The Atlantic*, 25 February 2015, https://www.theatlantic.com/technology/archive/2015/02/a-story-that-could-only-be-told-online/385895/.

36 Mordicai Knode, 'Homestuck is the First Great Work of Internet Fiction,' *Tor.com*, 18 September, 2012. https://www.tor.com/2012/09/18/homestuck-is-the-first-great-work-of-internet-fiction/.

37 Andrew Hussie, *Homestuck Act 4*, https://www.homestuck.com/story/1358/1.

38 Noelle Stevenson, *Nimona* (New York: Harper Collins, 2015).

39 Andrew Hussie, 'What is Homestuck,' MS Paint Adventures, http://mspaintadventures.com/scraps2/homestuckKS.html.

40 Michael Cavna, '"Homestuck" creator explains how his webcomic became a phenomenon,' *Washington Post*, 30 October, 2018, https://www.washingtonpost.com/arts-entertainment/2018/10/29/homestuck-creator-explains-how-his-webcomic-became-phenomenon/?noredirect=on.

41 Hussie, *Homestuck*, 3.

42 Hussie. *Homestruck*.

43 Miriam Johnson, 'What Is a Book? Redefining the Book in the Digitally Social Age,' *Publishing Research Quarterly*, 35, no. 1 (2019): 69.

44 Franco, 'Reinventing the Book,' 202.

45 Ryan Leach, 'Remediating the Book: Affordances, Symbolic Capital, and Co-mediation of Print and E-Books,' *Media Theory and Media Systems* (Spring, 2015): https://blogs.commons.georgetown.edu/cctp-748-spring2015/2015/05/04/remediating-the-book-affordances-symbolic-capital-and-co-mediation-of-print-and-e-books/.

46 Ian Sansom, *Paper: An Elegy* (London: Fourth Estate, 2012), 51.

47 Cathy Courtney and Roy Fisher, *The Looking Book: A Pocket History of Circle Press 1967–96* (London: Circle Press 1996) n.p.

48 Lucy Roscoe, 'A Thing to Hold: The Visual Language of the Book Form,' *Journal of Illustration* 6, no. 1 (2019): 78.

49 Steven Chen and Neil Granitz, 'Adoption, rejection, or convergence: Consumer attitudes toward book digitization,' *Journal of Business Research* 65, no. 8 (2012): 1219.

50 Chen and Granitz, 'Adoption, rejection, or convergence: Consumer attitudes toward book digitization'.

51 Hu Chen and Michael D Smith, 'The Impact of E-book Distribution on Print Sales: Analysis of a Natural Experiment,' *Management Science* 65, no. 1 (2019): 19–31.
52 Chin Ee Loh and Baoqi Sun, '"I'd Still Prefer to Read the Hard Copy": Adolescents' Print and Digital Reading Habits,' *Journal of Adolescent & Adult Literacy* 62, no. 6 (2019): 663–672.
53 Chen and Granitz, 'Adoption, rejection, or convergence: Consumer attitudes toward book digitization'.
54 Stevenson, *Nimona*
55 Kopas, *Videogames for Humans.*
56 'Subbed In,' https://subbed.in/.
57 'Community,' Viz Media, https://www.viz.com/community.
58 Andrew Smart, *Autopilot: The Art and Science of Doing Nothing,* (New York, O/R Books, 2013).
59 Frania Hall, 'Digital Convergence and Collaborative Cultures: Publishing in the context of the wider creative industries,' *Logos* 25, no. 4 (2014).
60 Richard Monson-Haefel, 'Steampunk Holmes,' Kickstarter, 30 July 2014, https://www.kickstarter.com/projects/369012565/steampunk-holmes-for-the-ipad.
61 Tamara Ashley, 'Mapping Lineage,' Indiegogo, n.d., https://www.indiegogo.com/projects/mapping-lineage-book-project--3#/
62 Kopas, *Videogames for Humans.*
63 Ryan, 'Transmedia narratology and transmedia storytelling,' 5.
64 James Lichtenberg, 'In from the Edge: The Progressive Evolution of Publishing in the Age of Digital Abundance,' *Publishing Research Quarterly* 27, no. 2 (2011) 105-106.
65 Franco, 'Reinventing the Book,' 203.

Bibliography

Ashley, Tamara. 'Mapping Lineage,' Indiegogo, n.d., https://www.indiegogo.com/projects/mapping-lineage-book-project--3#/.
Cavna, Michael. '"Homestuck" creator explains how his webcomic became a phenomenon.' *Washington Post*, 30 October, 2018. https://www.washingtonpost.com/arts-entertainment/2018/10/29/homestuck-creator-explains-how-his-webcomic-became-phenomenon/?noredirect=on.
Chen, Hu, and Smith, Michael D. 'The Impact of E-book Distribution on Print Sales: Analysis of a Natural Experiment,' *Management Science* 65, no. 1, (2019): 19–31.

Chen, Steven and Granitz, Neil. 'Adoption, rejection, or convergence: Consumer attitudes toward book digitization,' *Journal of Business Research* 65, no. 8, (2012): 1219–1225.

Cope, Bill, and Kalantzis, Diana. *Print and electronic text convergence.* C-2-C project. Altona: Common Ground Publishing, 2001.

Courtney, Cathy and Fisher, Roy. *The Looking Book: A Pocket History of Circle Press 1967–96.* Circle Press, 1996.

Cramer, Florian. 'Post-Digital Literary Studies,' *MatLit : Materialidades Da Literatura* 4, no. 1 (March 2016): 11–27.

Franco, Claudio Pires. 'Reinventing the Book : Exploring the Affordances of Digital Media to (Re)Tell Stories and Expand Storyworlds,' PhD Thesis, University of Bedfordshire, 2017, https://ethos.bl.uk/OrderDetails.do?uin=uk.bl.ethos.774224.

Freeman, Oliver. 'An Australian Perspective on the Future of Book Publishing,' *LOGOS: The Journal of the World Book Community* 23, no. 3 (Oct 2010): 34–47.

Hall, Frania. 'Digital Convergence and Collaborative Cultures: Publishing in the context of the wider creative industries,' *LOGOS: The Journal of the World Book Community* 27, no. 4 (2014): 20–31.

Hayles, Katherine N. 'Print Is Flat, Code Is Deep: The Importance of Media-Specific Analysis,' *Poetics Today* 25, no. 1 (April 2004): 67–90.

Howsam, Leslie. 'The study of book history,' In *The Cambridge Companion to the History of the Book*, edited by Leslie Howsam. 1–14. Cambridge: Cambridge University Press, 2014.

Hussie, Andrew. *Homestuck.* San Francisco: Viz Media, 2018, https://www.homestuck.com/.

Instar Books. 'About,' http://www.instarbooks.com/help/roach/7.html.

Jenkins, Henry. *Convergence Culture: Where Old and New Media Collide.* Rev. ed. New York: New York University Press. 2008

Johnson, Miriam J. 'What Is a Book? Redefining the Book in the Digitally Social Age,' *Publishing Research Quarterly* 35, no. 1 (March 2019): 68–78.

Kirschenbaum, Matthew G. *Mechanisms: New Media and the Forensic Imagination.* MIT Press. 2008.

Pearson, Roberta E, and Smith, Anthony N. *Storytelling in the Media Convergence Age: Exploring Screen Narratives.* London, New York: Palgrave Macmillan. 2015.

Knode, Mordicai. 'Homestuck is the First Great Work of Internet Fiction,' *Tor.com.* 18 September, 2019. https://www.tor.com/2012/09/18/homestuck-is-the-first-great-work-of-internet-fiction/.

Kopas, Merritt ed. *Videogames for Humans,* New York: Instar Books, 2015.

Lamb, Annette. 'Reading Redefined for a Transmedia Universe,' *Learning and Leading with Technology* 39, no.3 (Nov 2011): 12–17.

Lichtenberg, James. 'In from the Edge: The Progressive Evolution of Publishing in the Age of Digital Abundance,' *Publishing Research Quarterly* 27, no. 2 (June 2011): 101–112.

Loh, Chin Ee, and Sun, Baoqi. '"I'd Still Prefer to Read the Hard Copy": Adolescents' Print and Digital Reading Habits,' *Journal of Adolescent & Adult Literacy* 62, no. 6 (2019): 663–672.

Min, Lilian. 'A Story That Could Only Be Told Online.' *The Atlantic*, 25 February 2015. https://www.theatlantic.com/technology/archive/2015/02/a-story-that-could-only-be-told-online/385895/.

Monson-Haefel, Richard. 'Steampunk Holmes.' Kickstarter, 30 July 2014, https://www.kickstarter.com/projects/369012565/steampunk-holmes-for-the-ipad.

MS Paint Adventures. 'What is Homestuck?' n.d., http://mspaintadventures.com/scraps2/homestuckKS.html.

Murray, Simone. 'Charting the Digital Literary Sphere,' *Contemporary Literature* 52, no. 2 (2015): 311–339.

Ryan Leach. 'Remediating the Book: Affordances, Symbolic Capital, and Co-mediation of Print and E-Books,' *Media Theory and Meaning Systems*, (Spring 2015), https://blogs.commons.georgetown.edu/cctp-748-spring2015/2015/05/04/remediating-the-book-affordances-symbolic-capital-and-co-mediation-of-print-and-e-books/.

Ryan, Marie-Laure. 'Transmedia Narratology and Transmedia Storytelling,' *Artnodes*, no. 18 (November 2016): 1–10.

Ryan, Marie-Laure, and Jan-Noël Thon. *Storyworlds across Media : Toward a Media-Conscious Narratology*. Lincoln: University of Nebraska Press. 2014.

Roscoe, Lucy. 'A Thing to Hold: The Visual Language of the Book Form,' *Journal of Illustration* 6, no. 1 (April 2019): 77–98.

Sansom, Ian. *Paper: An Elegy*. Fourth Estate. 2012.

Sauerberg, Lars Ole. 'The Gutenberg Parenthesis - Print, Book and Cognition,' *Orbis Litterarum* 64, no.2 (2009): 79–80.

Smart, Andrew. *Autopilot: The Art and Science of Doing Nothing*, New York: O/R Books, 2013.

Stevenson, Noelle. *Nimona*. New York: HarperCollins, 2015.

Subbed In. n.d., https://subbed.in/.

Viz Media. 'Community.' n.d., https://www.viz.com/community.

Yao, Christine. 'Review of Videogames for Humans: Twine Authors in Conversation, edited by Merritt Kopas (Instar Books),' *hastac*, 8 June 2015, https://www.hastac.org/blogs/thevorpalblade/2015/06/08/review-videogames-humans-twine-authors-conversation-edited-merritt.

CHAPTER 9

Undisciplined Creation

Poetry on Tumblr

as Autoethnographic and Authorial Practice

ELOISE FAICHNEY

An Introduction to Tumblr: Welcome to the Fandom

this is the way the marble turns/i
open my eyes before you do
go to sleep before you do/&
in this way, i have always been
in your future [1]

When I joined Tumblr in 2012, setting up a blog under the nom de plume 'Delicious Interludes',[2] I had no intention of writing a book. Rather, I dreamed that one day I would write a book, but I had no idea where to begin. I was a former WordPress blogger working freelance as a copywriter in-between advertising agencies, and heard that Tumblr was a good place for writers; fiction writer and essayist, Jami Attenberg asserted that it was a great place to connect with readers[3] and lauded fantasy novelist Neil Gaiman also had a blog on the platform.[4] In retrospect, Tumblr has been a part of the origin story for many now established creatives: American singer and songwriter, Halsey; British-Somali poet, Warsan Shire, who worked on Beyonce's *Lemonade* album and short film; and many of the 'Instapoets' such as Rupi Kaur, Lang Leav, Pavana Reddy, R.M. Drake and Tyler Knott-Gregson.

I was late to the party. Tumblr was created in 2007 by a 20-year-old David Karp, whose laid-back, hoodie-wearing nonchalance set the tone for the site, focusing on individual 'tumblelogs' where users could create and 'reblog' short-form, mixed-media posts to curate their own blog. This practice, along with creating short 180-character statements on Twitter, became known as 'microblogging', a blogging behaviour characterised by short posts which users employ to broadcast 'information about their current activities, thoughts, opinions and status.'[5] The success of Tumblr was intrinsically tied with the demise of blogging platform LiveJournal, which after being bought by Russian media outlet SUP Media, banned sexual content on the site.[6] In response, many of LiveJournal's audience of fan fiction and fan art blogs jumped ship to Tumblr.[7]

Tumblr became synonymous with millennial narcissism and identity creation – a place for selfies, self-love and unselfconscious connection with other semi-anonymous users. Unconventional subcultures and fandoms abound on Tumblr – it is the seat of the now ubiquitous 'Daddy' culture,[8] a playground of diverse adult communities,[9] and a platform of origin for fan fiction and shipping culture.[10] Tumblr carries with it the subtext of countercultural deviance, and I have long joked that 'if you're into it, you'll find it on Tumblr.'

It was the semi-anonymity, perhaps, that drew me in. My creative writing style at the time was mainly limited to personal essays and poetry, although I had also attempted short fiction. I was looking for an escape from writing to an audience mostly comprised of my Facebook friends – my penchant for loosely fictionalising my real life had gotten me into trouble with people who recognised themselves in my words. The veil of anonymity given to me by my Tumblr blog was immediately freeing; I was able to breathe for the first time in my writing life. Julie Rak first explored the potential of 'queer blogging' as a site for the exploration of queer identity in a pre-Tumblr era,[11] and since then a number of scholars have looked at Tumblr in terms of a site of queer identity[12] and queer desire.[13] Like many LGBTQI+ users, blogging on Tumblr allowed me to explore aspects of my own identity outside of my 'real life', including my burgeoning queerness.

When I was asked to speak on a panel at a digital writing and publishing conference, halfway through my PhD, I began to connect my previous amateur digital writing – something I had been embarrassed about and kept fairly private – with my creative practice as a PhD student. The panel was about creative digital writing, featuring some highly established poets, published authors and myself. Consumed with imposter syndrome, I wondered why I had been asked. A smattering of my poems had been published in digital literary journals, but my current research focused on historical biofiction and women's life narratives. I did not feel qualified to speak on digital writing as a form with any authority. However, in writing my contribution to the panel, I was able to understand my four years of producing creative content on Tumblr in the form of poetry, prose, and autofiction, or autobiographical fiction,[14] as an autoethnography of my beginnings as a writer.

This essay documents my experience as a Tumblr writer and poet whose blog had 8,000 followers at its peak in 2014. After two years of sharing creative content almost daily to an engaged and critical audience of fellow writers and readers, I felt I had discovered a voice I wanted to explore further. This led to the decision to pursue creative writing within the university institution, first through a Masters by Research in Writing and then a PhD in Creative Writing. As a creative writer, I know that 'form should be an organic representation of the feelings of the core of the piece.'[15] As such, this practice-led essay is both personal and autoethnographic: it reveals its claims through the evidence of experience.[16]

Tumbling: Bricolage, Affect, Autoethnography and Authorial Subjectivity

consequence
was borne, & would
burn everything away;
yet the bones refused
to crunch or break
the skeleton reformed,
determined to birth again
my metempsychosis complete [17]

Life writing scholars, Sidonie Smith and Julia Watson, have characterised the behaviour of Tumblr users in terms of bricolage, or collection.[18] These techniques are well-known to creative writers, who gather pieces of information, images, threads of narrative from their own lives and the artistic work and lives of others. Observing and collecting shiny narrative objects like a 'magpie', the creative writer eventually weaves these together to create a whole, original piece of work. In this vein, the experience of creating a Tumblr blog, where 'self-making and visualisation combine found materials into a textual and visual melange that is interspersed with a blog',[19] lends itself well to creative writing practice.

Alexander Cho suggests that navigating Tumblr is a 'nonlinear, incoherent, and impermanent' experience, and argues that Tumblr trades in affect.[20] As a Tumblr user, Cho describes that 'you are the sum of your posts, which are a visualisation of your connection to others – a porous, living assemblage'[21] (2015, p. 45). For Cho, Tumblr is about curation, not creation. While Cho's evocative research explores the experience of being a Tumblr user who knits together reblogs to create a blog aesthetic that reflects one's emergent and mutable identity, there is little research into the practices of users, like me, for whom Tumblr is a place to make, share and cultivate original creative work.

Autoethnography, is a qualitative method that combines characteristics of ethnography and autobiography.[22] Autoethnographies often take the form of narrative reflections of one's own personal experiences. As Tess Muncey has discussed 'it is the complexity of individuals that autoethnography seeks to address.'[23] Practices of autoethnography include journal-keeping, sketching and recording one's own reflections about one's writing and/or research practice. I have used autoethnographical reflection in these ways to revisit my previous creative work, writing about how I felt at the time I produced a certain poem, recalling the research I undertook to approach a certain subject, or analysing the imagery and themes that come up repeatedly in my writing. This process creates a new text with which to understand how my creative process manifests: it is a resurrection.[24]

In this type of close, reflective reading of my work, I consider the scholarly, but also the personal and emotional. This kind of reflection is relevant to the work I have done within the PhD structure, where I have written the manuscript of a novel in the genre of biofiction, an entirely different creative process. Biofiction is 'literature that names its protagonist after an actual biographical figure',[25] and involves fictionalising the real-life experiences of biographical subjects. Examples of contemporary biofictions include Michael Cunningham's *The Hours* (1999), which fictionalised the life of Virginia Woolf as one of its narrative threads, and David Ebershoff's *The Danish Girl* (2000), which centred on a fictional imagining of the life of Lily Elbe, an artist and transgender woman who was one of the earliest recipients of gender confirmation surgery. Following this tradition, my unpublished novel fictionalises the experiences of two women: author, Naomi Mitchison and explorer, Zita Baker, who lived in Oxford between 1920 and 1940. In negotiating the problems that arise from biofiction – such as the issue of fact versus fiction, and the negotiation of gaps and silences in life narratives – I have realised that an understanding of my own authorial subjectivity is crucial.

An understanding of subjectivity, or selfhood, comprised of 'the narratives of personal memory, cultural history and desire'[26] is part of the autoethnographic process. Through autoethnographical reflections, I can see that the body of work I produced as a Tumblr writer contains the beginnings of many themes, images, techniques and overall writerly 'voice' I would develop further in writing my first novel as part of my doctorate in creative writing. For example, an analysis of my poems revealed the frequent use of the magnolia flower or tree in the imagery used, an image that recurred in the manuscript of my novel. On reflection, I remembered that my late grandmother's favourite flower was the magnolia, and that her house (which I frequently return to in my dreams) contained a garden with several magnolia trees. Thus this image, and the smell of magnolia flowers, is tinged with positive memory for me and has become a part of my creative language. These reflections help me to understand my authorial subjectivity, a framework I have defined as the worldview, or selfhood, of the writer – the filter through which decisions are made in the creative process. As Colm Tóibín has described, the author draws from this 'hidden self' in the process of creating their work:

> This is all a novelist needs, nothing exact or precise, no character to be based on an actual person, but a configuration, something distant that can be mulled over, guessed at, dreamed about, imagined, a set of shadowy relations that the writer can begin to put substance on. Changing details, adding shape, but using always something, often from years back, that had captured the imagination, or mattered somehow to the hidden self, however fleetingly or mysteriously.[27]

Of course, authorial subjectivity cannot divorce itself from one's identity as a whole. Tumblr is often credited as one of the origins of 'woke' millennial culture outside of the academy – the New York Times has reported on 'Tumblr Activism'[28] and Angela Nagle has suggested that 'Tumblr-liberalism' contributed to the online culture wars of the 2010s.[29] With its diverse user base and focus on social issues, Tumblr was the site I first learned about intersectional feminism[30] white privilege,[31] cultural appropriation,[32] the body positivity and acceptance movements, and police abolition[33] long before they became discourse *de jour* on Twitter. When I began postgraduate study, I found that I already had a grounding for some of these concepts, which helped me in approaching critical theory. I am not ashamed of this. As someone who came late not only to the Tumblr party but also to the academy, I understand that this lack of academic training makes me, as Sarah Schulman describes, 'undisciplined', and have come to embrace this as Schulman does in her own practice as a scholar and creative writer.[34] The context of a formative life and career outside the academy gives me flexibility, perspective and embodied knowledge that informs my writing.

'Validate me, Daddy': The Tumblr Writing Community

> *Self-awareness*
> *glittered on the windowsill*
> *close enough to spill its shimmer*
> *over your skin*
>
> *Instead, you lay in the dark*
> *making promises with your tongue*
> *that you knew your heart*
> *could not fulfill* [35]

Tumblr, and the Tumblr Writing Community (TWC), was formative in my practice as a writer, as it has been for many writers. The formation of the TWC began as more users across all of the platform's diverse subcultures began using tags to categorise their posts to reach certain audiences. In response, Tumblr launched the Featured Tag and 'tag-editor' system in 2010,[36] where users who interacted, posted or participated with certain tags became 'editors' of the tag. These editors were given additional permissions on their accounts, allowing them to promote certain posts to appear on the homepage of the tag, searchable through Tumblr's 'explore' function.

The now deleted writing blog, Spilled Ink, and its tag #spilledink, was an early gathering place for creative writers of poetry, prose and flash fiction on Tumblr. Spilled Ink was one of the first blogs on Tumblr to begin curating the work of other writers through reblogs, gathering thousands of followers who used it to discover the work of other writers on Tumblr, and to promote their own work. This system of reblogging and promoting new and established writers on the platform continued after the advent of the Featured Tag and tag-editor systems on Tumblr. The tags #poetry, #prose and #lit were chosen by Tumblr's staff to become part of the Featured Tag system, essentially creating a homepage for each tag, which featured the editors of the tag, and the top ten users who had contributed to the tag that day.[37]

These editors, seemingly bestowed with their powers at random (no explanation from Tumblr staff was ever communicated to these users – one day, they simply woke up to find their accounts were different), instantly became the tastemakers of creative writing on Tumblr. 'Getting featured' became the aim of all Tumblr poets and writers who interacted with the featured tags, no matter what your follower count. Flirting, or even pursuing relationships with the editors for validation and clout wasn't unheard of. The tag #TWC emerged around this time, and became the shorthand for the group of users who were sharing poetry, prose and flash fiction and developing critical friendships (and romantic ones) with one another through critiquing and appreciating each other's work. Further study into how these texts were circulated, how editors prioritised texts and how poets responded to each other's texts would be fruitful further questions to explore in subsequent research.

In an interview conducted four years after inception of the Featured Tag system, Tumblr poetry and prose editor, Jennifer Mueller of the blog 'Defenestrations'[38] described the ability for her account to promote 10 user posts per day under the #poetry, #prose and #lit tags.[39] Mueller spoke about the merging of the featured tags with the TWC itself:

> When I was first made a tag editor, I imagined I had all these responsibilities, all these duties to the writers and to the community as a whole. Over time, though, I've come to realize something: the featured tags are not community tags. They are part of Tumblr's explore system, created by Tumblr. As a tag editor (technically) your job is to promote things you think a Tumblr-wide audience would enjoy.[40]

Despite Mueller's distinction between featured tag and community, the TWC was very much in full bloom by 2012, when I stumbled into this circle of amateur digital writers.

Tumblr as Bildungsroman, or Imposter Syndrome, Creative Practice and the Narcissistic Musician We All Have to Date in Our Twenties

> *all the abuses i'd put*
> *the body through – every*
> *trespass the mind*
> *thought did not matter,*
> *(once i'd sinned,*
> *i crossed boundaries*
> *& over again) – the*
> *psyche soaked it all in* [41]

Jia Tolentino has described 2012 as the tipping point between Web 1.0 and 2.0 when 'the call of self-expression turned the village of the internet into a city.'[42] It was this lure to self-expression that made me begin blogging on WordPress, slyly working in nods to my tumultuous dating life and outbursts of early-twenties feminist angst among aesthetically pleasing imagery found on Weheartit.com. In hindsight, it is easy to frame the move to Tumblr as the call to produce art without the inherent self-censorship of a writer producing blogs for an audience of her friends, frenemies and exes; my ingress into the *écriture feminine*.[43]

Yet when I began writing this essay, here's how I remembered it: I started my Tumblr to impress a boy. A long-haired, poetry-scribbling, guitar-playing boy called Pete whose Twitter bio read, 'narcissistic jerk'. Pete was from Sydney, which seemed exotic enough to a bored 24-year-old who had always lived in Melbourne. He was effortlessly cool, he cared about the environment and he pursued me relentlessly, at first. The way I have always remembered it, I set up my Tumblr blog *after* Pete set up his, intoxicated by the fantasy of two young writers developing their craft in tandem, just like Henry Miller and Anais Nin.[44] Revisiting our email correspondence for the purposes of this essay, I was shocked to realise that I already had my Tumblr blog when I met Pete. It was he who followed me in becoming a Tumblr poet.

The early emails between us make me cringe; him, bent on emulating the style of Charles Bukowski, and me, fangirling over his ability to string swear words into his poetry. I couldn't see myself as possessing half of his brilliance, even as he assured me: '*you* are the one with the talent here. Stop second guessing yourself and forget everything you think you know. And write. And share.'[45] Success in the TWC was measured by hearts and reblogs – 'the major activity and almost-foundational logic performed on Tumblr'[46] – and for the first few months, his far outweighed mine.

My turn to be featured on the #poetry and #prose tags came around, and my followers grew, first into the hundreds and then into the thousands. I posted almost every day, ritualistically checking the featured tag homepages when I woke, seeing what had been posted by the members of the TWC, the majority of whom were American, roaming about freely on the platform while in Melbourne, Australia, I slept. Through Tumblr's messaging function I began corresponding with dozens of new writer friends. This did not please Pete, whose early success had started to wane.

> Babe, you're getting lots of great feedback. It's beginning to look as though I just fluked it on a couple. Interest now, is waning. It's good though. A testament as to whether I really am doing this just for me.[47]

Reader, it did not end well. After a year of torturous back-and-forth with this man, who would draw me in, only to reject me over and over again, I felt hardened; like Nin, I was 'effectively... cured of all emotional reactions.'[48] He was the first true creative I had dated and perhaps this is why it hit so hard; I had wound tendrils of my authorial subjectivity around Pete – he was in every poem, and the imagined reader of all I had written at this tender stage of my writing life. Luckily, there were several would-be writer lovers waiting to fill the void, setting up a pattern of behaviour where I would use my writing on Tumblr as a tool to seduce my lovers, but also to process my feelings about them as, and after, the relationship evolved.

In 2004, autobiography scholar Phillip Lejeune conceptualised the online blogger as 'cyberdiarist':

> Intimacy does not exist in solitude; it is always interiorized. The cyberdiarist indicates this [desire for] replies by including an electronic address, not as a betrayal of the secrets of the self, but as a way to accomplish his/her deepest wish, which is to have access to an alter ego, a synthesis between the diary and the letter. The internet is particularly well suited to the personal diary: brief texts, daily entries, pictures and photos.[49]

Twelve months into my Tumblr writing experiment, I had created LeJeune's cyberdiarist alter ego: a sexy poet woman who posed coyly in the occasional selfie and flirtatiously engaged with questions posed by the blog's followers. The poems and prose pieces flowed readily; I had given myself over more freely to the creative process, which Ellen Van Neervan calls 'a voice to throw belief at',[50] and yes, I was beginning to believe.

I made these poems and stories at breakneck speed, starting in Google documents. They could take up to a week to shape and edit, or sometimes just one day. Once I was satisfied with the first draft, I would read it aloud several times before I began assembling the poem in a Tumblr post: tinkering with the HTML to create emphasis; chunking; line spacing; and sometimes playing with form – for example, creating a shape that the poem would take upon publishing. The affordances of Tumblr as a platform affected the creative process. The 'preview' function was vital to witness how these manipulations would look when they were published on my blog homepage. I would breathlessly hover over the command before eventually pressing 'post'.

In the following hours, I would count the hearts and reblogs that appeared – perhaps 200 or so at the blog's peak. During my time on the platform, only one of my posts went viral, and it still does the rounds on Tumblr. I had deliberately copied a style I had seen on the blogs of the famous Tumblr poets such as Tyler Knott Gregson: the quote poem. The quote poem is published not as a post or an image, but using Tumblr's 'quote' function, and attributed back to my blog, 'Delicious Interludes.'[51] It is my most successful post to date, and has currently been reblogged 7,151 times (a pittance on Tumblr, where posts can get up to a million reblogs). After it had been published for a week or so and had good numbers, I received an anonymous message in my Tumblr inbox: 'what did you quote yourself for? You're not well known.'

The Tumblr Blockbusters and Instapoetry as Meme

I didn't mean to run you over with my power, honey.
I didn't mean to run you over.[52]

In 2017 in the United States of America, the printed work of Instapoets accounted for 47% of all poetry book sales[53] (NPD Group, 2018). It was the year that Rupi Kaur's *The Sun and Her Flowers* was published. Kaur's career trajectory is often attributed to its beginnings on the social media photo sharing platform, Instagram, but Kaur was posting her image-based poetry on Tumblr in 2009 before Instagram's emergence in 2010. Kaur's trajectory is well known in the publishing world: the Canadian poet's first collection of poems, *Milk and Honey,* outsold *The Odyssey* as the top-selling book of poetry.[54] Kaur, in particular, has been credited with breathing new life into poetry as a genre and bringing it to new audiences.[55]

Blogger, poet and photographer, Tyler Knott Gregson, who pioneered the 'typewriter' image style of poetry on Tumblr as early as 2007, has published four books of poetry and one children's book. It cannot be overstated how influential Gregson's poetry was in the TWC during my time on the platform. Although he wrote in a since-deleted post that he had no knowledge of the community and did not consider himself part of it, his work was all over our dashboards under the #poetry tag. Every time he would post a new poem in his typewriter series, it would go viral with thousands of hearts and reblogs. He also appears to be the first person on Tumblr who used images, rather than text posts, as a way to publish his poetry. While I have not done a systematic historical analysis of cultural forms on Tumblr, this would be a fascinating and useful future avenue for this research.

Another poet whose career blossomed from Tumblr is Lang Leav, an Australian poet and member of the TWC who self-published her first book of poems, *Love and Misadventure*, and sold over 10,000 copies before joining Writer's House. Leav describes the label of Instapoetry as 'silly':

> I think 'Pop Poetry' would be a far better description. If any comparison were to be made, look at the emergence of the Beat poets in the 1950's. This wave of poets, which included Jack Kerouac, Allen Ginsberg and William S. Burroughs, were basically anti-establishment. It was a literary movement born from a place of creativity and self-expression, by writers who tapped into the pulse of their generation.[56]

Despite such reflections on the form from a best-selling poet herself, the literary establishment regards Instapoetry as undisciplined and lowbrow, and scholars of the form have called it 'little more taxing to read than a meme.'[57] Perhaps this has something to do with the form's tendency toward free verse over metre, or the nature of the poets to be amateurs instead of freshly out of an MFA. Or perhaps it is because this is a space freely (as in, the work is offered for free) occupied by marginalised writers. In any case, the 'literariness' of poetic offerings from Tumblr and Instagram has always been in question.

Kathi Beren's work has described the ways in which Instapoetry, with its metadata and 'datafication of reader response'[58] is classifiable as e-literature, however she has also described what happens to the Instapoem when it is stripped of its metadata and printed naked on the page, arguing that its 'treacly insights'[59] are revealed as ordinary. This idea of the Instapoem as saccharin is notable. Is the appeal of Instapoetry, with its frequent descriptions of heartbreak, oppression, or healing from trauma, inherently tied to its appearance as self-help, as some scholars have suggested?[60] Does the appeal have to do with the simplification of the poetic form into free verse, which makes it more universally accessible? Or is it something about the fascination with the confession associated with Instapoetry, much like in memoir, where the poet writes themselves and their lived experience into a creation not only for 'others' enjoyment, provocation and education',[61] but their own? I am intrigued by the idea that an undisciplined poet, reflecting on their own marginalisation, relationships, joy and pain, is writing for themself an autoethnography of their life. Isn't that what poets have always done?

The Ballad of the Recovered Tumblr Poet

moments drowned in the neversaid
couldn't say, hadn't the character to confess
unfortunately, I'm in love with you
but I come by it honestly
embraced silence instead
finished crying with swift control
went to sleep and found 100
portraits of all the
lovers I almost took
awoke reverent, honoured
to have tasted the brine of their fingers,
Grateful for the words unsaid
for Leonard singing the gravel mantra
dance me to the end of love
and me writing it's over. it's over.[62]

The title of this section corresponds to the short contribution I made at the digital writing panel in 2018. The inclusion of 'recovered' speaks to my sense of embarrassment to be on the panel, and feelings of imposter syndrome to be sitting next to established digital writers and poets. 'I thought I could do what you do, once', it seems to say 'but don't worry, I am cured of that delusion, now'. The words of the anonymous messenger in my blog's inbox ring clear.

If the featuring system ended tomorrow, the TWC would still exist. In that sense, I suppose you could say Tumblr is but a means to an end – it provides the platform for us to share our work and gain a following of interested readers.[63]

As predicted by Jennifer Mueller, the Featured Tag system on Tumblr ended in 2015.[64] By this stage, I was writing less on the platform, pouring my creative energy into my Master's thesis instead – a manuscript of a young adult science fiction novella. However, my friends from the TWC had migrated into my real life. We were now connected via Facebook, Instagram and Twitter accounts, keeping in touch on Messenger, WhatsApp and Skype. I don't say this to suggest that the real TWC were the friends we made along the way, but to point out that writers need other writers. Writing is a solitary process and developing a trusted set of critical friendships, particularly as an amateur who doesn't have access to editors, publishers, or PhD supervisors, is a key factor in continuing to write.

In reflecting on the careers of Tumblr poets and fiction writers that formed part of my personal circle, around 15 have gone on to publish (and self-publish) works of poetry or fiction in print. For example, Nick Desjardins' of the Tumblr blog *A New American Classic*[65] released his debut novel, *In-Between Days* in 2017, published by Koehler Books. He is currently working on a second novel. Indo-Roman Tumblr poet, Scherezade Siobhan of the Tumblr blog *Scherezade Siobhan*[66] won the Berfrois Poetry Prize in 2016–17 and her third collection of poetry, *The Bluest Kali*[67] was published in 2018 by Lithic Press. Last year, Melissa Hem, a Khmer-American Tumblr poet, self-published a book of poetry, *Synchronicity*, in which she documents her three year relationship with her wife, Stephanie, through her poetry, Tumblr posts and diary entries.[68]

As these examples show, some Tumblr writers have used their digital creative practice to lead them to further work in the arts in a number of different ways. Some, like Desjardins and Siobhan, have attracted traditional publishing contracts for their work and in the case of Siobhan, received literary accolades. Others, like Hem, have self-published their work and created author profiles on social media that have attracted a high follower count. In my case, a career in academia presented itself after I followed my interest in creative writing, nurtured on Tumblr, into postgraduate study. These trajectories suggest that the possibilities of amateur digital creative practice are under-researched as a pathway to alternate careers as authors. Further, while studies of Tumblr users have grown in popularity in recent years, the work of these writers – the creators as opposed to curators – is an under-studied area and one that would yield insights into digital creative practice as methodologies such as autoethnography and the understanding of authorial subjectivity.

Endnotes

1   Faichney Eloise, 'Simple As,' *Delicious Interludes*, 2014, https://deliciousinterludes.tumblr.com/post/77897536314/simple-as.

2   Faichney Eloise, Delicious Interludes, 2012–2020, https://deliciousinterludes.tumblr.com/.

3   Jami Attenberg, 'Network: How to use Tumblr to connect with Readers,' *Poets and Writers*, 30 June, 2012, https://www.pw.org/content/network_how_to_use_tumblr_to_connect_with_readers_0.

4   Neil Gaiman, 'Neil Gaiman,' https://neil-gaiman.tumblr.com/.

5   Akshay Java, Xiadan Song, Tim Finin, and Belle Tseng, 'Why We Twitter: An Analysis of a Microblogging Community,' In *WebKDD/SNA-KDD '07: Proceedings of the 9th WebKDD and 1st SNA-KDD 2007 workshop on Web mining and social network analysis* (August 2007): 56–65.

6   Gita Jackson, 'In 2018 Tumblr is a Joyless Black Hole,' *Kotaku*, 3 July, 2018, https://www.kotaku.com.au/2018/07/in-2018-tumblr-is-a-joyless-black-hole/.

7   Ironically, this pattern would repeat itself to cause what has been called the demise of Tumblr (Leskin, 2019), which has historically been heavily dependent on its adult communities. In 2018, Tumblr, then owned by Yahoo's parent company, Verizon Communications, banned adult content – in particular, any images depicting 'real life human genitals or female-presenting nipples' (Tumblr, 2018). Page visits to Tumblr's login site by US users dropped by 49% after this date (Tiffany, 2019) and Verizon has since sold Tumblr to Automattic, the operator of WordPress.com.

8 Alana Hope Levinson, 'Fifty Shades of Daddy,' *Mel Magazine*, 2016, https://melmagazine.com/en-us/story/fifty-shades-of-daddy.

9 Casey Fiesler and Brianna Dym, 'Fandom's Fate is not tied to Tumblr's,' *Slate*, 5 December, 2018, https://slate.com/technology/2018/12/tumblr-fandom-adult-content-ban-livejournal.html.

10 Jackson, "Joyless Black Hole".

11 Julie Rak, 'The Digital Queer: Weblogs and Internet Identity,' *Biography* 28, no. 1 (2005): 166-182.

12 Parisa Zamanian, 'Queer Lives: The Construction of Queer Self and Community on Tumblr,' Masters Thesis, Sarah Lawrence College, 2014; Alexander Cho, 'Queer Reverb: Tumblr, Affect, Time,' in *The Making of the American Essay,* ed. Ken Hillis, Susanna Paasonen and Michael Petit (Cambridge: MIT Press, 2015), 43–58; Abigail Oakley, 'Disturbing hegemonic discourse: Nonbinary gender and sexual orientation labelling on Tumblr,' *Social Media + Society* 2, no. 3 (2016): 1-12.

13 Alessandra Mondin, '"Tumblr mostly, great empowering images": blogging, reblogging and scrolling feminist, queer and BDSM desires,' *Journal of Gender Studies* 26, no. 3 (2017): 282–292.

14 Serge Doubrovsky, *Fils* (Paris: Galileo Editions 1977).

15 Sarah Schulman, *Conflict is Not Abuse: Overstating Harm, Community Responsibility, and the Duty of Repair* (Vancouver: Arsenal Pulp Press, 2016): xv.

16 Joan W. Scott, 'The Evidence of Experience,' *Critical Inquiry*, 17, no. 4 (1991): 773–797.

17 Faichney, 'phoinix,' Delicious Interludes, 2014, https://deliciousinterludes.tumblr.com/post/85612289230/ph%C3%B3in%C4%ABBx.

18 Sidonie Smith and Julia Watson, *Reading Autobiography: A Guide for Interpreting Life Narratives* (Minneapolis: University of Minnesota Press, 2010).

19 Smith and Watson, *Reading Autobiography,* 186.

20 Cho, 'Queer Reverb,', 44.

21 Cho, 'Queer Reverb,' 45.

22 Steven Pace, 'Writing the self into research: Using grounded theory analytic strategies in autoethnography,' *TEXT* Special Issue no. 13 (2012): 1–15.

23 Tessa Muncey, *Creating Autoethnographies* (London: Sage Publications, 2010), xi.

24 Julia Kristeva qtd. in John Sutherland, 'The ideas interview: Julia Kristeva,' *The Guardian*, 15 March, 2006, https://www.theguardian.com/education/2006/mar/14/highereducation.research1.

25 Michael Lackey, *The American Biographical Novel* (New York: Bloomsbury Academic, 2016) 1.

26 Charles R. Garoian and Yvonne M. Gaudelius, 'Cyborg Pedagogy: Performing Resistance in the Digital Age,' *Studies in Art Education* 42, no. 4 (2001): 339.

27 Colm Toibin, *All a Novelist Needs: Colm Tóibín on Henry James* (Baltimore: The Johns Hopkins University Press, 2010) 111.

28 Valeriya Safronova, 'Millennials and the Age of Tumblr Activism,' *The New York Times*, 19 December, 2014, https://www.nytimes.com/2014/12/21/style/millennials-and-the-age-of-tumblr-activism.html.

29 Angela Nagle, *Kill ALL Normies: Online Culture Wars from 4chan to Tumblr to Trump and the Alt-Right* (London: Zero Books, 2017).

30 Kimberle Crenshaw, 'Mapping the Margins: Intersectionality, Identity Politics, and Violence against Women of Color,' *Stanford Law Review* 43, no. 6 (1989): 1241–99.

31 Peggy McIntosh, 'White Privilege and Male Privilege: A Personal Account of Coming To See Correspondences through Work in Women's Studies,' *Wellesley College Center for Women*, Massachusetts, 1998.

32 Susan Scafidi, *Who Owns Culture? Appropriation and Authenticity in African Law* (New Brunswick: Rutgers University Press, 2005).

33 Angela Y. Davis, *Abolition Democracy: Beyond Empire, Prisons, and Torture* (New York: Seven Stories Press, 2011).

34 Schulman, *Conflict is Not Abuse.*

35 Faichney Eloise, 'Shimmer,' Delicious Interludes, 2013, https://deliciousinterludes.tumblr.com/post/71410528802/shimmer.

36 Tumblr, 'A change to featured tag pages,' Tumblr Support, 26 October, 2015, https://support.tumblr.com/post/131976034667/a-change-to-featured-tag-pages-for-several-years.

37 Jennifer R. R. Mueller, 'Breaking down the wall: Interview six,' 2014, https://jayarrarr.com/post/55035886584/breaking-down-the-wall-interview-6-jayarrarr; Tumblr, "Featured Tag Pages".

38 Jennifer R. R. Mueller, 'Defenestrations,' https://jayarrarr.com/.

39 Mueller, 'Breaking down the wall.'

40 Mueller, 'Breaking down the wall.'

41 Faichney, 'phoenix,' Delicious Interludes, 2014, https://deliciousinterludes.tumblr.com/post/85612289230/ph%C3%B3in%C4%ABx.

42 Jia Tolentino, *Trick Mirror: Reflections on Self-Delusion* (London: 4th Estate, London, 2019).

43 Hélène Cixous, 'The Laugh of the Medusa,' translated by Keith Cohen and Paula Cohen, *Signs: Journal of Women in Culture and Society* 1, no. 4 (Summer 1976): 875–893.

44   Gunther Stuhlmann, *A Literate Passion: Letters of Anais Nin and Henry Miller 1932–1953* (London: Hardcourt Brace & Company, 1987).

45   Personal correspondence, 2012.

46   Alessandra Mondin, '"Tumblr mostly, great empowering images": blogging, reblogging and scrolling feminist, queer and BDSM desires.' Journal of Gender Studies 26, no. 3 (2017): 282–292.

47   Personal correspondence, 2012.

48   Gunther Stuhlmann, A Literate Passion: Letters of Anais Nin and Henry Miller 1932–1953. London: Hardcourt Brace & Company, 1987.

49   P. Lejeune, 'Le moi électronique,' 2004, http://www.autopacte.org/Cher-%E9cran.html.

50   Ellen van Neerven, *Throat*. (St Lucia: University of Queensland Press, 2020) 3.

51   Eloise Faichney, Delicious Interludes, https://deliciousinterludes.tumblr.com/.

52   Eloise Faichney, 'This love is over but it's useful,' Delicious Interludes, 2018, https://deliciousinterludes.tumblr.com/post/167797960875/this-love-is-over-but-its-useful.

53   NPD Group, 'Instapoets Rekindling U.S. Poetry Book Sales,' https://www.npd.com/wps/portal/npd/us/news/press-releases/2018/instapoets-rekindling-u-s--poetry-book-sales--the-npd-group-says/.

54   Faith Hill and Karen Yuan, 'How Instagram Saved Poetry: Social media is turning an art form into an industry,' *The Atlantic*, 15 October, 2018, https://www.theatlantic.com/technology/archive/2018/10/rupi-kaur-instagram-poet-entrepreneur/572746/; Rupi Kaur, *Milk and Honey* (Kansas City: Andrews McMeel Publishing, 2016).

55   Lili Pâquet, 'Selfie-Help: The Multimodal Appeal of Instagram Poetry,' *The Journal of Popular Culture* 52, no. 2 (2019): 296–314.

56   Lang Leav cited in Emma Wenner, 'A Modern Poet: PW Talks with Lang Leav,' *Publisher's Weekly*, 20 October, 2018. https://www.publishersweekly.com/pw/by-topic/authors/interviews/article/78075-a-modern-poet-pw-talks-to-lang-leav.html#:~:text=Lang%20Leav%20first%20shared%20her,publishing%20contract%20with%20Andrews%20McMeel.

57   Pâquet, 'Selfie-Help'; Kathi Inman Berens, 'E-Literature's #1 Hit: Is Instagram Poetry E-literature?' 7 April, 2019, *Electronic Book Review*, https://electronicbookreview.com/essay/e-lits-1-hit-is-instagram-poetry-e-literature/.

58   Berens, 'E-Literature's #1 Hit'.

59   Ibid.

60 Pâcquet, 'Selfie Help.'
61 Rak, 'The Digital Queer,' 22.
62 Eloise Faichney, 'omission,' Delicious Interludes, 2013, https://deliciousinterludes.tumblr.com/post/45163241771/omission.
63 Mueller, 'Breaking Down the Wall.;'
64 Tumblr, 'Featured Tag Pages.'
65 Nick Desjardins, 'A New American Classic,' https://a-new-american-classic.tumblr.com/.
66 Scherezade Shaubam, 'Scherezade Siobhan, https://viperslang.tumblr.com/.
67 Shaubam, *The Bluest Kali* (Colorado: Lithic Press, 2018).
68 Melissa Hem, *Synchronicity* (United States: Melissa Hem, 2019).

Bibliography

Attenberg, Jami. 'Network: How to use Tumblr to connect with Readers,' *Poets and Writers*, 30 June 2012. https://www.pw.org/content/network_how_to_use_tumblr_to_connect_with_readers_0.

Berens, Kathi Inman. 'E-Literature's #1 Hit: Is Instagram Poetry E-literature?' *Electronic Book Review*, 7 April, 2019. https://electronicbookreview.com/essay/e-lits-1-hit-is-instagram-poetry-e-literature/.

Cho, Alexander. 'Queer Reverb: Tumblr, Affect, Time,' In *The Making of the American Essay*, edited by Hillis, Ken, Paasonen, Susanna and Petit, Michael, 43–58. Cambridge: MIT Press, 2015.

Cixous, Hélène. 'The Laugh of the Medusa,' Translated by Keith Cohen and Paula Cohen. *Signs: Journal of Women in Culture and Society* 1, no. 4 (Summer 1976): 875–893.

Crenshaw, Kimberle. 'Mapping the Margins: Intersectionality, Identity Politics, and Violence against Women of Color,' *Stanford Law Review* 43, no. 6 (1989): 1241–99.

Cunningham, Michael. *The Hour*s. New York: Farrar, Straus & Giroux, 1998.

Davis, Angela Y. *Abolition Democracy: Beyond Empire, Prisons, and Torture*. New York: Seven Stories Press, 2011.

Desjardins, Nick. *A New American Classic*. https://a-new-american-classic.tumblr.com/.

Desjardins, Nick. *In-Between Days*. Virginia Beach: Koehler Books, 2017.

Doubrovsky, Serge. *Fils*. Paris: Galileo Editions, 1977.

Ebershoff, David. *The Danish Girl*, New York: Viking Press, 2000.

Faichney, Eloise. *Delicious Interludes*. https://deliciousinterludes.tumblr.com/.

Faichney, Eloise. 'Shimmer,' *Delicious Interludes*, 2013. https://deliciousinterludes.tumblr.com/post/71410528802/shimmer.

Faichney, Eloise. 'omission,' *Delicious Interludes*, 2013. https://deliciousinterludes.tumblr.com/post/45163241771/omission.

Faichney, Eloise. 'Simple As,' *Delicious Interludes*, 2014. https://deliciousinterludes.tumblr.com/post/77897536314/simple-as.

Faichney, Eloise. 'phoenix,' *Delicious Interludes*, 2014. https://deliciousinterludes.tumblr.com/post/85612289230/ph%C3%B3in%C4%ABx.

Faichney, Eloise 'This love is over but it's useful,' *Delicious Interludes*, 2018. https://deliciousinterludes.tumblr.com/post/167797960875/this-love-is-over-but-its-useful.

Fiesler, Casey and Dym, Brianna. 'Fandom's Fate is not tied to Tumblr's,' *Slate Magazine*, 5 December, 2018. https://slate.com/technology/2018/12/tumblr-fandom-adult-content-ban-livejournal.html.

Gaiman, Neil. 'Neil Gaiman,' https://neil-gaiman.tumblr.com/.

Garoian, Charles R and Gaudelius, Yvonne M. 'Cyborg Pedagogy: Performing Resistance in the Digital Age,' *Studies in Art Education* 42, no. 4 (2001): 333–347.

Gregson, Tyler Knott. 'I Am Tyler Knott Gregson,' n.d. https://tylerknott.com/.

Hem, Melissa. *Synchronicity*. Self Published, 2019.

Hill, Faith and Yuan, Karen. 'How Instagram Saved Poetry: Social media is turning an art form into an industry,' *The Atlantic*, 15 October, 2018. https://www.theatlantic.com/technology/archive/2018/10/rupi-kaur-instagram-poet-entrepreneur/572746/.

'Instapoets Rekindling U.S. Poetry Book Sales,' NPD Group, 5 April, 2018. https://www.npd.com/wps/portal/npd/us/news/press-releases/2018/instapoets-rekindling-u-s--poetry-book-sales--the-npd-group-says/

Jackson, Gita. 'In 2018 Tumblr is a Joyless Black Hole,' *Kotaku* 3 July, 2018. https://www.kotaku.com.au/2018/07/in-2018-tumblr-is-a-joyless-black-hole/.

Java, Akshay, Song, Xiadan. Finin, Tim and Tseng, Belle. 'Why We Twitter: An Analysis of a Microblogging Community,' *WebKDD/SNA-KDD '07: Proceedings of the 9th WebKDD and 1st SNA-KDD 2007 workshop on Web mining and social network analysis.* (August 2007): 56–65.

Kaur, Rupi. *Milk and Honey*. Kansas City: Andrews McMeel Publishing, 2016.

Lackey, Michael. *The American Biographical Novel*. New York: Bloomsbury Academic, 2016.

Lejeune, P. 'Le moi électronique,' 2000. http://www.autopacte.org/Cher-%E9cran.html.

Leskin, Paige. 'A year after Tumblr's porn ban, some users are still struggling to rebuild their communities and sense of belonging,' *Business Insider Australia*, 21 December, 2019. https://www.businessinsider.com.au/tumblr-porn-ban-nsfw-flagged-reactions-fandom-art-erotica-communities-2019-8?r=US&IR=T.

Levinson, Alana Hope. 'Fifty Shades of Daddy,' *Mel Magazine*, 2016. https://melmagazine.com/en-us/story/fifty-shades-of-daddy.

McIntosh, Peggy. 'White Privilege and Male Privilege: A Personal Account of Coming To See Correspondences through Work in Women's Studies,' *Wellesley College Center for Women*, Massachusetts, 1998.

Mondin, Alessandra '"Tumblr mostly, great empowering images": blogging, reblogging and scrolling feminist, queer and BDSM desires,' *Journal of Gender Studies* 26, no. 3 (2017): 282–292.

Mueller, Jennifer R. R. *Defenstrations. n.d.* https://jayarrarr.com/.

Mueller, Jennifer R. R. 'Breaking down the wall: Interview six,' *Defenstrations,* 2014, https://jayarrarr.com/post/55035886584/breaking-down-the-wall-interview-6-jayarrarr.

Muncey, Tessa. *Creating Autoethnographies*. London: Sage Publications, 2010.

Nagle, Angela. *Kill ALL Normies: Online Culture Wars from 4chan to Tumblr to Trump and the Alt-Right*. London: Zero Books, 2017.

Oakley, Abigail. 'Disturbing hegemonic discourse: Nonbinary gender and sexual orientation labelling on Tumblr,' *Social Media + Society* 2, no. 3. (2016): 1–12.

Pace, Steven. 'Writing the self into research: Using grounded theory analytic strategies in autoethnography,' *TEXT* Special Issue no. 13 (2012): 1–15.

Pâquet, Lili. 'Selfie-Help: The Multimodal Appeal of Instagram Poetry,' *The Journal of Popular Culture* 52, no. 2 (2019): 296–314.

Rak, Julie. 'The Digital Queer: Weblogs and Internet Identity,' *Biography* 28, no. 1 (2005): 166–182.

Rak, Julie. *Boom! Manufacturing Memoir for the Popular Market*. Ontario: Wilfrid Laurier University Press, Ontario, 2013.

Safronova, Valeriya. 'Millennials and the Age of Tumblr Activism,' *The New York Times*, 19 December, 2014. https://www.nytimes.com/2014/12/21/style/millennials-and-the-age-of-tumblr-activism.html.

Schulman, Sarah. *Conflict is Not Abuse: Overstating Harm, Community Responsibility, and the Duty of Repair*. Vancouver: Arsenal Pulp Press, 2016.

Scafidi, Susan. *Who Owns Culture? Appropriation and Authenticity in African Law*. New Brunswick: Rutgers University Press, 2005.

Scott, Joan W. 'The Evidence of Experience,' *Critical Inquiry*, 17, no. 4 (1991): 773–797.

Siobhan, Scherezade. *The Bluest Kali*. Colorado: Lithic Press, 2018.

Siobhan, Scherezade. *Scherezade Siobhan*. https://viperslang.tumblr.com/.

Smith, Sidonie and Watson, Julia. *Reading Autobiography: A guide for interpreting life narratives*. Minneapolis: University of Minnesota Press, 2010.

Stuhlmann, Gunther. *A Literate Passion: Letters of Anais Nin and Henry Miller 1932–1953*. London: Hardcourt Brace & Company, 1987.

Sutherland, John. 'The ideas interview: Julia Kristeva,' *The Guardian*, 15 March, 2006. http://www.guardian.co.uk/education/2006/mar/14/highereducation. research1.

Tiffany, Kaitlyn. 'Tumblr's First Year Without Porn: The engine of internet culture chugging along, changed,' *The Atlantic*, December 4, 2019. https://www.theatlantic.com/technology/archive/2019/12/tumblr-year-review-2019-nsfw-ban-memes/602911/.

Tolentino, Jia. *Trick Mirror: Reflections on Self-Delusion*. London: 4th Estate, London, 2019.

Tóibín, Colm. *All a Novelist Needs: Colm Tóibín on Henry James*. Baltimore: The Johns Hopkins University Press, 2010.

Tumblr. 'A change to featured tag pages,' Tumblr Support, 26 October, 2015. https://support.tumblr.com/post/131976034667/a-change-to-featured-tag-pages-for-several-years.

Tumblr. 'Adult Content.' n.d. https://tumblr.zendesk.com/hc/en-us/articles/231885248-Adult-content.

Van Neervan, Ellen. *Throat*. St Lucia: University of Queensland Press, 2020.

Wargo, Jon M. '#donttagyourhate: Reading collecting and curating as genres of participation in LGBT youth activism on Tumblr,' *Digital Culture & Education* 9 no. 1 (2017): 14–30.

Wenner, Emma. 'A Modern Poet: PW Talks with Lang Leav,' *Publisher's Weekly*, 20 October, 2018. https://www.publishersweekly.com/pw/by-topic/authors/interviews/article/78075-a-modern-poet-pw-talks-to-lang-leav.html#:~:text=Lang%20Leav%20first%20shared%20her,publishing%20contract%20with%20Andrews%20McMeel.

Zamanian, Parisa. 'Queer Lives: The Construction of Queer Self and Community on Tumblr,' Masters Thesis, Sarah Lawrence College, 2014.

Contributor Biographies

Kate Cuthbert is the Program and Partnerships Manager at Writers Victoria, and previously ran Escape Publishing, an imprint of Harlequin Australia. She is a PhD candidate with the University of Queensland, with research interests in popular fiction, publishing, and paratexts.

Alexandra Dane is a Lecturer in Media and Communications at the University of Melbourne. She is the author of *Gender and Prestige: Contemporary Australian Book Culture* (Palgrave Macmillan, 2019).

Eloise Faichney is a novelist, academic and editor. Her work has been published in *Foundation: The Science Fiction Journal*, *The Medical Journal of Australia*, SMUT zine, Bukker Tilibul, *Stormcloud Poets Anthology* and others. Eloise's research interrogates notions of authorial subjectivity, the gaps and silences in women's life narratives and digital life narratives. She is currently working on a novel about the lives of author Naomi Mitchison and explorer Zita Baker.

Airlie Lawson is a literary cartographer, book industry researcher and a Postdoctoral Research Fellow at Melbourne Law School, the University of Melbourne, working on 'Untapped: the Australian Literary Heritage Project'. She is the author of *Don't Tell Eve* (Vintage, 2009), a satirical novel set in the world of publishing.

Sarah Layton has a Masters in Publishing and Communications from the University of Melbourne. Her research interests interrogate the connections between book history and digital book forms. She has been published in *Voiceworks* and *Antithesis Journal* and edited these publications. She currently works as a customer service agent for Cengage, reviews books at www.litsponge.com and tweets @SlmLayton.

Kenna MacTavish is PhD candidate in Publishing and Communication at the University of Melbourne. Her research interests include contemporary book culture, genre, and social platforms. Kenna's thesis-in-progress is titled 'Organising Books: Creative and Connective Systems of Classification in the Twenty-First Century'.

Claire Parnell is a PhD candidate, lecturer and research assistant at the University of Melbourne. Her research focuses on the platform-isation of publishing and cultural inclusion in romance fiction. Claire's thesis-in-progress is titled 'Media Ecologies, Digital Publishing Platforms and Inclusivity in Romance Fiction'. Claire is the author of 'Mapping the Entertainment Ecosystem of Wattpad: Platforms, Publishing and Adaptation' published in *Convergence* 2020.

Millicent Weber is a Lecturer in English at the Australian National University. Her books include the monograph *Literary Festivals and Contemporary Book Culture* (Palgrave Macmillan, 2018), and essay collections *Book Publishing in Australia: A Living Legacy* (Monash University Publishing, 2019) and *Publishing Means Business: Australian Perspectives* (Monash University Publishing, 2017).